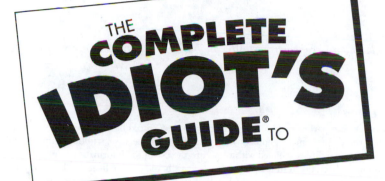

THE COMPLETE IDIOT'S GUIDE® TO

Quilting

Illustrated

Second Edition

by Laura Ehrlich

ALPHA

A member of Penguin Group (USA) Inc.

To my loving and supportive family, my husband Elliott, daughters Jamie, Jessica, and Amanda, and son-in law Ed.

Publisher: *Marie Butler-Knight*
Product Manager: *Phil Kitchel*
Senior Managing Editor: *Jennifer Chisholm*
Senior Acquisitions Editor: *Randy Ladenheim-Gil*
Development Editor: *Tom Stevens*
Senior Project Editor: *Billy Fields*
Copy Editor: *Tiffany Almond*
Illustrator: *Richard King*
Cover/Book Designer: *Trina Wurst*
Indexer: *Angie Bess*
Layout/Proofreading: *Rebecca Harmon, Donna Martin*
Graphics: *Tammy Graham, Laura Robbins, Dennis Sheehan*

Contents at a Glance

Contents

Foreword

Welcome to the world of quilt making! It's a wonderful world with a distinguished history that has risen from humble beginnings to a multi-million-dollar industry. As Laura explains in her first chapter, the idea of stitching two or three layers of fabric together is certainly not new. Ancient Egyptians did it to create covers for extra warmth, and bits of fabric sewn together to form a whole cloth are found in early Oriental, Middle Eastern, and European textiles. Today, quilt making, a cherished part of our own country's heritage, is as popular around the world as it was centuries ago.

One reason for its popularity lies in the intrinsic beauty of the quilt itself. The exciting color combinations, the intriguing patterns, the textural surface designs—just feast your eyes on the quilts in this book! Another reason quilt making has remained so popular is that a quilt is easy to make, especially when you have Laura by your side every step of the way. Believe it or not, the aptitude to shop for fabric (a most pleasant experience), the talent to cut the fabric into pieces (you know how to use scissors so this step is a cinch), and the ability to sew pieces together (a simple straight stitch by hand or machine does it) are really all the technical skills needed to create a quilt.

As you begin to create your first quilt, you begin your exciting journey into the wonderful world of quilt making. In addition, with Laura as your personal guide, you'll explore every realm from planning your quilt to displaying it on your bed or wall. On each page, Laura shares many years of quilt making and teaching experience so you can learn everything you need to know about making a quilt, including things you didn't know enough to ask about.

By the end of the book and upon the completion of your first quilt, you will have learned the most important lesson of all: Quilt making is not just another craft. It's a means of creative expression. It's an art form. It's a quiet street you stroll along to savor solitude. It's a bustling boulevard along which you encounter the friendliest folks. It's the adventure of a lifetime. It's a lifetime of adventure. It's everything you are now and everything you can be. It's a state of mind. It's a wonderful world, and you are part of it. Welcome!

Jan Burns
Editor, *Creative Quilting* magazine

Introduction

I always get a comfortable feeling when I look at a room that has a quilt in it. There is nothing like a quilt to add warmth and beauty to a room. Quilts have an appeal that has lasted through centuries. Some people regard quilts as an investment and collect antique quilts. Nowadays we are valuing quilts more and more as works of art. You can see quilts displayed in museums and art galleries as the new textile art. Most people, however, just like quilts because they are beautiful to have around.

If you are someone who loves quilts and has decided to join your heritage and create your own quilt, you have many decisions to make. Quilts come with a variety of different names, designs, and options that make the quilting process complicated enough, without throwing in the dilemma of choosing colors. Where do you begin?

I began by looking through quilt books for inspiration. Then I walked through craft stores and linen departments to see what I liked. Finally, my friend Linda twisted my arm and I took a class in beginner quilting. I loved the class—especially the creativity and productivity! At the end of 10 weeks, I had lots of squares of quilt block designs but did not know what to do with them. It bothered me that putting these blocks together into a quilt was only briefly discussed in the class. That is where the idea for offering my own class and writing this book came into being.

This book will take you from start to finish in making a quilt. It will give you a basic understanding of quilts—their history, types, and names. You'll learn about quilt components and quilt construction. I will take you step by step through all the decisions you have to make. You will learn how to plan the quilt, buy the materials, piece the quilt top, quilt, and sign your work of art.

What You'll Find in This Book

Beginners need to be realistic. Quilts vary in size, and the designs range from easy to very challenging. I encourage beginners to experiment with a variety of simple designs for a small project. The best way to learn quilting is to make a Sampler quilt. The Sampler quilt combines different designs, both pieced and appliquéd. You can pick and choose blocks, starting with the easy ones and then, as you become more accomplished, go on to make more challenging ones. Here's how you do it: Follow this book from Part 1 to Part 5, then choose a project in Part 6—the Make It Your Way section—and you will have a quilt you're proud to display.

Part 1, **"Getting Ready to Quilt!"** gives you a general understanding about types of quilts and how our ancestors developed them. There are many decisions to make, so first take some time to look at the quilt patterns throughout this book and choose the quilt you would like to make. We'll take the mystery out of planning the size and selecting colors to make your quilt one that you will want to live with for a lifetime.

In **Part 2, "Get Set—What You Need to Start,"** you'll learn about equipment and materials. There are certain supplies that you will need to get started. I have listed the necessities—you'll find many of them around the house, but there are some neat gadgets that could help you in your quest for the perfect quilt. Probably the scariest part in making a quilt is purchasing the fabric. There are so many choices it boggles the brain. Knowing the type of fabric and how much you need will help put your mind at ease.

Part 3, "We're Home and Ready to Go," provides you with a general knowledge of fabric characteristics. Templates or quilt patterns must be made and transferred onto the fabric. You'll discover how to cut your fabric and put the pieces of the quilt together.

The chapters in **Part 4, "Let's Put It All Together,"** include step-by-step instructions of the stitches that will help your quilt be durable and hold up to every day usage. We also don't forget the quickness and practicality of machine-made quilts. Once your blocks are made, it's time to put them together and frame them out into your quilt top.

By **Part 5, "Making the Quilt Sandwich and Keeping It Together,"** you need to know about the filling batting and a backing. How much and what type to purchase for your quilt is examined. Holding this quilt sandwich together in wrinkle-free layers is imperative—basting is your key to success. Can you believe we are more than halfway through this book and we're just starting to quilt? Decide how to give your quilt the three-dimensional life it deserves by tying, hand quilting, or machine quilting. We need to address the finishing touches. You'll find out how to eliminate all those frayed edges. Artists sign their creations and so should quilters. After all the time, work, and love you have put into your quilt, you'll learn how to take care of it with tender, loving care.

In **Part 6, "Make It Your Way Projects,"** you'll find all types of projects. Through my years of teaching, I have a whole file cabinet of projects that my students have requested to make, and have loved them. Sometimes you only want to make a small project. I'll explain how to make a pillow and wall hanging from start to finish. There are all different techniques, regular piecing, appliqué, and machine piecing. Lastly, there are all levels of difficulty. Choose one project and happy quilting!

Extras

There are many steps involved in making a quilt. This book is designed to make it as easy as possible and help you avoid any problems. Sidebars are scattered throughout the book and will highlight things I feel are important for all quilters to know.

Scraps and Pieces

This box offers a variety of different quilt stories, historical tidbits, or just interesting information about quilting.

Don't Get Stuck!

Throughout my many years of teaching beginner quilters, I have discovered many different pitfalls that may occur. Hopefully the hints in these boxes will help you avoid these problems.

Quilting Bee

Sometimes there is an easy way of doing something, and these tips are ones that you would learn at a quilting bee.

Quilt Talk

Quilters seem to have a language of their own. Any new and unusual words will be explained.

Acknowledgments

Many people have contributed to this quilting guide. First of all I would like to thank my husband Elliott, and my girls, Jamie, Jessica, Amanda, and son-in-law Ed for encouraging me, helping me with all my computer glitches, and putting up with me in general. Here's to all the times you've forgiven me when you've stepped on runaway pins while I was working on a quilting project. I'll always be grateful to my mother, Tony Mangano, for giving me an appreciation of fabrics and taking me all over the state looking for fabric when I first started sewing. Thanks especially to Linda Mayer, my wonderful friend who twisted my arm and made me take my first quilting class, and to Debra for allowing me to teach quilting in her store. A thank you to Lori Groveman for helping me to overcome my computer phobia.

I am especially appreciative of all my "quilting ladies" who have given me insight and taught me as much as I taught them. Thanks for all the wonderful years of finding new and unusual quilts for me to draft, create, or figure out how to assemble. It has always been fun.

A special thanks to Randy Ladenheim-Gil and Tom Stevens, my editors, for making sense out of my words; Nita Munson, my technical editor, for her vast knowledge of quilt history, exquisite antique quilt collection, and making sure I was technically accurate and counted all parts of the quilt blocks correctly; Marie Varner, quilter and friend who supported me throughout the writing process; and all of the New Bridge Quilters, who were so helpful during the photography by loaning, carrying, and holding all the quilts. Special thanks to the following quilters for allowing me to advise them on their wonderful quilts and letting me use their quilt pictures in my book. Special thanks to: Doris Bobek, Robin Bogert, Holly Ciccorico, Maureen Fetko, Mari Garcia, Nita Munson, Maureen Mueller, Marsha Oakes, Rosetta Tiendeau, Sara Reiss, Pearl Roth, Elaine Saigh, Kathy Stehle, and Tippi Ulman.

Special Thanks to the Technical Reviewer

The Complete Idiot's Guide to Quilting Illustrated, Second Edition, was reviewed by an expert who double-checked the accuracy of what you'll learn here, to help us ensure that this book gives you everything you need to know about quilting. Special thanks are extended to Nita Munson.

Trademarks

All terms mentioned in this book that are known to be or are suspected of being trademarks or service marks have been appropriately capitalized. Alpha Books and Penguin Group (USA) Inc. cannot attest to the accuracy of this information. Use of a term in this book should not be regarded as affecting the validity of any trademark or service mark.

In This Part

Part

Getting Ready to Quilt!

There are many decisions for all beginner quilt makers to make, and I suggest you first acquire a general understanding about types of quilts and how our ancestors developed them. Then take some time to look at the quilt patterns throughout this book and choose the quilt you would like to make. We'll take the mystery out of planning the size and selecting colors to make your quilt one that you will want to live with for a lifetime.

In This Chapter

◆ Letting your creative spirit out, making a quilt

◆ Understanding what a quilt is

◆ Learning a brief history of quilts

◆ Exploring types of quilt projects

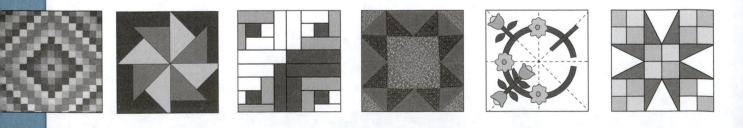

Chapter 1

The Who, What, When, and Where of Quilts

I have been quilting for 25 years! I actually can't believe that it's been that long. It has been a long journey of planning, buying and using fabrics, pins, needles, and thread to make a quilt. My love of quilting is still evolving. There are always new quilts and techniques to be learned. Quilters are so creative. Do your research. There are new books being published each day, one more exciting than the next. Go to quilt shows. They always make me wonder why didn't I think of that pattern, or use those colors or that fabric.

As a beginner, I learned that there are three basic components involved in making a quilt:

1. Sewing the quilt top out of many small pieces of fabric
2. Attaching the fluffy inside layer
3. Securing the backing fabric that holds the quilt together

This chapter deals with the who, what, when, and where of quilting. Learn the basics, then branch out with new quilts using your own imagination.

The Who Is You

You can do this. Bring your likes and dislikes, your favorite colors, and your abilities together to make a quilt. If you are a beginner, start simple. This book has many projects that you can choose from to make a quilt, pillow, or wall hanging. Just decide on a project, start at the beginning, and you can follow from start to finish. You won't even have to make any complicated decisions, it's all planned out for you. If you want, I'll even make suggestions you might follow to make them truly unique and your own.

If you are looking for a creative outlet, quilting may be for you. Quilts are used as an art form, not only decorating your walls but the walls of offices, corporate headquarters, and art galleries. Make a quilt and let the artist out. To continue to have quilt inspirations and to improve your techniques, read quilt magazines and/or sign up for a course at an adult school to fine-tune what you will learn from this book. Join a quilting group. Remember those quilting bees the women attended during the pioneer days, they still have them but now they are called guilds. Make a quilt and let the artist out.

What—It's Not a Blanket?

Here's the answer to that question: A blanket is a single layer, a quilt is not. A quilt is not a blanket. There, I have said it. A blanket is necessary on your bed for warmth, but a quilt, while adding warmth, is also decorative. You can find quilts throughout the house on chairs, on the backs of sofas, and on your walls.

A quilt consists of three layers: the quilt top, which is the right side displaying the pattern designs; the batting or filling substance; and the backing, most often one solid piece of fabric and usually considered the "wrong" side. All of these three layers have to be held together. Quilters have learned to prevent shifting of the warm stuffing by either tying the layers together or by quilting. Technically, quilting is a running stitch that goes through all layers, holding the batting in place. Believe it or not, quilting is one of your last steps in the preparation of a quilt.

See how a quilt can make a room feel comfy and homey.

When—the History of Quilt Types and Names

It is believed that quilted fabric dates back to the Egyptians. Do you think that Cleopatra wore a quilted vest for warmth or beauty? Then there is the theory that knights on the Crusades liked the idea of wearing quilted garments under their armor for comfort. (Wouldn't you want some padding under that heavy metal suit?) Europeans have used bed quilts for warmth since the fourteenth century. However, American quilters have expanded the purpose of quilts. Quilts not only are utilitarian but also add beauty and individuality through creative patterns on the quilt top. Quilting has become an art form that spans the ages and world—Colonial Sampler quilts, Victorian Crazy quilts, Amish quilts, Baltimore Album quilts, Texas Lone Star, Hawaiian quilts, Hmong needlework, and Japanese Sashiko quilts.

Scraps and Pieces

In order to provide warmth for their bed coverings, colonial women would sandwich and stitch together a large length of fabric; a layer of cotton, wool, rags, or even newspapers for the stuffing; and another large piece of fabric for the backing—thereby deriving the name "whole quilt." As scarcity of fabric became a problem, scraps of clothing were used, making it a necessity to use smaller pieces that evolved into patchwork.

One of the most interesting, but also most bewildering, aspects of quilting is the multitude of quilt names. There are books with hundreds of patch diagrams and names that can be very confusing for beginners. The names of the patchwork designs follow the story of our forefathers. Let's wander through a history of quilt names and see how they mirror pioneer wanderings. Starting in England, the colonists began their trip to America. They named quilt blocks for their experiences: London Road, Ocean Waves, Mariner's Compass, and after arriving in America, Log Cabin, Virginia Star, and Ohio Star. Religion was an important part of colonial America as quilt patches such as Church Steps or Star of Bethlehem exemplify. Quilters even entered the political arena by designing quilts named Tudor Rose, Clay's Choice or 54 – 40, or Fight. Quilters have used their lives and surroundings to name quilts. It is not important to remember all the names, but it is fun to get into the quilters' minds and understand how they devised the making of their quilts.

Here is an example of a Baltimore Album Quilt block made by Pearl Roth.

Where—Where Can You Use Quilts?

Quilts may be used throughout your house. They are not only for the bedroom. I've taught my students many different projects throughout my years of teaching quilting. You may also use quilt blocks as pillows, table runners, pocketbooks, tote bags, pot holders, aprons, Christmas decorations, and quilts as wall hangings, or lap quilts thrown over chairs or sofas.

Will your quilt be the center of attention? I sure hope so. Look around the room that your quilt will live in. Do you want it to be the focal point of the room or blend with the surroundings? It's all up to you where your quilt will go.

You can make a quilt highlight a room, as Robin Bogert has done with her nautical-themed room and her lighthouse quilt.

The Least You Need to Know

- A quilt is composed of three layers—a quilt top, a fluffy filling, and a backing fabric—which is secured by small running stitches.

- People have made quilts throughout the ages in different regions of the world.

- Discovering the names of quilts and how they evolved can be fun and educational.

- Quilts can be found all around the home and even adorning walls in museums and corporations.

In This Chapter

◆ Learning the difference between piecing and appliqué

◆ Finding out how quilt tops can be designed and assembled

◆ Choosing different types of quilt setups

◆ Understanding the parts of a quilt

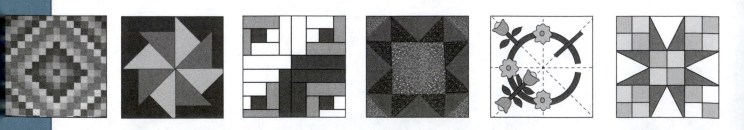

The Building Blocks of Quilts

Let's examine the various methods for constructing quilt tops. A patch, or a portion of a quilt, can be made either by piecing or appliquéing the top, or face, of the quilt into designs using a variety of different-size pieces. Quilters can then assemble these sections of the quilt, starting with a single length of material, and work their way up to creating overall designs using thousands of pieces of one shape. Don't stop reading when you see "thousands of pieces" because beginners start with the building blocks of quilting.

Piecing and Appliqué

We're going to use fabric to create your quilt top. Just as women apply lipstick or blush to their faces, we're going to apply our fabrics to the quilt face by sewing together pieces of fabric with different colors and designs. You can choose to sew quilt tops together by piecing or appliqué. Each uses a different technique and stitch and the resulting quilts have a distinctive look. We'll learn how to make the stitches in Chapter 11—right now, let's look at quilts in each of the different techniques.

Pieced Quilt: Geometry Lesson

In a *pieced* quilt block, the pattern is divided into geometric shapes—usually squares, rectangles, triangles, and diamonds. When various shapes are sewn, it is like putting a fabric jigsaw puzzle together.

> ### Quilt Talk
>
> **Piecing** is the cutting out of fabric shapes and sewing them together two pieces at a time with a small running stitch. Then they are combined with another shape to form a larger section until the block or square is completed.

In more challenging patches, you can use hexagons, pentagons, and weirdly shaped rhomboids. Doesn't this sound like a high school Geometry class? Drafting your own patchwork patch uses geometric skills to get the pattern pieces to fit together like an intricate puzzle. If one pattern piece is cut slightly wrong, the alignment of the entire quilt will be off.

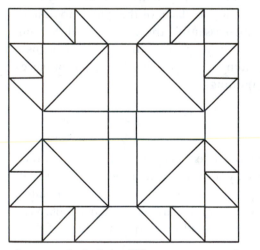

See if you can find all the different geometric shapes in this pieced patch.

Appliqué Quilt: Drawing Pictures

Appliqué quilts always seem more feminine than the angular pieced patchwork quilts. The pattern pieces of an *appliqué* block may be free-form or portray a specific object.

Some of my students make quilts with appliqué shapes in the form of hearts, flowers, birdhouses, roosters, moose, and Santa Claus.

Traditionally, the oldest appliqué quilts are of flowers. Other quilters have appliquéd historically important buildings, churches, and even family crests. The shaped pieces can be attached using a special appliqué stitch, a hemming blind stitch, or by machine zigzagging. You can also use black embroidery thread to decorate the design with a blanket stitch. (These stitches are discussed in Chapter 11.)

> ### Quilt Talk
>
> **Appliqué** is the technique of applying a shaped piece of fabric onto a larger contrasting piece of base or background fabric. The edges of the applied design are turned under and sewn down.

Notice the appliquéd pieces that actually look like leaves and flowers in the American Wreath block.

If you love the hearts-and-flowers look of appliqué patches but are leery of making an appliquéd quilt, don't be afraid of appliqué. Getting a flower to look like a flower can be intimidating but if you follow the step-by-step directions in Chapter 14, your fabrics will lay down perfectly. Beginners should experiment with both techniques in pieced and appliqué blocks in order to become a well-rounded quilter.

Cutting Your Quilt Top into Designs

Another method of categorizing quilts is by the way a quilt top is designed. Examine quilts and notice if there is one central design, several smaller repeated designs, or many small shapes that form an overall pattern. Quilters can start by planning a quilt top with one large piece of fabric or by cutting the material smaller and smaller until the quilt top is composed of thousands of fabric pieces.

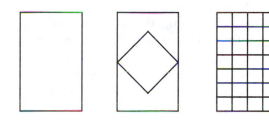

Examine how these five quilt tops are divided into smaller and smaller pieces.

When designing a quilt, a quilter can start with the whole cloth quilt, as discussed in the first chapter. As the name implies, you use only one length of material for the quilt top. Now I know you're saying, "Wow, what a great quilt, no sewing little pieces together." Before you start one of these quilts, however, be aware that they usually involve elaborate quilting designs that can be very tedious for beginners.

The medallion quilt has one large central-pieced or appliquéd design with strips of fabric or borders to finish out the top. A Lone Star is a good example of a medallion quilt.

The quilt face can also be divided into squares or blocks of patterns. This is the most popular method of designing or planning a quilt. The pieced or appliquéd blocks can be attached together or framed out with a piece of fabric called a lattice or sashing. Because the block method is the easiest for beginners, the patterns I have included in this book are all 12-inch blocks of designs.

Scraps and Pieces

Blocks developed and flourished because they were easy for our pioneer ancestors to carry from house to house to work on at quilting bees. Each individual would make a square block and then all the blocks were assembled to create the quilt top. Now, that's what you call teamwork.

The last way a quilt top can be drafted is with an overall design. A quilt top can consist of all squares, as in the Trip Around the World quilt; or hexagons, for example, like Grandmother's Flower Garden; or diamonds, exemplified by the Baby Block quilt. You can realistically have a thousand pieces of all of the same fabric in one quilt top.

After examining and drafting many entire quilt tops using each of these categories, I have found the easiest for a beginner is definitely the block method. Blocks are the building blocks of many quilts. They can have all the same design with one block repeated throughout the quilt, or you can assemble a Sampler quilt where each block or square has a different design. It's great fun.

This Trip Around the World quilt illustrates an overall design using hundreds of squares.

The Quilt Setup

It's important to understand the language of quilting. Before you start planning your quilt, look at the diagram of a quilt top and learn the parts of the quilt. Understanding these terms is important because I will be discussing their construction for the quilt top throughout the rest of the book.

- ◆ **Block.** A square of pieced or appliquéd patchwork, also called a square, that is put together with other blocks to make a quilt.

- ◆ **Lattice.** A strip of fabric that frames each block in a quilt. The strip can be a solid strip or it can have small squares at the corner of each block. The lattice is also sometimes called sashing. I will discuss this part of a quilt in Chapter 17.

- ◆ **Border.** A length of fabric that frames the outside edge of the quilt top. Borders can be as simple as solid strips of fabric or as complex as intricate geometric patterns or appliqués. We'll learn about borders in Chapter 17.

- ◆ **Batting.** The inner lining between the top, or face, of a quilt and the bottom layer, or backing, that gives the quilt its fluffiness and warmth. Back in the "good old days," stuffing or filling was anything to fill the middle layer in a quilt. It could be cotton picked in the fields and stuffed into the quilt, or the cotton could have been carded or combed to smooth it out. Sometimes old, worn-out quilts were used as the middle layer, or old, discarded men's suits were cut up and used. Cotton batting purchased in a store was used for many years in the early twentieth century. Polyester batting bought either in packages or from a giant roll dates from the 1970s.

- ◆ **Backing.** The bottom part of a quilt that sandwiches the batting with the quilt top. It is often considered the "wrong" side of the quilt.

- ◆ **Binding.** The folding of the backing or a long strip of bias fabric that finishes off the edge of a quilt.

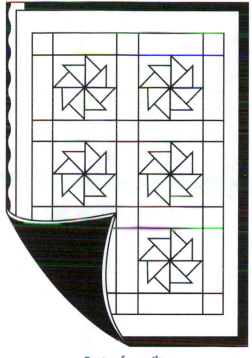

Parts of a quilt.

Now you know about all the parts of the quilt top. Let's start planning which designs to create for your quilt.

The Least You Need to Know

◆ Quilt tops are either pieced or appliquéd.

◆ Pieced quilts are usually geometric or angular, while appliqué can be rounded or picture a specific object.

◆ Quilt layouts are categorized by the manner in which the quilt tops are assembled: whole cloth, medallion, or block to an all over design.

◆ A quilt top can be made up of blocks, lattices, and borders.

In This Chapter

- ◆ Understanding the decisions you will make in planning your quilt

- ◆ Choosing a quilt based on your ability, likes, and use

- ◆ Is machine piecing for you?

- ◆ Hints on machine piecing

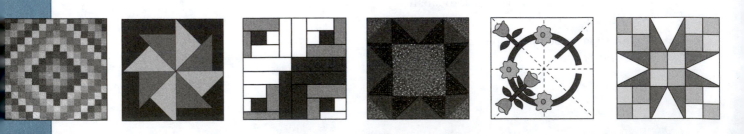

Chapter 3

Let's Plan Your Quilt

Now that we've learned about quilt blocks and quilt construction, it's time for you to start your plans like our ancestors did. Novice quilters wonder—how do you start? What do you consider? How do you undertake such an overpowering task? My recommendation is to start small: a pillow, baby quilt, or lap quilt. With the block method, you can add or subtract squares to suit your needs and ambitions. Several years ago, one of my "Quilting Ladies" wanted to make placemats, but once she started she liked piecing so much she ended up making a queen-sized quilt. Quilts can grow right before your eyes.

As I grew to love quilting, I envisioned hundreds of quilts, and I wanted to make them all. Unfortunately, most of us can't devote 10 hours a day to quilting. When I started a project, I seemed to forget my housework, cooking meals, my family, and so on. The sewing machine seemed to be the answer. I was able to produce quilts at a quicker pace and keep the rest of my life together, which made my family happy. Many of the quilt projects in this book are specifically made for machine piecing, to give you a jump start. It's your choice: machine or hand piecing.

This book will make your life easier. Most of the planning is done for you, the templates, instructions and fabric requirements are all included. However, make the quilt your way; these quilts can be changed. Colors, the actual type of blocks, and size are all your choice.

This is where we really begin!

There are several factors to think about before choosing your quilt. First of all:

What Do You Want to Make?

Almost everyone wants to make a bed quilt to show off their workmanship. If you are a novice quilter, I do not suggest this. A quilt of that size may take you more than a year to complete, which can be very discouraging. I suggest working on a project that you can finish quickly. You need the positive reinforcement of accomplishment—a pillow, a wall hanging, or a *lap quilt* are perfect small projects. Check out the easy projects in the back of this book.

Quilt Talk

A **lap quilt** is a small quilt put together with six to nine blocks; the finished size is usually between 36 × 60 to 60 × 60 inches square. I like to drape one over a sofa or at the base of the bed and use them when I'm cold.

A quilt isn't meant only for the bed. Here is an example of a beginner's Sampler quilt made by Marie Varner. She uses it as a wall hanging in her living room.

Who Is Going to Use This Quilt?

Is the quilt for you? What style of pattern do you like: geometric or curvy? Is there any quilt pattern that you just love and must try to make? All these are questions to ask yourself.

Another important question is: If the quilt is a gift, who is it for? Will the quilt be used or abused?

If you are making a baby quilt, you have to be sure to use fabrics that are durable and totally washable. Don't make something that is so difficult and time consuming that when something happens to it (they are children you know), you will not be offended. And you do want to give it to the child while they are still a child. One of my ladies is making a train-patterned quilt. It was supposed to be done for a boy's first birthday; unfortunately, his second birthday is in two months and she is still working!

Another question to ask is if the person receiving the quilt will appreciate it. It is very annoying to spend a year on a project and then see the quilt folded in a closet or being used as a blanket with people sitting on it at a picnic. A simple machine-made design may be the answer.

Will Your Quilt Be the Center of Attention?

Look around the room your quilt will live in. Do you want it to be the focal point or blend in with the surroundings? Bright dynamics colors will ensure that everyone's eyes will be on your masterpiece. Check out the room décor. Scrap quilts look great in a Colonial house but not in a Danish Modern. You may want to carry out a motif that is already in the room. If you have a flowery wallpaper, you also may want your quilt to have appliquéd flowers. Blend or contrast, it's your decision.

Aren't your eyes drawn to Mari Garcia's patriotic flag quilt?

Machine or Hand? What's Your Choice?

Many of the projects in this book are put together by hand piecing, but some use machine techniques. I love the whole tactile process of working with fabrics, marking, cutting, pinning, and the careful stitches of seaming and quilting. I enjoy sitting and piecing quilt blocks while my husband watches his sports on television. I feel I've accomplished so much and yet can spend time with him. There is a relaxing pleasure in the joy of working with fabrics.

Nevertheless, you may not find hand piecing as enjoyable as I do, or may be impatient; if so, then machine piecing is for you. When I think of all the quilts I want to make, and when I'm rushed for time, I turn to my sewing machine. Machine piecing and quilting is much faster, but you need to have a good relationship with your sewing machine. Accuracy is difficult unless you are experienced. I'd like to show you several tricks for using the machine because certain quilts are more conducive to machine stitching. So read Chapter 12 and decide.

Can you rev up your sewing machine and start sewing? I think so.

The Least You Need to Know

◆ Decide who will use the quilt and how it will be used.

◆ Machine piecing is a quick way that quilts can be made.

◆ Decide what your preferences are and whether you want the quilt to be the focal point or not.

In This Chapter

- ◆ Survey pattern designs and choose a pattern equal to your abilities

- ◆ How to use a color wheel

- ◆ Understand how colors affect one another as well as your emotions

- ◆ Learn how to choose pleasing color combinations

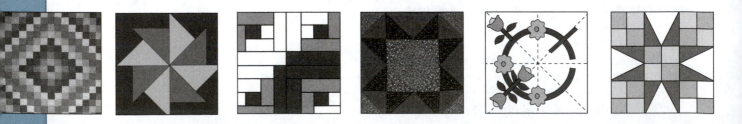

Chapter 4

Now to the Drawing Board

I hope you are sitting at home, starting to plan your actual quilt. The past and present are meeting. Years ago, women traded quilt designs with their friends, or bought them from newspapers. Now our world is slightly different, we still can get patterns from friends, but there are also books (like this one), quilt magazines from all over the world, and even the Internet. (Quilt chat rooms are very popular.) Our drawing board is diverse.

One of the considerations in planning quilts is deciding on the specific quilt design or pattern. You can choose either individual blocks or an overall design. Then comes a roadblock for some quilters: how to color in these designs. The designs and patterns in this book are varied. Some are easy, others are challenging. There are individual blocks for Sampler Quilts and some overall designs. Some are sewn by hand while others are machine pieced. The shading of these designs with your favorite color schemes can sometimes be scary. I hope this chapter will help.

Quilt Designs

There are several quilt projects in this book designed for beginners, and other projects that are for quilters that want more of a challenge. I feel that novice quilters should start with a Sampler quilt. Look at the pictures in the color section. There are several Sampler quilts so you can appreciate the variety of blocks.

Since each block is different, you can start with easy ones and then choose blocks that are more difficult as you gain confidence. There is a challenge in combining a variety of different patterns and colors.

Quilt Talk

A Sampler quilt combines blocks of different types of patterns. Each block is often framed by a strip of fabric called a "lattice" or "sashing." Some blocks are easy; others are more advanced and showcase the quilter's expertise.

Easy Pieced Quilt Blocks

12-inch block

◆ Churn Dash
◆ Ohio Star

◆ Eight Point Star
    Dutchman's Puzzle Variation
    Old Maid's Puzzle
    Windmill

16-inch block

◆ Amish Square in a Square

Don't Get Stuck!

When a beginner makes a Sampler quilt, make sure the block sizes are all the same. It's difficult to match up a 12-inch block to a 16-inch one without a lot of planning.

Churn Dash

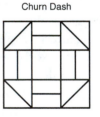

Ohio Star

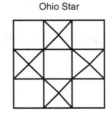

Dutchman's Pinwheel

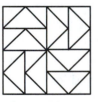

Eight Point Star

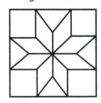

Amish Square in a Square

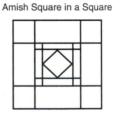

Windmills

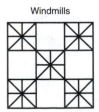

Old Maid's Puzzle

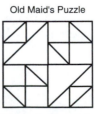

Easy blocks have fewer pieces and easy construction.

Pieced Blocks—Up for the Challenge?

As you examine these challenging pieced blocks on this page, you can see that the blocks are divided into many, smaller pieces and the designs are more intricate. Many of the blocks have special cutting and piecing know-how so you will have to pay special attention to them.

12-inch block

- ◆ Blazing Star
- ◆ Crazy Ann
- ◆ Pinwheel
- ◆ Rolling Star
- ◆ Starflower
- ◆ Virginia Star
- ◆ Waterwheel

Appliqué Patterns and Specialty Blocks

Traditionally, appliquéd blocks have separate pieces of fabric that, when positioned over a base fabric in a specific pattern, form a picture or design. These blocks below start easy but become increasingly difficult, depending on the size of the appliquéd pieces. The last block, the Flower Block, has a pieced base and *Yo-yos* appliquéd onto it.

12-inch square

- ◆ Hearts and Squares
- ◆ Dresden Plate
- ◆ American Wreath
- ◆ Yo-Yo Flower Block

Blazing Star

Rolling Star

Old Tippecanoe

Pinwheel

Crazy Ann

Star Flower

Virginia Star

Water Wheel

These blocks will challenge your cutting and piecing ability.

Hearts and Blocks

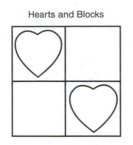

Dresden Plate

Stripped Heart

Trip Around the World

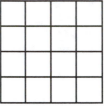

American Wreath

Yo-Yo Flower Block

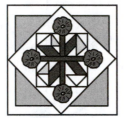

Appliquéd and specialty blocks.

Log Cabin

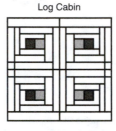

You can sew these in a "sec" with your sewing machine.

Quilt Talk

A **Yo-yo** is made from small, circular pieces of fabric that have been gathered around the outside edge. The gathering thread is pulled to form a flat circle of fabric that resembles a Yo-yo.

Start Your Machines

The last category of patterns in this book are for those people who love and know how to use their sewing machine. These machine-pieced quilts have special shortcuts that will help you finish in a jiffy.

- Striped Heart Quilt
- Log Cabin
- Trip Around the World

Color—Your Wheel of Fortune

You have seen the linear patterns and designs. You have chosen your pattern that you want to begin to make. Now the next big decision is upon you, and that one may be quite intimidating. The design may be perfectly pieced, but the color is what first catches your eye. It is probably the most important element of a quilt. Whenever my class goes to a quilt show, our eyes are always pulled to the quilt with vibrant colors or a pleasing color combination. Once we are closer to the quilt, we start to notice the patterns, designs, and techniques. The colors give us an impression that lasts. (Even if the pattern is not one of your favorites, you may like a quilt because of a pleasing color combination.)

Colors—They're Emotional

Colors affect our emotions. Attractive color combinations make us happy. Let's examine the facts and the characteristics of color relationships. Scientists found that the colors of the spectrum are at their strongest intensity or brightness. Maybe that is why rainbows are so dramatic and pleasing and make everyone feel happy. There are three primary colors: red, yellow, and blue. Yellow, orange, and red colors are considered warm. What sunny, happy colors—they seem to explode right out at you. A color scheme using these colors will brighten up a dark room. Now look at the colors green, blue, and purple. The difference is amazing—now calm and tranquility prevail. When these colors are combined in a quilt, the warm colors advance at you while the cool colors recede. Knowing this will help you choose your colors and their amounts of fabric for your quilt.

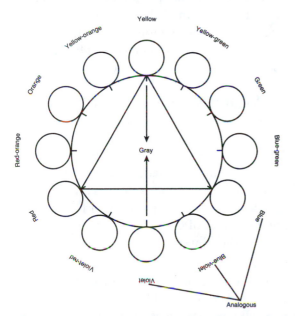

The primary colors form a triangle within the wheel. Arrows show complementary colors positioned opposite each other, and analagous colors that are next to each other.

Do You Have Values? Color Values That Is!

Although there are 12 colors on the color wheel, there are thousands of colors that can be blended by mixing colors with a neutral. A neutral can be either white, black, or gray.

With respect to *values*, everything is relative. A range of color values add contrast and depth to your quilt. We need to look at a color in comparison to those around it. Fabrics can be divided into lights (*tints*), mediums (*hues*), or darks (*shades*).

A light color may actually become a medium tone if a white or lighter color is introduced. Our eyes perceive differences when the background color changes. Take a piece of medium-colored green fabric and place it on top of a white fabric. The colors pop out at you. On the other hand, if you place the same medium-colored fabric onto a black fabric, the black sinks away from you.

Quilt Talk

Hue is the name of a specific color, for example, navy blue or magenta. **Value** is the lightness or darkness of a color. There are either **tints** or **shades**. Tint is a hue that contains more light or white. Pink is a tint of red. A shade is a hue that has been blended with black or a darker color. Cranberry is a shade of red.

Even more mystifying is the effect of complementary colors. When these colors are put next to each other, each color seems brighter. Think of a tree with red apples on it. The apples jump out at you. Red and green colors complement each other and the brightness of each is brought out.

Marsha Oakes monochromatic quilt has shades of
blue, giving it a soft, soothing affect.

Quilting Bee

The complementary colors of blue
and orange may be too strong for you,
but peach and colonial blue are beautiful
together. Red and green may look too much
like Christmas, but a forest green quilt with
cranberry flowers can be used all year.

Dominant or Contrasting: Blending It All Together

Now that we have a color sense and have learned
about the color wheel, color schemes, moods
and symbolism, tints, and shades and values, it's
time to choose your colors. Decide on a color
scheme, or find a picture in a catalogue or book
that appeals to you. I usually begin with the
quilt's surroundings to start this process. Because
the walls of my bedroom are blue and the rug is
cranberry, that's probably a good color combination to start with. I need to decide on the
dominant or main color. Do I want the quilt
more blue or more cranberry? I chose blue. That
was my dominant color. It should be found in
almost every quilt block, and possibly also in
the lattice and the border. The contrasting color

will then be cranberry. The contrast color is
used as an accent and should be in most of the
patches and the corner blocks.

Don't Get Stuck!

Be sure to choose a color scheme
that you want to live with for a while.
I have several quilts in avocado green and
gold that were popular in the '70s. As a
beginner, by the time I finished the quilts,
the color combination was passé. So you
have to either learn to like it or learn to quilt
faster!

Now you have both ends of the color
scheme—the dominant and contrasting colors.
When purchasing your fabric, choose a large
printed fabric that includes both of those colors. It could be floral, paisley, or an abstract
design. I call this the *blender fabric*. The blender
fabric creates a harmonious bridge between the
dominant and contrasting colors. The most
important blender fabric is one that has both of
the colors from your color scheme. I was able
to find a floral fabric that contained cranberry
and blue. It was a medium shade of the colors
and blended both perfectly. You will notice that
fabric manufacturers have developed patterns
with quilters in mind, having coordinated combinations of popular colors in the same material.
Don't forget to choose a variety of fabrics with
different values of each color in your color
scheme to add interest to your quilt.

Find blender fabrics in different values. Some
fabrics should appear as a tint or lighter color,
while a darker-colored blender fabric will give
you a full range of values. In my cranberry-and-
blue quilt, I was able to find fabrics that blended
together but gave the quilt variety in colors. I
started by choosing a fabric with an off-white
background and small navy-blue-and-cranberry

flowers, giving the impression of a light tint. Then I found a navy fabric with an overall design of small white flowers and leaves. Even though this fabric had a navy background, it was a medium value because it contained so much white. When you squint at the fabrics you can see the values. Lastly, looking through the fabric store, I found a cranberry fabric with pin dots (small dots about an inch apart), which I used for my dark color.

At least one fabric should contain your dominant and contrasting colors. Other fabrics should harmonize with your color scheme but do not have to contain all the colors. When these fabrics are put next to one another, they should give you a range of values. Get your value out of your colors!

Now that you have thought about your color scheme, the dominant color, contrasting color, a blender fabric, and approximately three fabrics in a variety of values from tints to shades, it's time to move to the next step: How much to buy?

The Least You Need to Know

- ◆ Know your ability and choose a quilt design that you will be able to finish.
- ◆ Sampler quilts are the best learning experience.
- ◆ Colors can be warm or cool and evoke different emotions from us.
- ◆ Color your quilts with a variety of light values (tints) or darkness (shades) to provide contrast and depth.
- ◆ There should by a dominant color, contrasting color, and blender colors in your quilt.

In This Part

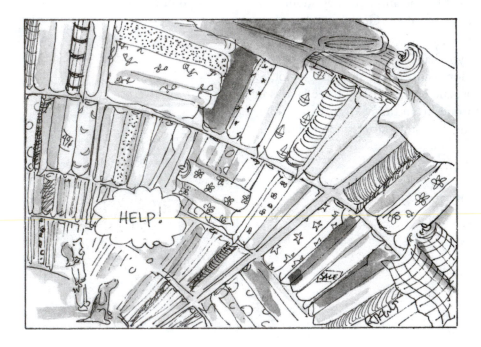

Part 2

Get Set—What You Need to Start

Now that you have a general idea of the type of quilt you want to make, it's time to go shopping. Before you go, let's take a moment to talk about what you need. Unlike pioneer women who did not have the advantage of all our craft and quilt stores jam-packed with supplies and fabrics, we can easily go into shopping overload. If you have trouble making decisions, these next chapters will help.

Some supplies can be found around your house. A few will be essential for beginning your project; others can wait until later, when you have a handle on quilting.

"Help!" This is what most beginners say when it's time to buy fabric. Put your mind at ease. Suggestions on types of fabric and tips on what to avoid will make your shopping easier. To make it even easier, exact fabric amounts are provided with each specific project, but when you branch out and make your own quilts, I'll furnish you with a chart to help you estimate the amount of fabric for each part of your new design.

In This Chapter

- ◆ Finding the basic supplies you really, really need
- ◆ Choosing the materials that best help you
- ◆ Super cool gadgets to spark creativity
- ◆ Keeping it all together

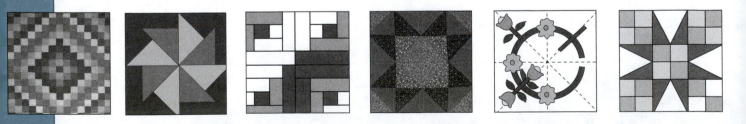

Chapter 5

Tools of the Trade

Most quilters collect more supplies than they really need. I have many ladies in my quilting class who bring in new gadgets each week. Some are good, some are bad, and some are useless.

This chapter is about the supplies that every quilter needs in order to make a quilt. Some of the items listed are necessities. But because everyone has different preferences and abilities, I will give you many options and suggestions. Some supplies you will need right now, some you will need at a later time, and others you may want but will never need.

We will start our supply list with things you can find around your own home, then get into the materials that you will need to purchase in a craft store or specialty quilt store. When you go to a quilt store that sells supplies, do not be intimidated by the multitude of "stuff" that is displayed. Start with the basics. Do not be encouraged or persuaded to buy something that a beginner may not need. As you work on your quilt, you will discover what will help *you*.

The Necessities: Supplies You Need Right Now

There are many things listed below that you will be able to find right around your house. Look at the list and see what you can find before you go out to the store. Some things may seem very strange but I will address each item and explain it.

- ◆ Pencils: number 2 lead and a variety of colored pencils
- ◆ Ruler: 12 or 18 inches long
- ◆ Straight pins
- ◆ Paper scissors

- Fabric scissors
- Quilting needles: betweens and embroidery needles
- Quilting and regular thread
- Poster board or oak tag paper
- Rubber cement
- Medium sandpaper
- Seam ripper
- Thimbles

Pencils

Number 2 lead pencil: Quilters use this type of pencil to draft *templates* and trace these patterns onto the wrong side of the fabric. Do not use a softer pencil because you will be forever sharpening it. This pencil can also be used to lightly mark your quilt designs onto the right side of the quilt top.

Quilt Talk

A **template** is a pattern of the exact size of each design element, usually made with cardboard or plastic. A block may have several shapes of templates incorporated into the square; for example, the Ohio Star block is composed of two templates— a square and a small triangle.

Colored pencils: There are many fabrics that are dark in color (navy, red, and especially black) or have a design so busy that a pencil mark does not show. If this is the case, turn your fabric to the wrong side and try whichever colored pencil shows the best. Colored pencils are also helpful in planning the colors of your quilt blocks.

Rulers

I usually have a variety of rulers that I use. The best all-around ruler is one that is see-through plastic, 12 or 18 inches, and has parallel lines running the length, marking every quarter inch. This will be very useful in marking long seam allowances on your fabric and testing to see if your borders or lattices are even. I sometimes also like to use a small plastic 6-inch ruler because it is easier to maneuver around the templates. There are other rulers that are optional and will be discussed later.

Straight Pins

I use regular old straight pins (1-inch long pins used by dressmakers) when I am piecing my patches. For pin-basting your quilt top we will discuss other options (see Chapter 18).

Paper Scissors

Paper scissors are necessary when we make the templates. Templates are made from cardboard and sandpaper, or a plastic sheet. If you use good fabric scissors on the template material, they will not be good for long.

Quilting Bee

My favorite scissors are Ginghers, and they can be purchased at most quilt stores or through dressmaker catalogues.

Fabric Scissors

There are many different types of scissors or dressmaker shears that you can purchase. Fabric scissors are sharper than paper scissors and are usually made of lighter-weight steel. Prices vary greatly. As a beginner, do not buy really expensive scissors. Eventually, if you become addicted to quilting, you will need scissors that cut through the fabric easily—when working on large projects I've had blisters pop up on my fingers as my scissors got dull. There are also scissors that can cut through several layers of fabric at a time.

A pair of small thread-cutting scissors is also useful. The best practice is to hang them on a ribbon around your neck. It makes them easier to find while you are working.

Bent dressmaker shears with a protective nylon sheath and thread nippers are your best bet for scissors.

Needles

Quilters use "between" needles to piece their projects. A between needle is short and has a small round eye. The larger the number, the smaller the needle size. Size 10 is smaller than size 6. I had one student who said that compared to quilting needles, her needle was like a crowbar!

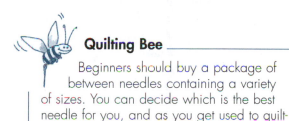

Quilting Bee

Beginners should buy a package of between needles containing a variety of sizes. You can decide which is the best needle for you, and as you get used to quilting you may go for the smaller size.

When you become experienced, there are also quilting needles that are even shorter than betweens. These are specifically used for quilting. Quilters have learned that the smaller the needle, the smaller and more durable the quilting stitches. Occasionally you will need to use embroidery needles when basting your quilt together, decorating your appliqué block with embroidery stitches, or tying your quilt (sometimes knots can be used instead of quilting stitches to hold together the three layers).

Here is a package of quilting betweens size 8, which is a medium-size needle.

Quilting Bee

Buy beeswax that is in a holder, because the holder will make it easier for you to run the thread through the beeswax and will keep it neat and clean.

Thread

For piecing or quilting, use a cotton-covered polyester quilting thread. This thread is superior to the 100 percent polyester thread that is usually on sale. Quilt thread is heavier and does not tangle or knot when used. Try to purchase a color that blends well with your fabrics. For example, if your background fabric is muslin, purchase a thread that is ecru; if your background is white, use a white thread; or if the background is navy, buy a navy quilting thread. If you can't match the color with a quilting thread, you can use a regular cotton-covered polyester thread. In order to keep this thread from tangling, run each length of thread through beeswax.

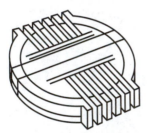

This container of beeswax makes it easy to run your thread through it.

Poster Board or Oak Tag?

You can purchase poster board or oak tag paper at stationery, craft, or five-and-dime stores. This weight of cardboard is the best for making templates. I've even used gift boxes in a pinch, just don't use thick cardboard because it is difficult to cut accurately.

Rubber Cement

Rubber cement is used to make templates and for gluing together the poster board and sandpaper. Do not use white school glue or craft glue because it makes your templates ripple and they will not dry flat.

Sandpaper

Not all templates need sandpaper, but it helps beginners trace around the pattern accurately. Buy a medium-weight sandpaper that is approximately 8×10 inches in size. This will be used for the backing of your templates.

Don't Get Stuck!

One of my quilting students has a problem because her dog loves to chew her leather thimble, so she has to buy several! Keep them out of harm's way and

Seam Ripper

I hate to even mention ripping seams, but everyone makes mistakes, and seam rippers remove your boo-boos quickly and safely. A seam ripper is a small pen-like tool that allows you to put a sharp point under the "bad" stitches, carefully breaking the thread. Look for a seam ripper that is a medium size. When a seam ripper is too small, it gets lost in the shuffle. If it is too large, it is harder to manipulate under the line of stitches.

Thimbles

Most quilters or seamstresses insist on using a thimble. A lot of people do not like the needle pricking their finger every time they take a stitch. Unfortunately, I have never felt comfortable wearing one. Many quilters wear a thimble on the third finger of the hand that holds the needle. Some wear thimbles on both hands. There are many types of thimbles. The most common is the metal thimble. Try one out and see how it feels. If it is uncomfortable, there are newer types of finger guards available. One very popular type is a leather thimble.

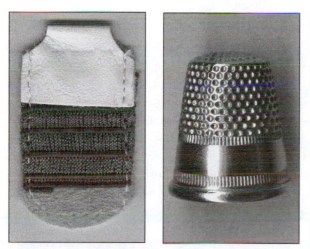

These are both thimbles. The right is the traditional, metal thimble and the left is a leather finger guard.

Things You Will Need Later

You will need the items already on this list once your quilt top is completed. You have pieced or appliquéd, then set the blocks together and framed them out with borders. Certain supplies will be necessary for joining the three layers of the quilt together. Never purchase your batting until the face of the quilt is complete—you may get carried away and your quilt plan may grow.

◆ Batting: The thimbles, types, and specific amounts of *batting* needed for your projects will be discussed in Chapter 18.

◆ Marking equipment: Don't buy these yet!

◆ Quilt stencils.

◆ Quilt hoop: There are many types and everyone has different dexterity and preferences. Hoops will be discussed in Chapter 19.

Quilt Talk

Batting is the middle or filling part of the sandwich that makes up the quilt. It is the material that makes a quilt puffy and adds the warmth.

Marking and quilting equipment will be discussed in detail in Chapter 19. Sometimes you have to see the finished quilt top to decide on the type of quilting you want and the pattern of the quilting stencil. As you learn to handle fabrics, you will discover what equipment will work for you. There are different types of hoops. The hoop is necessary to hold the quilt in place and smooth while you quilt. I suggest purchasing your hoop after you are more experienced, and by the time you're ready to quilt, you will be experienced!

Optional Supplies That Are Neat

Through my years of experience I've found the items on the "neat" list to be helpful. They are not really necessary for a beginner to own, but if you become a serious quilter, these tools and supplies may assist you with certain projects.

◆ Graph paper: four squares to the inch

◆ Quilter's quarter

◆ Rotary cutter

◆ Cutting mat with grids

◆ Ruler with a lip

◆ T-square ruler

◆ Quilting pins

Now for an in-depth discussion of each gadget, and how you use it.

Graph Paper

Graph paper is helpful when making patterns or templates that have right angles: squares, rectangles, and triangles. It will help you see if your template is true to shape. Be sure to purchase graph paper that has four grids to the inch. It is easier to compute enlarging or transferring patterns. One-fourth increments are easier to calculate than one-fifth inch grids. Try to fold anything into five sections!

Quilting Bee

Be sure to purchase a quilter's quarter that is made of colored plastic. I have searched many an hour trying to find a clear quilter's quarter in my sewing supplies.

Quilter's Quarter

A quilter's quarter is a ¼-inch × ¼-inch × 8-inch piece of plastic that is used to mark the ¼-inch seam allowance on your fabric. This tool makes marking very quick and accurate, so beginners like to use it.

Don't Get Stuck!

Be careful, rotary blades are very sharp. Be sure to always close your cutter as soon as you've finished each and every cut.

Rotary Cutter

A rotary cutter is a great tool for cutting straight lines on your fabric. It looks very similar to a pizza cutter. If you are very careful, it can cut through several layers of fabric at a time. The rotary cutter is used mainly when you are making a quilt that is strip-pieced by machine and can be used when you are cutting lattices and borders. One drawback: You can't cut on curves, and you always need a ruler to guide the rotary blade.

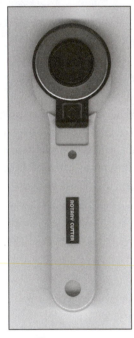

Rotary cutter.

Cutting Mat with Grids

Rotary cutters should always be used with a cutting mat that is "self healing." The plastic mat is strong enough to not be damaged by the sharp blade. These mats are marked with ¼-inch hash marks on the sides and also 1-inch grids over the whole surface. There should also be two bias diagonals over the grid as well. Buy a mat that is at least 18 × 24 inches. I have just discovered cutting mats that have a handle opening cut right into the plastic. It makes it easier to carry! You can even buy a cutting mat that rotates so you don't have to continually turn your fabric as you cut (I usually walk around the table).

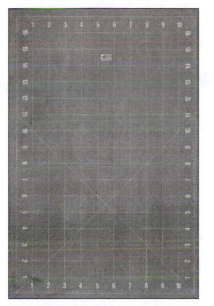

A self-healing cutting mat comes in a variety of sizes.

Ruler with a Lip

There are many see-through plastic rulers with grids that are heavy enough to withstand rotary cutters. Rulers come in all sizes and shapes, and the one you purchase will depend on the quilt you are making.

I personally like a plastic ruler with a lip for use with the rotary cutter. It has a clear plastic piece under the ruler that allows you to wedge it against the cutting mat so your cut is accurate. Some rulers even have markings for left handed use.

T-Square Ruler

A metal or heavy-duty plastic T-square is used for squaring off the patches.

Quilting Bee

Get on a list for a sewing and quilting supply catalogue. You are sure to find a gadget to help in your quilt making.

Quilting Pins

These pins are 1¼-inches long and have brightly colored heads. They are really great for pin-basting your quilt top, batting, and backing together, and many quilters feel they are a necessity when assembling a quilt.

Your Supplies: Get Them All Together

Quilters need to keep all their supplies in one place. There is nothing worse than running around your house looking for something. Many people use boxes to store their things. See-through plastic boxes with a lid are probably the most popular. I've also seen cigar boxes or unused pizza boxes filled with supplies going back and forth to class. I personally like fabric bags to hold my tools. You do have to keep certain things, like scissors, in a smaller bag to keep the sharp point from cutting the fabric. Be sure to hide your fabric scissors amongst your supplies so the rest of the family doesn't use them for cutting paper.

The Least You Need to Know

◆ Check over the supply list and look around your house before going shopping.

◆ Get all your necessary materials before starting your project.

◆ Experience piecing blocks before buying specialty gadgets.

◆ Keep all your supplies together.

In This Chapter

- ◆ Popular quilt sizes
- ◆ How to calculate the amount of fabric needed for a pattern piece
- ◆ Estimating fabric amounts for a particular part of a quilt
- ◆ Table for computing the amount of fabric to buy for an entire quilt

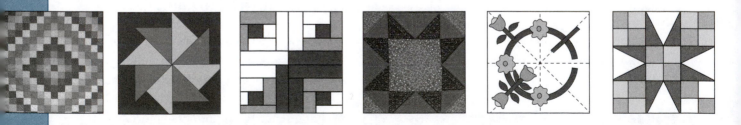

Chapter 6

Materially Speaking, How Much Do You Need?

In the Make It Your Way Project part, each quilt has all the fabric amounts listed for you. It makes it very easy—no muss, no fuss, no math. Eventually you will want to branch out and design and plan your own quilts or will want to change the size of one of the book's projects. If so, then this chapter will help you.

There are two theories in making a quilt:

◆ You can plan, plan, plan, and get all your fabrics before you actually start (which is the preferred method).

◆ Or let your quilt evolve as you go along.

One of my beginning students wanted to make four placemats. After constructing two patches, she was hooked and bought enough fabric for a lap quilt. A few weeks later, she decided to make a full-size quilt, so back to the store she went. At the end of the session, she had made a terrific full-size quilt top. This was a success story, but be warned: If you don't purchase enough fabric at the start, when you go back to get more, it's often gone! Let's figure out how much fabric you need before you get started.

This chapter is arranged in three sections. The first segment deals with quilt sizes. So get out your tape measure and calculate the exact size that you need. I still advise you to start small for your first project. In the second section, I'll show you a method of calculating fabric amounts for a specific pattern piece of a quilt pattern. If you are making a quilt with only one pattern, there may be hundreds of the same pattern piece. So it would be smart to be able to estimate how much fabric you will need to purchase. I'll explain how to make those calculations later.

The third section explains two ways to consider fabric amounts. I have developed a table showing how much fabric you will need to buy for your whole quilting project. You can also purchase material for a specific part of your quilt; for example, you may need to buy fabric just for the borders. If that is the case, I have a table to help you determine that amount. So let's start measuring and discovering how much fabric to buy.

Quilting Bee

Remember that a lattice is the fabric frame around each quilt block. It can also be called sashing. The corner squares are squares where the lattices meet, and the borders outline the entire quilt. If it is very wide, the border may be divided into a border A and B.

Your Quilt's Dimensions

It's important to know the size of a finished quilt. I had a student who made a twin-size quilt but it wasn't quite large enough. She had an antique bed that stood high off the floor, therefore the quilt was too short. Please don't let that happen to you. Choose a quilt size and check your dimensions carefully.

Lap Quilt

A lap quilt can have many purposes. It's a great size for a baby's crib quilt, for hanging on the wall, or, my favorite, for putting over your lap when you're cold.

- ◆ Finished size: 40 × 56 inches
- ◆ Six blocks (12-inch squares)
- ◆ Lattice: 3 inches wide
- ◆ Corner squares: 3 inches
- ◆ Border: 4 inches wide

Twin Size

- ◆ Mattress size: 39 × 75 inches
- ◆ Finished size: 68 × 94 inches
- ◆ 15 blocks (12-inch squares)

Full Size

- Mattress size: 52 × 75 inches
- Finished size: 80 × 103 inches
- 15 blocks (12-inch squares)
- Lattice: 4 inches wide
- Corner squares: 4 inches
- Border: 14 inches, broken down into 6 inches and 8 inches

Queen Size

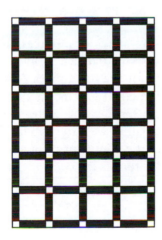

- Mattress size: 60 × 80 inches
- Finished size: 83 × 103 inches
- 24 blocks (12-inch squares)

- Lattice: 3 inches wide
- Corner squares: 3 inches
- Border: 10 inches wide

King Size

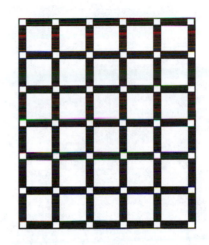

- Mattress size: 72 × 84 inches
- Finished size: 100 × 116 inches
- 30 blocks (12-inch square)
- Lattice: 4 inches wide
- Corner squares: 4 inches
- Border: 8 inches wide

Estimating Fabrics, or How Many Pieces Can I Get from a Yard?

There will come a time when you will have to calculate how much fabric you need to purchase for a quilt project. One quilt block may have many pattern pieces that fit together to make the 12-inch square. The following strategy will help you calculate the amount you need for each pattern piece in a quilt block. If you are creating a quilt that repeats one type of block, you will have many similar pattern pieces (for example, when making a Double Nine Patch lap quilt, pictured below). It has 4 four-inch squares of the dominant color and 4 four-inch squares of the accent color. Let's figure out how much fabric you will need of each fabric.

A Double Nine Patch lap quilt.

1. Count the number of pattern shapes you need for one block. Measure and add on the ¼-inch seam allowances to get the true size. (For each Double Nine Patch you need four 4½-inch squares of the dominant color and four 4½-inch squares of the accent color.)

2. Determine how many of these pattern pieces you will need for the entire quilt. (There are four squares of dominant colors in each block of the Double Nine Patch, and there are six blocks in the quilt, so you'll need 24 4½-inch squares.)

3. Measure the width of your fabric. Usually it's 44 inches.

4. Find out how many pattern pieces (with seam allowances added on) will fit across the fabric width. Divide the fabric width by the width of the pattern piece. (Forty-four inches divided by 4½ inches of the Double Nine Patch square is 9.7—but wait—you can only fit nine whole square pattern pieces in the width.)

5. To determine the length of fabric needed and how many rows needed to fit all the squares in, first divide the total number of pattern pieces by the number of squares that fit across the width of the fabric. (Remember, we need 24 squares for the lap quilt, and 24 divided by 9 is 2.6 rows. You'll have to allow for three whole rows of fabric.)

6. Then multiply that number of rows by the length of the pattern piece, including the seam allowance. (Multiplying the 4½ inches of the Double Nine Patch square by three rows yields 13½ inches.)

7. To figure out how many yards are needed, divide the total inches by 36 inches (for the yard). Add on a 4- or 5-inch "fudge factor" to allow for mistakes. (For the Double Nine Patch, 13½ inches are needed for the rows plus a 4-inch fudge factor to equal 17½ inches. So approximately 18 inches divided by 36 inches equals half a yard. You will need half a yard of the dominant color and half a yard for the accent color.)

See how many Double Nine Patch squares will fit on the fabric.

Do Your Math: Calculate the Right Amount

Now that we know the fabric yardage, you need to buy for a specific pattern piece or template of your quilt, let me show you how these amounts can be put together. There are ways that you lay out your patterns, dovetailing them with borders and lattices to save fabric. I try to use every scrap of my material. When we get to the chapter about cutting out the templates, I will show you some handy hints to reduce fabric waste. It is difficult to estimate the exact amount of fabric for a sampler quilt, because each patch is different. The following table gives you an educated guesstimate for fabric yardage. Backing and batting are not included, but will be discussed in Chapter 18.

Fabric Guesstimates to Purchase for Entire Project

Quilt Size	Color	What Is Included	Fabric Yardage*
Lap	Dominant	Blocks, lattice	2
	Contrast	Blocks, borders	2
	Blenders	Blocks (two fabrics)	½ each
		Blocks and corner squares (one fabric)	¼
	Background	Blocks	1
Twin	Dominant	Blocks, lattice, border B	4
	Contrast	Blocks, border A	3½
	Blenders	Blocks (two fabrics)	¾ each
		Blocks and corner squares (one fabric)	1
	Background	Blocks	1¾
Full	Dominant	Blocks, lattice, border B	4½
	Contrast	Blocks, border A	3¾
	Blenders	Blocks (two to four fabrics)	¾ each
		Blocks and corner squares (one fabric)	1
	Background	Blocks	1¾

continues

Fabric Guesstimates to Purchase for Entire Project (continued)

Quilt Size	Color	What Is Included	Fabric Yardage*
Queen	Dominant	Blocks, lattice, border B	5
	Contrast	Blocks, border A	4
	Blenders	Blocks (two fabrics)	1
		Blocks and corner squares (one fabric)	1⅛
	Background	Blocks	2
King	Dominant	Blocks, lattice, border B	5½
	Contrast	Blocks, border A	4½
	Blenders	Blocks (two fabrics)	1¼ each
		Blocks and corner squares (one fabric)	1¾
	Background	Blocks	2½

Remember, these are estimates—not everybody cuts wisely.

Sometimes it's necessary to know the amount of fabric to purchase for a specific part of your quilt. I can't tell you how many times I've had to go back to the store and buy a different fabric for a lattice or border because the one that I purchased wasn't quite right. Occasionally some quilters wait to see how the patches look before choosing the border fabric. If that happens to you, I've calculated how much fabric you'll need for each section of your quilt. So get out your pad and pencil and let's see what you'll need.

To use this table, locate the section of the quilt that you need to purchase fabric for, perhaps it's the lattice. Then look for the quilt size you are making, let's say full size, and determine the yardage you should buy.

In your quilt, you may have several blender fabrics. One blender fabric should include all the colors of your color scheme. Others will be of different values of the dominant and accent colors. You can have as many blenders as you want; I've suggested the minimum.

We've discovered three different methods of calculating fabric yardage. You can determine the fabric requirements of a specific pattern piece or template in a patch, figure out yardage for the entire quilt, or find the yardage amounts for one particular part of the quilt. Let's decide on your project, do the arithmetic, and calculate the amount you need to purchase before going to the store. Next stop—the fabric store.

Yardage for a Specific Part of a Quilt

Part	Quilt Size	Number Needed and Size	Yardage
Lattice	Lap	17 (3" × 12")	¾
	Twin	38 (3" × 12")	1½
	Full	38 (4" × 12")	2
	Queen	58 (3" × 12")	2¼
	King	71 (4" × 12")	2¾

Part	Quilt Size	Number Needed and Size	Yardage
Corner Squares	Lap	12 (3" × 3")	¼
	Twin	24 (3" × 3")	½
	Full	24 (4" × 4")	⅝
	Queen	35 (3" × 3")	⅝
	King	42 (4" × 4")	¾
Borders	Lap	4"	1
	Twin	10" or	2½
	A: 4"	1½	
	B: 6"	1¾	
	Full	14" or	3
	A: 6"	1¾	
	B: 8"	2½	
	Queen	10" or	3½
	A: 4"	1¾	
	B: 6"	2	
	King	8" or	3½
	A: 3"	2	
	B: 5"	2½	
Background Fabric	Lap	6 blocks	1
	Twin	15 blocks	1¾
	Full	15 blocks	1¾
	Queen	24 blocks	2
	King	30 blocks	2½
Blenders	Lap	2 or 3 fabrics	½–¾ of each
	Twin	3 fabrics	¾–1 of each
	Full	3 to 5 fabrics	¾–1 of each
	Queen	3 to 5 fabrics	1 of each
	King	3 to 5 fabrics	1½ of each

The Least You Need to Know

◆ Know the dimensions of the finished size of the quilt.

◆ Measure the width of the fabric in order to calculate the number of templates that will fit.

◆ Check the charts and plan the amount of fabric needed, but remember, you may need more.

◆ Be realistic—start small.

In This Chapter

- Understanding the type of fabric appropriate for making quilts

- Knowing which fabrics to avoid

- Choosing fabrics with variety in scale and pattern

- Choosing fabric to blend in with your color scheme

- Determining the best places to purchase fabrics

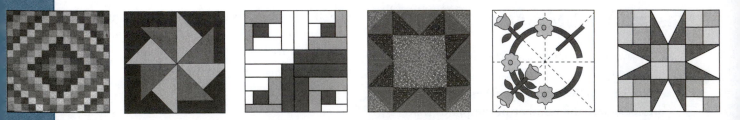

Chapter 7

Time to Purchase Your Fabric

Every quilter accumulates a stash of fabrics. Your leftovers will grow with each project. After quilting for 25 years, I have a great fabric collection. One of my students bought me a bumper sticker that said, "The quilter who dies with the most fabric wins." Actually, everyone in my class seems to be vying for that title.

Purchasing the appropriate fabric for your project can be intimidating, but this chapter sets out guidelines to follow to make it easier. Today we are fortunate to have a variety of sources to obtain fabric. We take fabric for granted, while our ancestors used their fabric with reverence, using every scrap. Let's start our modern-day quest for the perfect fabric, and you may become a "fabriholic," too.

What Type of Fabric?

Without a doubt, the best type of fabric for beginners to use is 100 percent cotton. Cotton has been proven through the test of time to be easy to work with and also durable. The material shouldn't ravel or stretch, since these characteristics make it difficult to work with. Your fabric should be colorfast and washable. To check out your fabric, look at the end of the *bolt* in the store.

Synthetic fabrics, such as polyester, are more difficult to control. The fibers themselves are slippery and stretchy, and the cloth frays easily—three very problematic factors. Many quilters will use polyester fabrics when the fibers are blended with cotton. Make sure there is an equal or greater percentage of cotton to polyester. The fabric should be called cotton/polyester, not polyester/cotton. The end of the bolt will state the exact percentage of cotton to polyester, so be sure to look. You can also buy fabric from precut yardage found folded on tables in many stores; but be sure to ask a salesperson for the fabric's fiber content.

Quilt Talk _____

A **bolt** is the fabric that is rolled around a cardboard base. The end of the bolt has a great deal of information: fiber content, colorfastness, finish (permanent press), and, of course, the price.

There are certain fabrics that beginners should avoid. Knits, corduroys, ginghams, stripes, and fabrics with _nap_ or one-way designs are all materials that are difficult to handle. Fabrics with tulips all standing in a row are just more complicated to cut and sew together into blocks. If you are not careful, some tulips will be on their sides, upside down, or if you are lucky, they will be standing up straight.

Quilt Talk _____

Nap has nothing to do with sleeping. It's the short, fuzzy ends of fibers on the surface of cloth. The nap usually falls in one direction, as it does on velvet. When you look at velvet one way it's one color, but turn it around and the color darkens depending on the way the fibers are brushed. I extend this definition to include patterns with one-way designs, such as tulips all in a row.

Even though I tell you to avoid these fabrics, quilters do make quilts using these fabrics with great success. I just feel that beginners should stick with basic cotton. Slippery satins and napped velvets are used beautifully in crazy quilts. Stripes can be extremely effective as borders, or specially cut in your patches, if you know how to "fussy cut" them. It takes experience and extra planning to work with fabrics that aren't cotton or that have special cutting needs.

Where to Get Your Fabric

Where do you get your fabric? There are plenty of ways to acquire your material. Of course, the best place for a beginner to go is to a fabric store that specializes in quilting fabric. The shopkeepers are only too anxious to help beginners plan their quilts. I have a favorite fabric store where the staff helps you choose the fabric, cuts swatches from each piece and pins it on a sheet of paper, and lists where you will use it. Now that is service. Quilt shows offer great selections of fabrics and even have special lengths of fabrics called _fat quarters_, used just for small accents in your quilt.

Quilt Talk _____

A **fat quarter** is one quarter of a yard of fabric. However, instead of the salesperson cutting ¼ yard the normal way across the width of the fabric (9 inches × 44 inches), she cuts the yard in half lengthwise and then across the width (18 inches × 22 inches). These pieces are great because you can fit larger pattern templates on them.

It's so much fun going to quilt shows and seeing all the booths with new gadgets and fabrics. Many merchants have fabrics that are specially dyed and bundled into coordinated fabrics. That really makes it easier to purchase your material.

Now for some unconventional ways to get fabric. There are catalogues that sell supplies and fabrics, so you can buy from your own home. I love to feel the fabric, so I usually don't use catalogues to buy fabrics. They do have an assortment of selections, and the quality is top-notch. When you need small amounts of a fabric, it's fun to have a swap with your friends.

Garage sales and rummage sales are also good sources for fabric, although unfortunately you won't know the fiber content in most cases.

Lastly, before you go fabric shopping, look around your house to see what you already have. Remember you can use fabric from old projects or garments as long as the fabric is cotton and is the right weight.

Quilting Bee

A quilter went shopping for fabric at a rummage sale at her church and saw a table of old clothes. She knew shirts are a great weight for quilting fabric, so she purchased some. When she brought them home, her husband remarked that they looked familiar. Upon examination, they noticed the dry cleaner's marking with their name on the collar! She had bought back her husband's shirts!

Put Your Fabric on a Scale, Then Do a Background Check

There are very few quilts that are created from only solid fabrics. There needs to be patterning to make your quilt visually interesting. Let's examine how you can add variety to your fabrics. One of the most important dimensions, besides the color value of a fabric, is the scale of the design. Prints that are all the same size are dull and boring. Little calico prints are nice in small doses but choosing five calicos of all the same design is monotonous. You should choose small-, medium-, and large-size prints for your quilt. Pin dots and little flowers are examples of small-scale prints—I've even bought fabrics with little spools of thread. Small-scale material appears almost

solid. Large-size prints have motifs of 3 or 4 inches in size, and the large design patterns can be an overall floral or paisley or any other large figure.

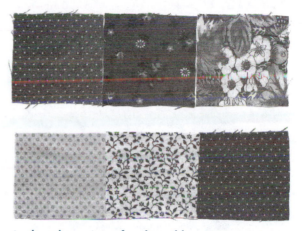

Look at the variety of scale and how it is more interesting than fabric with a one-size scale.

Look at the motif of the fabric and keep in mind who will use the quilt. One of my students spent all her time making patches for a baby quilt. When her quilt top was completed, she found a really cute, colorful, frog fabric for the backing. Of course her nephew loves the back of the quilt, not the front that she toiled over. You can see that fabric patterns are a crucial consideration when buying fabric for your quilt.

There is one more important factor in purchasing your fabric, and that is the background of a fabric. The background or ground color of the material is the hue on which the design is placed. For example, a fabric may have red and pink hearts on a white background, or you may have red and white hearts on a pink color. Same colors, different fabric appearance. Be sure that the background coordinates with all your fabrics. For example, if all of your fabric motifs but one are on an ecru background, a white one will stick out like a sore thumb. The value of the background hue will help blend with your other fabrics.

Blending Your Fabric Together: Dominant and Contrasting

Now it's time to select your fabric. Most fabric stores have their cottons, many times advertised as *calico*, in one section with all similar hues arranged together, almost like a rainbow.

Quilt Talk

The term **calico** today is used to describe quilt fabrics that are 100 percent cotton or cotton/polyester blends. At one time, calico pertained to a process of printing designs on a cotton fabric by using a roller. The patterns were usually small florals.

I start by going to the row that has the dominant color I'm looking for. Let's say I've chosen a color scheme of red and blue, with blue being the dominant color. I first try to find a fabric that blends all the colors of my color scheme—in other words, red and blue. It should be in a large-scale overall pattern. This is the blender fabric.

Scraps and Pieces

Be sure the blender fabric is really the color you want. Many times beginners are so close to the fabric that they see one color, but from afar it may appear a different hue. If the fabric design is red and blue flowers with green leaves, be sure the fabric gives a red and blue look, not green. Do what I call the "squint method." Stand back from the fabric bolt, look away, then turn back and squint at it. The first impression of color is how it will appear in your quilt.

Once this blender fabric has been chosen, I then pull out bolts of the dominant- and contrasting-colored fabrics that coordinate with the blender fabric. Next, decide on a lighter or darker value of the dominant and contrasting colors. That brings your fabric total to five, which is perfect for beginners. Lean your bolts of fabric against a wall, one next to another. Step back and do the squint method to evaluate your fabrics. Is there variety in the values of light and darkness of the fabrics? Do you have a good mixture of patterns and scale of designs? Most important, do you like it? This quilt will reflect your personality—can you live with it? If the answers are yes, let's pick out the background fabric.

The background fabric is the material that surrounds the main design of a patch. For example, in the Eight Point star, the star motif is made up of the dominant, contrasting, or blending color and appears to be laying on top of the background. This background fabric traditionally was a solid color so it would not detract from the pattern. You have to decide on the intensity of the background: Do you want a white, ecru *muslin*, or even a hue of the dominant color?

Quilt Talk

Muslin is a plain weave cotton fabric, generally used as the background fabric for your patches or appliqué. Muslin comes in a variety of different shades of beige (unbleached is ecru or beige) and if the manufacturer bleaches the muslin, it will appear whiter. Today there is even a permanent-press muslin that will not wrinkle. Since muslin comes in a wide range of weights, be sure to buy a good quality.

Notice how each star motif looks distinctive with different background fabrics.

Remember that a plain white fabric makes a strong contrast against your color scheme. Sometimes a neutral-color muslin makes your quilt colors appear softer. Recently quilters have started using a solid print for the background. This material should have a motif so small that from a distance it appears solid, but as you get closer the fabric adds texture to your patch. The white, tan, or gray fabric may have swirls, flowers, or a paisley motif in the same subtle shades of neutral colors. These are known as white-on-white fabrics.

Don't forget you can also use a color or black for the background. Amish quilts with black backgrounds are extremely dramatic.

The salespeople at the fabric stores usually hate to see me coming because I take out bolts and bolts of fabric to get just the right color combinations. Be nice and put back all the bolts that you're not buying.

Now that I've given you some guidelines to help in your quest for the perfect fabrics, choosing your fabrics should be exciting and fun. Buy the best fabric that you can afford. We want this to be a family heirloom and last a lifetime. Now go out and buy.

The Least You Need to Know

- Do not choose fabrics with all the same scale of patterns.
- Avoid problem fabrics such as corduroy, ginghams, napped fabrics, one-way designs, and striped fabrics.
- Line up all your fabric bolts, step back, and squint to make sure the colors blend.
- The best source for beginners to purchase fabric is a specialty quilt shop where you will get the most help.
- The choice of background fabric of the patch can change the effect from subtle to dramatic.
- Buy the best fabric that you can afford.

In This Part

Part 3

We're Home and Ready to Go

Washing, organizing, and storing fabrics will keep them in perfect condition. Knowing the characteristics of fabrics—especially the straight-of-fabric grain—makes cutting and sewing your quilt easy.

Templates are used as patterns for quilts. Accuracy is extremely important. You transfer the template shape onto the wrong side of your fabric. Once each fabric has its pieces marked, you add the seam allowances and cut. Then you make your fabric pieces into a block. Be sure to organize all your fabric pieces to avoid losing any.

You may have hundreds of pieces to assemble to make up your quilt top! Where do you start? Simple strategies make hand piecing easy. Pressing gives your quilt a professional look and sometimes irons out your mistakes!

In This Chapter

- ◆ Preshrinking your fabric before you start your quilt
- ◆ Testing to see whether fabric is colorfast
- ◆ Organizing and storing your fabrics
- ◆ Understanding the terminology of woven fabrics

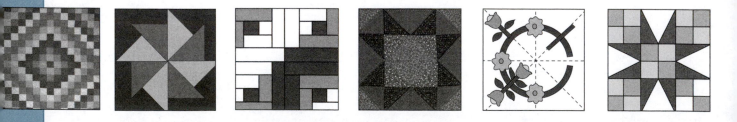

Chapter 8

Knowing and Taking Care of Your Fabric

We've bought our fabrics and supplies at the store and now we're home. Where do we start? I like to prepare and organize my fabrics first. Fabric has to be preshrunk and tested for colorfastness before you can start working with it. Then you need to have an orderly and systematic approach to storing your collection. As you create more and more quilts, there will be additional fabric to store. Our quilting ancestors saved every scrap—we don't want to squander our fabric!

Fabrics have certain characteristics—I feel that fabrics have a life of their own. Some are stiff, wrinkly, stretchy, or raveled. And the same length of fabric can react in a different way just by holding it differently. Knowing these factors will help you manage your fabric and make your quilt last a lifetime. Let's jump in and get our fabric wet!

Don't Forget to Wash!

As soon as you get home from the store, wash your fabrics! This way you don't have to wonder later if you washed them or not. Two qualities of fabrics may give you difficulties: (1) shrinking and (2) fading or running when washed. Both have to be addressed before making your quilt. A friend forgot to wash a red fabric, and after making 15 patches and stitching them together, she started to quilt. Then she wanted to take off a little stain. Unfortunately, as she applied water, the stain got worse—the red fabric started bleeding into the white background fabric. She had to wash the entire quilt and the white background turned a pale shade of pink. You know what happens when a red sock is put in with your white clothes.

Quilting Bee

You can tell if a fabric runs if the water turns color. You can also put a small piece of a white fabric in to see if it discolors. I've had many blues and reds that tend to not be colorfast and bleed onto the white.

Check to see if your fabric is colorfast. Even if the bolt at the store says that it's colorfast, don't trust it. I divide my fabrics into darks and lights, and soak them in a sink of warm water to see if they run.

Quilting Bee

Small quarter-yard cuts of fabric will get tangled in the dryer, so let them line dry.

Keep changing the water until it remains clear. After four times of doing this, if the dye still comes out, then desperate measures need to be taken. I soak the fabric in a sink filled with very hot water that has two cups of white vinegar added to it. Keep the fabric submerged for about 30 minutes. Then try the colorfast test again, soaking your problem fabric with a scrap of white fabric. If after several times of doing this the color is not set, I would advise not using your fabric.

Besides making sure that the colors are set, let's preshrink the fabric. All fabric has some residual shrinkage. To prevent shrinkage, treat your fabrics as you would a finished quilt. I put the fabrics in warm water and even throw them into the dryer.

Don't Get Stuck!

Sometimes when you take your fabric out of the dryer, the fabric is very stiff and wrinkled. If you use this same fabric in your quilt, after washing your quilt, it will have this same appearance. You may not want to use this fabric. Remember, quilts cannot be ironed once they are completed—the inner puffy batting will compress and become flat.

If one material shrinks and the others don't, then the quilt top will pucker wherever that fabric is used. Actually some people like that puckered look, because they feel that it gives their quilt an antique look. My advice to you is to buy your fabric, come home, and shrink and wash your fabric that same day. Then you'll know the qualities of your fabric and you'll be ready to go.

Keep Your Fabrics Dry!

I always have wistful feelings when I read quilt books with chapters on planning your quilting studio. If you are like me, you can only wish for a separate room for your projects. But no matter how small your working space, organizing your fabrics is a necessity.

To keep your fabrics "healthy," be sure to store them away from light and dampness. There is nothing worse than thinking you have leftover scraps of the perfect fabric only to find that it faded or has that moldy smell. Keep fabrics more than half a yard folded with similar colors. Stack these folds of fabric in full view on shelves, so you can easily see your stash. If you don't have a spare closet or bookcase, store similar colors of fabric in those clear plastic boxes that fit under a bed. Avoid storing fabric in the basement or any place with high humidity. Mildew and a musty odor are almost impossible to remove.

Quilting Bee

Keep snippets of fabric for a quilt project in progress on a small index card and carry this around with you for reference. You never know when you will find a terrific additional fabric or accessory that will be perfect with your quilt.

I also keep little scraps smaller than a fourth of a yard in a separate bag. You never know when you need just a few inches of that perfect color for a pillow. Never throw away that last little smidgen of a material. Save it so you can match the color or design if you need to buy more. I also keep a bag of novelty fabrics, like velvets, satins, and laces, for projects like crazy quilts. Whenever I shorten a velvet dress, I save the material I cut off from the hem.

Save your scrap fabrics for a rainy day when you don't want to run out to the store. It's just more economical to reuse your leftovers. So set up your studio!

The Straight- and Narrow-of-Grain Line

Have you noticed the different ways that fabric feels, drapes, and reacts? There are certain characteristics of fabrics that will determine how you use them. The most important factor is the fabric *grain*. This determines how your fabric reacts and needs to be handled. There are several types of grain. When fabric is pulled in different directions, it reacts differently. Each grain or direction has a specific name and characteristic.

Quilt Talk

Grain is the direction that the threads are woven into fabric. Fabric is made up of threads that run perpendicular to each other on a loom. There is a **lengthwise grain**, which runs the length of the fabric, and a **crosswise grain**, which is woven at a right angle to the lengthwise thread.

The threads that run the whole length of the fabric are called the lengthwise grain and need to be very strong in order to endure the weaving process. Because of their strength, they have very little stretch. The direction that runs parallel to these threads is called the *lengthwise grain*. The crosswise threads, or *crosswise grain*, are not quite as strong and have some "give."

Where the crosswise threads turn around the outer side of the fabric is known as the *selvage* or selvedge.

Quilt Talk

The **selvage** is the outer finished edge of your fabric. It is the edge that doesn't ravel and is more closely woven than the rest of the fabric.

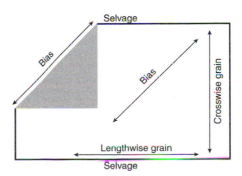

Look at the directions of the different lines of grain.

Because the selvage is thicker and has a denser thread count than the rest of the fabric, it reacts differently. The selvage shrinks and puckers and is very difficult to sew through. Many quilters cut the selvage off as soon as they wash the fabric, but I like to keep it on so I can tell the lengthwise grain. The lengthwise grain is also known as the straight of the grain, as it runs parallel to the selvage.

The tried-and-true technique has templates (quilt patterns) put in a particular direction so that the fabric is easy to handle. The straight of grain is the strongest direction and each template will have a straight-of-grain arrow that should be placed parallel to the selvage. We'll talk about marking templates on your fabric in Chapter 10.

The last type of grain is known as *bias*. Bias is the diagonal direction of fabric. True bias is at a 45-degree angle to the grain lines.

The bias direction has quite a bit of stretch and is more difficult to handle. Some blocks have a bias piece on the outside edge, and if you are not careful when ironing, it will stretch out of shape. Quilters use bias for preparing the outer binding, because the binding needs to conform to the outer curves, and bias strips make it easy.

Now that you have washed and organized your fabrics and learned about certain fabrics' characteristics, we're ready to move to the next level: making templates.

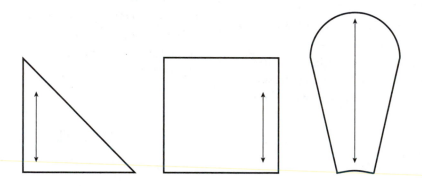

Illustrated are several templates with the straight-of-grain arrows indicated.

The Least You Need to Know

◆ All fabrics have residual shrinkage.

◆ Wash your fabrics to check for shrinkage and colorfastness.

◆ Lengthwise grain is stronger than cross-wise grain, and templates should be put on the straight of grain.

◆ The bias direction is stretchy and more difficult to handle but is useful in making bias tape.

In This Chapter

- ◆ Learning about the different materials for making templates
- ◆ Transferring templates from books
- ◆ Preparing templates for hand piecing
- ◆ Preparing templates for machine quilting

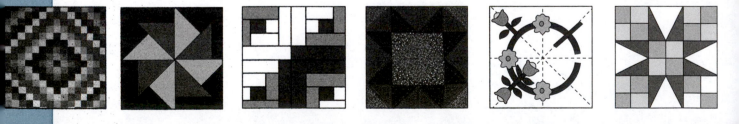

Chapter **9**

Words to Live By: Templates Are the Patterns of Success

Look in the color photo section. In a quilt like the Trip Around the World, how do you cut all those squares neatly? Quilters use templates. A template is anything you draw around to mark pattern pieces for your quilt. Templates can be made of many different materials. Appliqué quilts can use heart-shaped cookie cutters for templates. I've even used a quarter to mark a center of a flower.

Now that you've chosen a quilt block to piece, you're ready to start the quilting process. You can draft the templates yourself, but it is very tedious and time-consuming. When I first taught beginners, I had them draft a Double Nine Patch made of two squares: a 4-inch square and a 1⅓-inch square. Even using graph paper, it took almost the entire two-hour class. That's why all the patterns in this book are full-size and ready to copy.

Machine-sewn quilts use different templates than handmade quilts and both will be discussed. Templates can also be purchased from quilting catalogues or specialty quilt stores. Let's find out how to make our patterns of success.

Materials for Making Templates

A template or pattern must be made for each shape in your quilt block.

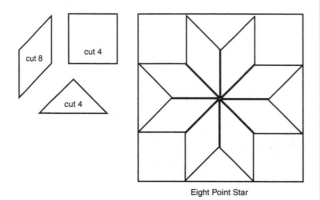

These three shapes make up the Eight Point Star block.

Patterns for quilts are totally distinct from patterns with which you sew clothing. If you are used to sewing clothing, quilt patterns or templates may seem very unusual. Commercial clothing patterns are made from printed tissue paper with seam allowances marked on each pattern piece. Quilting patterns have to be extremely accurate in order to have the parts of the block fit together like a jigsaw puzzle, so the templates are made the exact size of the shape in the hand-pieced block. We will add the seam allowances on the fabric later in Chapter 10.

Because many quilts have hundreds of pattern pieces to draw, templates must be durable. Usually templates are made of cardboard or plastic sheeting. You can find cardboard around the house: file cards, gift boxes, even cereal boxes that are cut apart. Optimally, oak tag or poster board are the best weight—easy to cut but durable. As you mark your fabric by drawing around these templates, the points on cardboard templates tend to wear away. If you know that this may be a problem, plastic sheeting

may be advantageous. The plastic sheets can be found in craft stores. A student who was a nurse used exposed X-ray sheets for templates. The most durable template I've seen was purchased at a booth at a quilt show and constructed from metal with sand glued onto the bottom.

Don't Get Stuck!

You can photocopy your pattern pieces, but beware: If the page is not flat against the machine, the patterns will be skewed. Many copying machines enlarge the pattern very slightly. Even $\frac{1}{16}$ of an inch makes a difference in a quilt. It's best to trace the patterns.

Accuracy Counts

If one patch is crooked, then your whole quilt is out of alignment. Does that frighten you? It need not. If your templates are precise, then your quilt will be, too. The best type of templates for beginners are made from cardboard and sandpaper. The following are some guidelines to help in the quest for accurate templates:

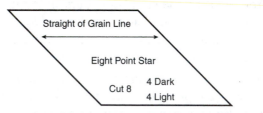

This is the diamond template from the Eight Point Star. It is important to include the name of the block, the number of pattern pieces you need to cut, and the straight-of-grain arrow.

1. Choose a block. (That's easy enough!)
2. Copy each pattern of the block. Either use tracing paper to redraw the patterns or carefully photocopy the page. Be sure to mark the name of the block, the number of blocks you need to cut, and the straight-of-grain arrow.

Quilting Bee

I know you are asking, "Why glue sandpaper to the template?" The reason is that the sandpaper keeps the template from sliding around while you are marking the fabric.

3. Use rubber cement to affix medium-weight sandpaper to the cardboard. Be sure to apply the rubber cement to the smooth side of the sandpaper.

4. Glue copied patterns onto the cardboard/sandpaper with rubber cement. The template has the copied pattern on top and the rough sandpaper on the bottom.

5. Now it's time to cut very carefully around the outer edges through all three layers—pattern, cardboard, and sandpaper.

6. Test for template accuracy by putting your template over the book's pattern. If it is inaccurate, carefully recut it.

7. Store all your templates for each block together. I like to use zippered plastic bags for each individual block. Be sure to label the block name—you do not want to mix them up!

Don't Get Stuck!

Be sure to use rubber cement and not any other type of glue because only rubber cement dries flat and won't make the cardboard ripple. If your template is not flat, it will not be accurate.

Remember, accuracy counts. The outside of these templates will mark the sewing lines on your fabric, and when sewn, these pieces must fit together perfectly like a jigsaw puzzle.

That doesn't seem too hard, does it?

Templates for Machine Piecing

Templates for machine piecing are slightly different from those for hand quilting. The ¼-inch seam allowances are included in the template. The cutting line is drawn on your fabric—not the sewing line.

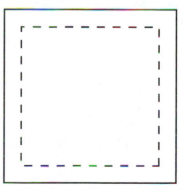

Quilting Bee

Sometimes when you try to cut small slivers off the templates, you only make it worse by cutting too much. To straighten an uneven edge, file it down with sandpaper or an emery board. You have more control.

When machine sewing quilts, the cutting edges are aligned and pinned together. The seam line is determined by the sewing machine's ¼-inch presser foot, not by a line drawn on the fabric as in hand quilting. Accurate cutting is extremely important for machine piecing.

A template for machine piecing has the ¼-inch seam allowance incorporated in the template.

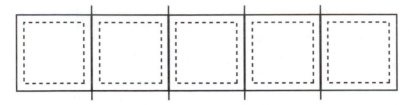

Multiple templates drafted together in a row.

Sometimes machine-sewn quilts have multiple templates (templates that are drawn in a long line). It saves time to mark and sew multiple templates rather than marking and sewing each separate template. The Trip Around the World and Lone Star quilts are examples of quilts with multiple templates. Although I have taught how to make them many times, it still seems like magic when all these templates come together. There are several books that deal specifically with this method.

Many machine-made quilts don't have special templates, for example, the Rail Fence. A fabric strip of the correct width is cut from selvage to selvage and sewn together in the *strip-pieced* method, then cut apart and re-sewn to form a block. The blocks are sewn together to form the quilt top.

The Rail Fence and Log Cabin blocks will be discussed in depth in Chapter 16.

Quilt Talk

Strip piecing is a method of creating quilts by taking long strips of fabric and sewing them together in a set sequence. This newly combined material is then cut apart and re-sewn to form a part of

Remember, no matter whether you are hand or machine quilting, you must be sure your

templates are exact. Any deviation will cause your quilt not to line up. Check all templates for accuracy against the patterns in the book, and use a T-square ruler for testing right angles in squares and rectangles.

Be sure to keep templates sorted by blocks. I always have at least one student who tries to put a Double Nine Patch square into an Eight Point Star corner. The templates may look the same, but there is a ¼-inch difference in size, and no way to fit them. So keep them separated in envelopes or my favorite—zippered plastic bags.

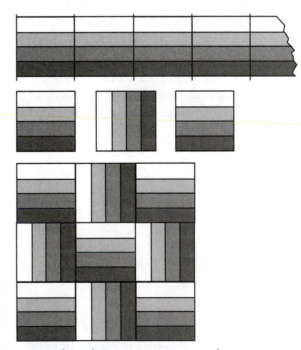

Notice how the strips are sewn together, cut apart, then re-sewn to form a Rail Fence block.

The Least You Need to Know

◆ Templates for hand piecing are pattern pieces that are the exact size of each element in a block.

◆ Templates for machine-sewn quilts have the ¼-inch seam allowance included so that only the cutting line is drawn on the fabric.

◆ The best templates for beginners are made from cardboard and sandpaper glued together.

◆ All markings must be transferred to the templates—be sure to include the name of the block, cutting directions, and straight-of-grain arrow.

◆ Draw and cut templates accurately; then check them for preciseness.

In This Chapter

- ◆ Choosing the correct equipment to mark on fabric
- ◆ Tracing around the template carefully
- ◆ Economizing on fabric
- ◆ Cutting out the pattern pieces
- ◆ Organizing and storing fabric pieces

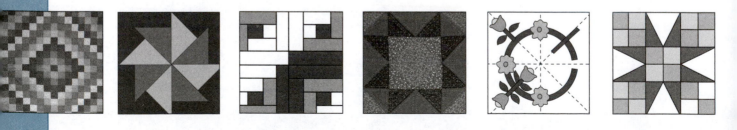

Chapter 10

On Your Mark, Get Set, Cut!

We've spent a long time making perfectly accurate templates, now it's time to transfer those shapes onto the material. Can you believe that we draw right on the wrong side of the fabric? Using the correct equipment will help your "markability."

Templates for hand-sewn quilts have no seam allowances. The traced shape is the exact sewing size. We need to draw them onto the fabric after the template is marked. Proper placement of the patterns will help economize the fabric. With all these marked lines, you should think before you cut. Think twice, but cut once.

In short, templates make fabric pieces, those pieces make up a block, and blocks make up a quilt. If there is only one block repeated throughout your quilt, there may be hundreds of cut pieces of fabric. How do you keep them all together and not lose them? Keep reading and you'll find out.

Equip Yourself

There are several considerations to make before marking your fabric. Choose a tool that is easy to see, marks finely and accurately, and does not run or bleed into the fabric. A number 2 pencil is usually best. Because the wrong side of the fabric is a lighter color than the right side, lead pencils make terrific fine, visible lines. If the fabric is a dark color or has a busy pattern, you may have to use a white, silver, or yellow pencil for the lines to be seen. I usually keep a variety of colors with my supplies to test which color pencil is best.

Quilting Bee

I really prefer an artist's pencil over the ones made for marking quilts. Some pencils are too waxy, make a line too thick, break easily, and need to be sharpened too often—you know, like eyebrow pencils. Avoid those pencils.

Some quilters use ballpoint pens for marking. Be very careful to test if the pen markings are permanent. Avoid them if they bleed when wet—the color will stain a light-colored fabric.

Be sure your pencil is sharp! You don't want a thick line. Even that small difference multiplied over hundreds of pieces will change the alignment of your quilt. Keep your sharpener handy.

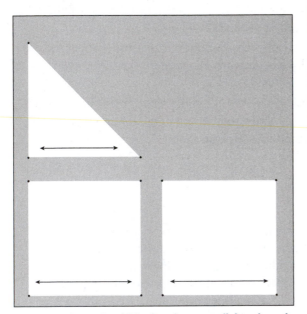

Your templates should be lined up parallel to the selvage of your fabric. Draw dots in each corner of the template.

Quilting Bee

It is easy to tell the wrong side of a printed fabric—the design is fuzzier and lighter in color. With solid fabrics, both sides seem to be the same color. There may be a slight difference in values, so make sure you use the same side consistently. I sometimes put a pin or masking tape on the wrong

It's as Easy as Drawing from Dot to Dot

It's time to mark our fabric! Here are some simple steps to follow:

1. Be sure the fabric is preshrunk and colorfast.

2. Choose the template and the fabric. Turn the fabric to the wrong side.

3. Find your selvages—these finished edges are your guidelines to pattern placement. Place the straight-of-grain arrow parallel to the selvage. This makes your quilt more durable and the fabric easier to work with when placing it on the lengthwise grain.

Don't Get Stuck!

Do not use the selvage—it continues to shrink after the rest of the fabric has been preshrunk and will make your quilt pucker. Also, because the selvage is thick, it is extremely difficult to sew and quilt through.

4. Start by placing a template ½ inch away from the selvage with the straight-of-grain arrow parallel to it.

5. Put a dot in each corner of the geometric shape of the template. You will use the dots to help maintain accuracy. This is very important—so make those dots!

6. Carefully draw around the outside edge of the template, connecting the dots. Take care not to press down too hard with the pencil because it drags the fabric and the markings will be out of shape. Lift the template and check for accuracy. Redraw if necessary.

One template down, how many to go?

Cut Between the Sewing Lines

Now that you have drawn your sewing lines, let's draw the cutting line. Don't forget to add the seam allowances onto the outer edge of the markings. Seam allowances for hand-pieced quilts are ¼ inch (not ⅛ inch as is typical in commercial clothing patterns).

Before you cut, you must make some additional marks on your fabric:

1. Draw a line ¼ inch around the marked seam line. Beginners sometimes use a colored pencil to mark all the cutting lines. This way there is a real visible difference. Use a ruler or *quilter's quarter* to measure the ¼ inch.

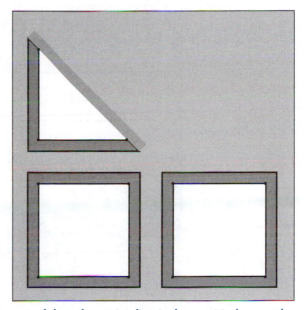

Look how the cutting line is drawn ¼ inch around the seam lines.

2. Place the next template on the fabric, making sure to leave enough room for the seam allowance.

3. Check that you drew the correct number of pattern pieces, and be sure you drew all the seam allowances.

4. Cut out fabric pieces on the cutting lines. Use sharp scissors to avoid blisters on your hands.

There is a perfectly logical reason for a ¼-inch seam allowance. The ¼-inch seam allowance is enough to keep the quilt from raveling, but not too large that you would have to quilt through it. Those pioneer women really thought this through.

There are strategies to marking fabrics that help you economize fabric usage. The first approach is to start at the selvage side and mark the patterns side by side, only ½ inch apart. If you start marking in the middle of the fabric and then place the other templates in no particular order, you waste much of the fabric. Be methodical, and mark across the fabric from selvage to selvage or up the side of the selvage.

Quilt Talk

The **quilter's quarter** is an 8-inch-long four-sided rod of plastic that is ¼-inch wide. It is very easy for beginners to line up this ruler with the seam line in order to draw the cutting line.

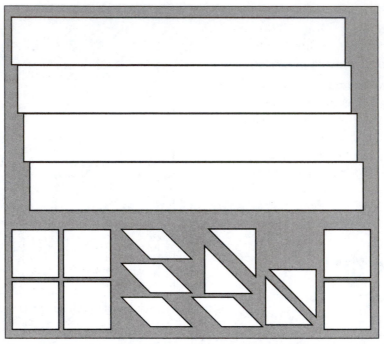

You can utilize all your fabric by thinking ahead.

You may want to mark up the side of the selvage if you need the length of the fabric for borders. Another idea is to dovetail pattern pieces. Dovetailing means fitting odd-shaped pieces like triangles or wedges into one another. Remember: Plan ahead.

If you are preparing a quilt with repeated blocks, make one patch before you cut out the rest of the quilt. Sometimes you decide to change the color combination or move the placement in the block. Once the block is perfected, it's time to cut out the rest of your blocks.

Stack and Store

There are two methods of storing fabric pieces. For example, an Eight Point Star has three pattern shapes—a diamond, square, and triangle. Some quilters keep fabric pieces of each template shape in separate plastic bags—one bag for the diamonds, a second for the squares, and a third for the triangles. Other quilters like a

plastic bag with all the fabric shapes for one block together. If you are making a lap quilt, you may have six plastic bags that contain the diamonds, squares, and triangles that will be pieced together for one block. This is great if you want a portable project. Pick up a bag and take it with you—all the pieces you need are in one bag.

Quilting Bee

All patterns for templates in this book do not have the seam allowance included. In other quilting books, sometimes the ¼-inch seam allowance is included in the drawn template, and sometimes it has to be added. Templates with included seam allowances usually have a dotted line indicating the ¼-inch seam line. If done consistently, it won't matter in the templates or cut pattern pieces.

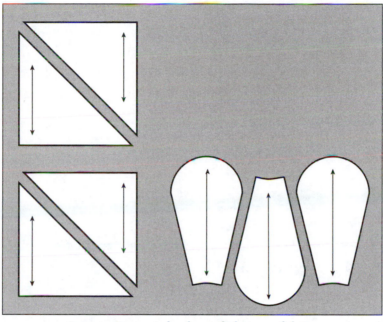

Pattern pieces can be dovetailed to save fabric.

If you don't like the bag method, you can baste your fabric pieces together. Take a long piece of thread with a knot on the end, and stab this through a stack of similar pieces. Don't knot both ends. You can just pull off one piece at a time as you need it. I usually put two threads through a stack just in case one breaks!

If you are making a Sampler quilt, each block will be different and created one at a time, so patches will be cut and sewn as you go along.

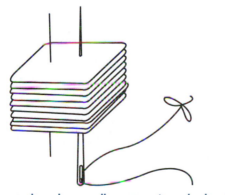

You can stack and store all pattern pieces by basting them together.

The Least You Need to Know

◆ A number 2 pencil is best for transferring templates onto the fabric, but try a different color if the pencil line is hard to see.

◆ Mark on the wrong side of the fabric.

◆ Place templates with the straight-of-grain line parallel to the selvages.

◆ Put a dot in each corner of the template, then connect the dots.

◆ Hand-sewn quilt templates do not have seam allowances; you must add ¼ inch all around the outside for the cutting line.

◆ Check twice, then cut on the cutting lines.

In This Part

Part

4

Let's Put It All Together

Time to make your first patch! You have gathered your supplies, decided on a project, chosen a color scheme, bought your fabric, and, I hope, practiced the piecing stitch on scraps of fabric. It's now time to put your quilt together. Machine or hand piecing, it's your choice.

You should have a stack of finished blocks ready now to assemble into a quilt top. There are many ways to set together your quilt and your decisions will change the look of the quilt and the manner you attack its construction. Then we will frame your quilt face with borders to complement and accentuate your work of art.

So choose and let's get started.

In This Chapter

- ◆ Sewing the piecing stitches and appliqué stitch
- ◆ Understanding how fabric pieces are seamed together
- ◆ Strategies of piecing blocks
- ◆ Pressing quilt blocks

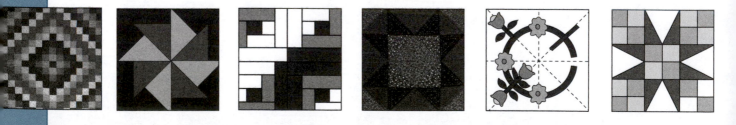

Chapter 11

Be a Sew and Sew

Depending on the type of quilt you have chosen, you may have hundreds of fabric pieces to assemble or as few as 13 pieces for one block. If you are a novice, please let me remind you to start small and cut out pieces for one block only.

It's time to sew your pieces of fabric together! There are certain procedures that make piecing logical and easy. We'll start with just two pattern pieces and learn to sew them together effortlessly. Continue sewing until a row is formed, then seam the rows together to form a square block. When you have completed your block, it's time to give your patch the professional look by giving it a real press job. Get your needle and thread—let's start.

Know Your Stitches

We'll examine hand-piecing stitches and the appliqué stitch. When these blocks are sewn, the resultant patches are contrasting in appearance. Compare the angular Ohio Star in Chapter 12 and the rounded Tudor Rose in Chapter 15. The stitches that put these patches together are totally different.

Piecing Stitch—Know the Ins and Outs

Beginners are always amazed that the stitching for hand-pieced blocks is so easy. It's a simple running stitch where the needle goes in and out of the fabric. Start with a quilting needle and quilting thread. Remember to choose the smallest size needle that you can work with confidently. Our quilting ancestors discovered that smaller needles made smaller stitches. Be sure to use quilting thread—it's thicker, more durable, and doesn't tangle. Then follow these steps:

Don't Get Stuck!

Don't make the type of knot that I use for making hems (wrapping the thread around my finger and rolling it back and forth till it forms a massive ball of a knot). If you make a knot like that, it may rub against the fabric of your quilt and wear a hole. We want our quilts to be heirlooms.

1. Cut quilting thread about 2 feet in length. Any longer and it's awkward and tiring to pull the thread through. Any shorter and you have to constantly re-thread the needle, and that gets annoying.

2. Put a single knot in the end of the thread. I make a loop with the thread and put the needle through the circle, and pull it through. It should form a little knot with a ¼-inch "tail." The tail keeps the knot from unraveling.

3. Place the two fabric pieces, right sides together, matching the sewing lines. This is it—our first piecing stitch. Poke the needle down through the fabric right on the sewing line and then up through the fabric about ⅛ inch down along the seam line. It's simply a running stitch using an in-and-out motion that is sewn right on the seam line.

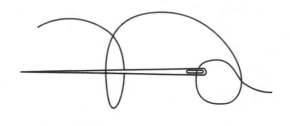

Make a loop with the thread and pull the needle through, leaving a small knot with a tail.

Running stitches used for the piecing stitch are very small.

Draw a pencil line on the wrong side of a scrap of fabric and practice the piecing stitch. In and out—it's easy.

Scraps and Pieces

Quilts have a rich history of superstitions. The most universal bit of folklore confirms that each quilt should have a small mistake in it, either a piecing or appliqué mismatch or a quilting faux pas. My theory is that once a quilt was completed and the quilt maker discovered the mistake, she developed the idiom that "the quilt is supposed to be like that since only God is perfect." Of course I do not recommend making mistakes in your quilt, but this does make a great explanation.

Appliqué Stitch

Beginners also need to learn the appliqué stitch. In appliquéd blocks, a fabric motif is cut out, layered, and stitched invisibly onto the background of another fabric. Several different techniques make these stitches almost invisible to the eye. In true appliqué we want to see only the design, not the stitches.

Scraps and Pieces

There has recently been a revival of folk art. The quilt is the most popular example of traditional American crafts. Quilters used the medium of fabric to make pictures of their world. This was the original folk art. Pioneer women would appliqué stylized people (Sunbonnet Sue), animals, flowers, and farm scenes in a primitive style. In these homespun-style quilts, the appliquéd pieces are embroidered with a decorative blanket stitch. This method will be discussed in Chapter 15.

This is the appliqué stitch that I was taught and it has worked for me. I'll illustrate how to appliqué a heart motif. The appliqué stitch leaves a small, visible dot of a stitch.

Quilt Talk

Basting is a large, temporary running stitch that is sewn to hold down the raw edges or hold two pieces of fabric together. You should use a contrasting color so it is easy to see and remove after you have finished appliquéing.

1. Start with your quilting needle and knotted quilting thread in a color that blends with the appliqué motif.

2. Prepare the design by *basting* under the raw edges.

3. Baste the fabric motif into position on the background fabric. Now let's appliqué.

4. Start with the needle under the background fabric. Push it up through the background and the edge of the appliqué motif. Pull the thread through.

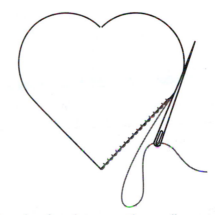

Only a dot of stitch is seen. The needle goes down through the background fabric and up into the edge of the appliqué piece.

5. Position the needle right next to where the thread came up but on the background only. Take a ⅛-inch stitch through the background and come up at the edge of the appliqué motif.

6. Continue appliquéing stitches all around the fabric design, ending underneath the background on the wrong side. Knot off.

The appliqué stitch does seem more time-consuming. The first appliqué block that a beginner creates is a slow go, but you soon develop a rhythm of stitching that makes your block sing.

Don't Get Stuck!

Be sure to mark the dots at each corner of your templates so you know where to start and end your seam lines.

How Does It Seam?

"Where do I start?" is a question all beginners ask. The answer is with just two fabric pieces, three pins, and your needle and thread. We're going to seam the pieces together using the hand-piecing stitch. Let's take two pieces and turn them right sides together so the penciled seam lines can be seen on both sides of the pieces.

The dots marked at each corner of your templates will be the beginning and end of your seam lines. Stab a pin right into the dot of the top piece into the dot of the bottom fabric. Both dots are matched. Match up and pin the dot at the other end. Put another pin in the seam line in the middle of the pencil line.

Don't Get Stuck!

Check for accuracy before you sew. Gather several stitches on your needle, but don't pull the thread through. Turn the piece over and check to see if your needle is exactly on the line—if not, take the needle out and shift the seam line.

Get out your quilting needle and thread and make a knot. Put the needle in the seam line ⅛ inch from the right-hand dot (if you are right handed, the left-hand dot is just the opposite) and take a *backstitch* into the dot. Then sew the piecing stitch along the seam line.

Quilt Talk

A **backstitch** is a stitch taken backward from the direction you are sewing to reinforce the seam.

Continue sewing to the end of the seam line, bringing the needle right into the end dot. Take a backstitch ⅛ inch in reverse and back into the dot. I do not knot this end (knots can rub against and wear out material) but take a 90-degree turn into the seam allowance, make two stitches, and cut off the thread.

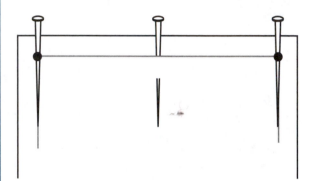

Sew right on the seam line with the hand-piecing stitch.

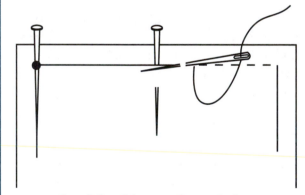

Pin each end dot of the seam line and place one pin in the center of the seam line.

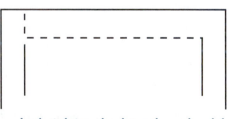

Take a backstitch into the dot at the end and then take two stitches into the seam allowance.

Put Your Blocks Together: Sew Row by Row

Didn't that "seam" easy? There are certain strategies that make it easier for you to piece your block. First, lay all your block pieces on the table in front of you. Put them in the same position as your finished block. Doesn't it look great? It is easy to decide where to start sewing and then to check if you've pinned correctly.

Quilting Bee

One student often had to put her work away then set it up again, so she laid out her pieces on a piece of felt or flannel. It was easy to fold up her work, then pull it out again later. The fuzzy nap of the felt kept the pieces in place even when the felt was folded up.

Each block has specific directions on sewing procedures, but here are some hints. Start by sewing the smallest pieces together to form a larger unit. Those small scraps of fabric are very easy to lose. Stitch pieces together into rows. One student sewed pieces across and then down in an L-shaped angle instead of sewing rows. She came to me and asked, "How do I put in the middle piece?" Don't sew yourself into a "jam." Sew row by row.

Let's learn how to sew rows together. It is important to have the seams match at intersections. Do not start sewing from one end of the row to the other side. Make sure that the seams align, sewing from the middle out. Pin the dots at each end of the row and at each seam intersection.

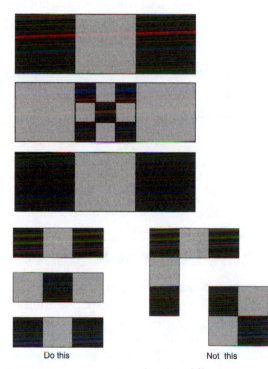

Do this   Not this

It's easy to sew rows together, but difficult to sew a piece into an angle.

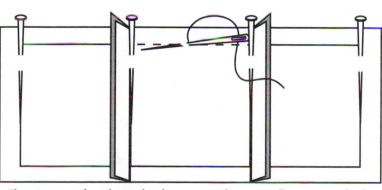

The pins are placed into the dots next to the seam allowances. Check out the direction you should sew.

Don't pin or sew down the seam allowances—you'll need to press them in any direction. Start at one of the center seams, backstitch into the dot, and sew to the end of the seam line. If you have to cross a seam line, sew right up to the dot but stand the seam allowance up and pass the needle through it and continue stitching to the end of the row. Backstitch into the dot and take two stitches into the seam. Sew all of the rows in the same manner, and "Hooray," we have a block.

Don't Get Stuck!

Even if only one of your fabrics is a cotton-polyester blend, press your block at the lower synthetic setting to prevent scorching it.

Ironing Out Your Mistakes

When your block has been pieced, it's time to press it to get a professional look. Wait until the patch is completed to see the optimum way to press. I like to use a steam iron set to either cotton or the synthetic setting depending on your fabric's type.

Quilting Bee

The seam allowances are pressed to one side, not open as in dressmaking. When seams are pressed together, they are stronger.

Here are some guidelines to follow for pressing your block:

1. Iron on the wrong side of the block, with all seams pressed to one side—NOT OPEN.

2. Press the seam toward the darker color. If you press in the direction of the lighter color, a dark shadow will appear on the quilt top. Sometimes the weight of a fabric will force you to press the seam in one direction, no matter how you try to press it the other way. Then let the fabric win.

3. If there are any puckers or your block seems out of alignment, use a wet press cloth to smooth it out.

Be careful to move the iron, lifting it up and down. Sometimes pressing back and forth causes the edges of the patch to stretch. Use a light touch. Many times my students come to me with wrinkled patches and are amazed how terrific they appear after pressing. You can definitely iron out your mistakes.

The Least You Need to Know

◆ Thread your needle with quilting thread and make a single knot at the end.

◆ Pin into the dots at each end of the seam line and pin the seam line in the middle.

◆ Use the hand-piecing stitch for pieced patchwork blocks and the appliqué stitch for appliqué blocks.

◆ Sew your blocks together row by row.

◆ Don't sew down intersecting seam allowances; this way you can press them in any direction.

◆ Press seams to one side, not open.

In This Chapter

- ◆ Getting your sewing machine ready for quilting
- ◆ Choosing and modifying patchwork patterns for the machine
- ◆ Hints on machine piecing
- ◆ Directions for joining blocks by chain and strip piecing

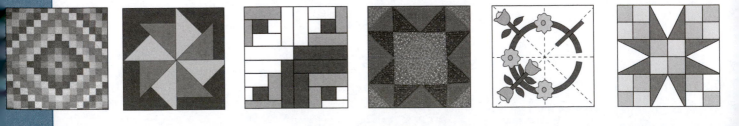

Use Your Sewing Machine

As I grew to love quilting, I envisioned hundreds of quilts, and I wanted to make them all. Unfortunately, most of us can't devote 10 hours a day to quilting. When I started a project I seemed to forget my housework, cooking meals, my family, and so on. The sewing machine seemed to be the answer. I was able to produce quilts at a quicker pace and keep the rest of my life together, which made my family happy.

To create machine-made quilts you first have to really be proficient, and second, enjoy using the sewing machine. It is more difficult to handle piecing the blocks—you will need sound eye-hand, and even eye-foot, coordination. To make your life easier, choose a patch that lends itself to machine sewing, and modify the templates by including the ¼-inch seam allowances. There are special techniques, like strip piecing and chaining, that make machine piecing even faster. If you know how to sew and enjoy it, this chapter is for you.

Pressure but No Pain—Your Machine Tension

Knowing your sewing machine and its proper use is utmost in the piecing and quilting process. Be sure your machine is in good working order. Let's learn about parts of the sewing machine so we know the proper terminology. I hate to be talking about the feed dogs and have you think this book is about animals! Get out your owner's manual and compare the diagram of my machine to yours.

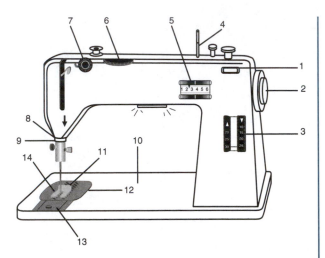

1. Power Switch
2. Hand Wheel
3. Stitch Length Regulator
4. Spool Pin
5. Needle Position
6. Stitch Width Regulator
7. Tension Dial
8. Thread Cutter
9. Pressor Foot Lifter
10. Bed
11. Presser Foot
12. Throat Plate
13. Slide Plate
14. Feed Dogs

Compare this sewing machine to yours.

Let's Start at the Top

Here are some important parts of the machine that you can easily see. I'll be talking about them in this chapter, so make sure you can identify them:

◆ Power on-off switch.

◆ Hand wheel: Raises or lowers the needle.

◆ Stitch length regulator: Changes the length of the stitch.

◆ Stitch width regulator: Determines the width of zigzag stitches.

◆ Spool pin: Holds the spool of thread on top of the machine.

◆ Needle position: Most new machines have this selection. Check to see if your needle is set on the left, center, or right. It can affect the size of your seam.

◆ Tension dial and disc: Control the top thread tension. Tension is the balance of the tightness of the top thread to the bottom bobbin thread. If the tension is unbalanced, the seam will pucker.

 Quilting Bee

The width of the stitch will make the stitch zig and zag. A zero stitch width is a straight stitch; usually the larger the number, the bigger the zigzag.

◆ Thread cutter: Cuts threads at the ends of the seams.

◆ Presser foot lifter: Lets you raise and lower the presser foot and is found at the back of the machine.

◆ Presser foot: Holds the fabric against the bed as the fabric is fed through the machine.

Under the Bed

The following important parts of your sewing machine are not easily seen but are just as important in accomplishing your sewing projects.

◆ Bed: Now is not the time to take a nap, the bed is the work surface at the base of the machine.

◆ Throat plate: Supports the fabric during sewing and has seam line guides for different widths.

◆ Slide plate: Opens for easy removal and replacement of the bobbin.

◆ Feed dogs (or feed system—I just liked the term because it helped jog my home economics students' memories): These teeth move the fabric under the presser foot.

◆ Bobbin case: Under the slide plate, it holds the bobbin, which contains the bottom thread of the stitch.

The lists of sewing machine parts are not intended to teach a novice to sew, but just to acquaint you with common terminology.

Now it's time to start sewing. When you sew the seam, put the right sides together and line up the side of the presser foot with the raw edge. Measure the width of the seam—usually the presser foot when lined up in this manner makes a ¼-inch seam—perfect for quilting. If aligning the presser foot along the raw edge does not produce a ¼-inch seam, then measure ¼-inch from the needle and place a narrow piece of masking tape on the throat plate for your guideline.

Now your seam should be perfect; let's look at the stitches.

Practice stitching two pieces of scrap fabric together to guarantee that the seam line is not *puckered* and has no *skipped stitches*.

Quilt Talk

A **puckered** seam looks almost gathered, with wrinkles under the stitches even when pressed. A seam with **skipped stitches** has missing stitches, giving the seam large stitches and low durability.

Look in your sewing machine instruction manual to fix your stitches. When there is a problem, always check out whether you have threaded the machine correctly, and then remove and replace the bobbin to see if it is inserted properly. If there is still a problem, here are some hints to troubleshoot when your machine isn't up to the quilt experience.

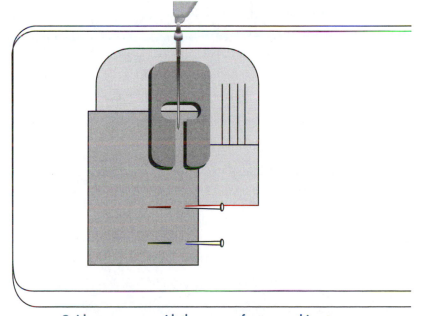

Guide your seam with the presser foot or masking tape.

If you have skipped stitches, check to see if your needle is dull, or if you are using the right thread.

When your seam line is puckered, you may have to change the tension by turning the tension regulator slightly, but read your manual. The tension is very important. You may even need a tune-up for your machine if you can't correct it.

a) top too loose

b) top too tight

c) in balance

When your stitches are in balance, it's time to sew!

Hints for Machine Piecing

My students complain that I make machine sewing look too easy. I always apologize to them, but it is easy if you pin accurately and work slowly and carefully. I don't think you should try machine piecing until you have done hand piecing. Once you are familiar with the order of piecing and techniques, you can attempt it on the machine.

Quilting Bee

Choose a thread that is 100 percent cotton or an all-purpose, cotton-wrapped polyester. Do not use 100 percent polyester (the type that is usually in the sale bins at craft stores) because it knots and breaks too easily.

The first modification can be in changing your templates. As with hand piecing, you can use the typical template and add on the ¼-inch seam allowance when marking the fabric. Or to save time, you can make the template with the ¼-inch seam allowance already included. Since the presser foot measures the ¼ inch, you don't have to mark the seam line. There is a problem, however, because there are no dots to match up—so this method is not as accurate as hand piecing.

Quilting Bee

Sometimes as you are pinning, you can have trouble getting seams to match. You may have been inaccurate in marking, so take out your template, redraw the seam lines, and mark the dots. Then re-pin and sew.

To sew basic seams by machine, put the right sides of the fabric together, pin at each end and at every few inches on the seam line. Insert your pin perpendicular to the seam line. For regular piecing, there is no need for backstitching. In most cases, the seam is strong enough. Start at one end, and with the presser foot aligned with the raw edges, sew to the other end. Machine piecing diamonds is a little tricky. When you align the pieces without dots, there is a tendency to pin them incorrectly. You must have ¼ inch of the tip of the diamond or triangle sticking out for the seams to line up.

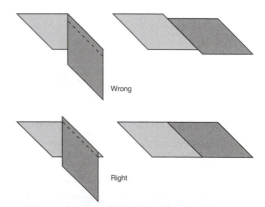

Wrong

Right

Look how the diamonds for the Virginia Star are aligned for sewing.

Another piecing problem for the sewing machine is inserting right-angled pieces. With this type of piecing, start sewing ¼-inch away from the end of the seam allowance, as if there was a dot. Move the hand wheel so that you can position the needle right into the seam, then release the presser foot. Sew from the inside of the angle to the outside. Look at the Eight Point Star. The diamonds are sewn together and it is time to put in the squares and triangles. Position the block on the bed of the sewing machine, and make sure that the fabric is flat with no folds underneath. Sew slowly and carefully, pulling out pins as you sew.

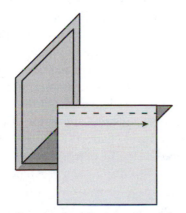

In the Eight Point Star, for inserting right-angled pieces, pin and sew from the inside out.

When machine sewing intersecting seams together, it is best to press as you go. This is different from hand piecing where you press when the patch is done. Think before you press. It is smart to butt the seams so that as the machine sews over them, the fabric of the top seam is pushed against the bottom seam and is held in place.

Pin into the seam of the intersecting seam lines. The seam allowance of the top should be ironed in one direction and the bottom pressed the opposite way. When you seam over these lines of stitching, the seam allowances will lay in opposite directions. Look how intersecting seams should be pressed for easy sewing.

Quilting Bee

When butting intersecting seams of two rows, the seams of the top and bottom rows are pressed in opposite directions. This yields less bulkiness than having both seams on top of one another.

The secret to accurate machine piecing is to pin and press carefully. Sew slowly and make sure that the pieces seamed together have no tucks or puckers. Take out your pins as you go.

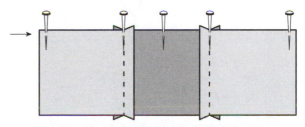

Press the seams that meet in opposite directions.

Quick Methods for Joining Blocks

Now for some quick method strategies. There are so many creative, smart quilters who have developed these methods. Obviously they were in a hurry and needed to finish their quilt by a deadline, like most of us. Check out how to sew in chains and strips and try them out on the blocks in this chapter.

Chain Piecing

I'm for anything that saves time, and sewing fabric pieces in a production line makes sense. Chain piecing makes sewing several blocks at a time easy. I hate cutting threads and restarting seam lines, especially when half of the time when I start the seam, the needle unthreads because I didn't have the needle at the highest point. It's so annoying to have to rethread the needle. With chain piecing, you sew the first two fabric pieces together, but do not cut the threads at the end of the seam line. Instead, you sew two or three stitches more, and then put the next set of fabric pieces by the presser foot and continue the same seam line. Do this for all the fabric pieces, forming a long string of pieces.

Chaining together a long string of fabric pieces.

This technique is perfect to practice on the Log Cabin block because there are four units in one patch. You can string together four centers to template A, then cut the line of units apart. Position the first unit right sides together with template B and seam all four units. Cut them apart, and sew each template in a spiral manner until the unit is totally complete.

Chaining together the Log Cabin.

It may sound confusing, but when you take the templates one at a time, it really does make sense to chain yourself to this method.

Strip Piecing

My favorite quick sewing method is strip piecing. I have made many different types of quilts with this procedure—sewing squares of the Trip Around the World, Boston Commons, Double Irish Chain, and even the diamonds of the Lone Star. When I teach this technique, I tell my students, "Trust me, it's like magic, it just works!" Blocks are analyzed and long strips of fabrics are sewn together in set patterns. There may be one, two, or three different units of strips. These units are then sliced apart and combined to make a row. Then different row units are pressed and sewn together to form the block. There are many great books that give specific instructions on this technique.

There are many great blocks that use the strip-quilting method. You can practice on the Rail Fence with the patterns and directions in this chapter, and then you'll be ready to strip your quilts.

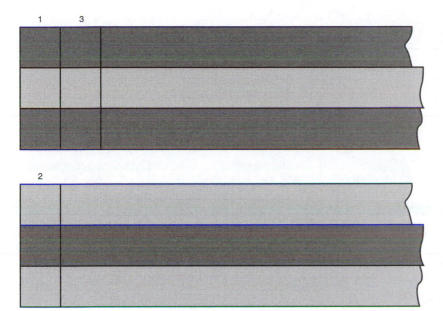

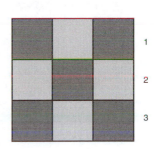

See how easy the center of the Double Nine Patch can be made if you strip piece?

Scraps and Pieces

The Seminole Indians in Florida first developed the technique of strip quilting. The Indians were given sewing machines on their reservation at the beginning of the 1900s. They perfected the strip method and made long narrow rows of small, intricately pieced squares and triangles. These strips were not used in bed coverings but to adorn colorful clothing. Solid, bright-colored fabric is used. Quilters now use their procedure to make blocks.

Quilting Bee

Fabric always stretches on the bias; but if it stretches along the straight of grain, you will have trouble sewing with the zigzag stitch. On the other hand, do not use a fabric that is too thick, like broadcloth or poplin, because it will be too thick to quilt.

Let's Zig and Zag Your Appliqué Blocks

It is very durable and fast if you appliqué by sewing machine. The look is folksy and homemade, if this is the look you prefer. If you choose to machine appliqué, there are several modifications to consider before starting your appliqué patch.

I think one of the most important things to remember is to be sure to use a fabric that is sturdy and will not ravel. Use a material that is 50 to 100 percent cotton and is densely woven.

The thread for your machine should be a cotton-wrapped polyester or 100 percent mercerized cotton. You can use a thread color that blends into the appliqué motif to give it a softer, more polished look. On the other hand, if you choose a contrasting thread, your eye will be drawn to the zigzag stitch, which will give it a real country look. Be sure to have your bobbin thread the same color as your top thread.

Don't Get Stuck!

Be sure to choose a fusible webbing like Wonder Under or Stitch-witchery and not a fusible interfacing. The webbing totally dissolves and glues your appliqué design to your background fabric. I've used these several times; but be careful, it is really difficult to quilt through this glue if you are planning to hand quilt.

It's time to cut out your fabric designs and place them on your patch. There are two ways to do this. If you choose a fabric, such as felt, that doesn't ravel, you don't even have to add on the seam allowances or turn them under. This is a real time-saver. The second way is similar to the traditional appliqué method, in which you mark and cut out your appliqué designs, adding on the seam allowances. Baste the seam allowances under and pin them into position.

Keeping these designs flat and in the correct place is really a challenge. I baste, baste, and more baste the designs onto the background. Your machine has a tendency to drag the fabric out of place very easily. You can even use a fusible webbing or a glue stick to hold these designs down.

Cut the sheet of webbing the same size as your template.

Place the fusible webbing between your appliqué design and the background fabric. Then it's as easy as pressing to fuse these pieces into place. Now for the zig and the zag.

I've talked about the sewing machine and how to use the straight stitch to piece your blocks. Now it's time to learn how to use the other optional stitches on your machine. Experiment with your sewing machine, changing the stitch width regulator and the stitch length. Choose a zigzag satin stitch that is so densely sewn that you will not see the fabric through it. The width of the stitch is your preference, but I find that a more narrow stitch width is easier to maneuver around your design. Allow the machine feed dog to push your fabric through—be sure not to pull the fabric or your stitches will be uneven. Make sure the stitches land exactly on the edge. If the stitches pucker, change the tension on your machine.

Position the zigzag stitching to land on the edge of the appliqué.

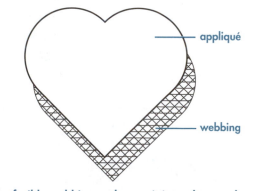

appliqué

webbing

Cut the fusible webbing and press it into place under the appliqué designs.

The Least You Need to Know

◆ Properly using and caring for your machine is important for perfect stitches.

◆ Use your presser foot or place a piece of masking tape on the throat plate of the sewing machine to mark the ¼ inch for seam allowances.

◆ When chain piecing a quilt with one block, you can sew all the patches together at the same time in a production line.

◆ Strip piecing means sewing long strips of fabrics together into several patterns that, when cut apart and re-sewn, form blocks.

◆ Position the zigzag stitches so that the stitches land on the edge of the appliqué design.

In This Chapter

◆ Positioning and balancing colors and designs

◆ How placement of blocks can change a quilt's look

◆ Piecing blocks into a quilt top

◆ Framing out the quilt top with borders

◆ Mitering corners

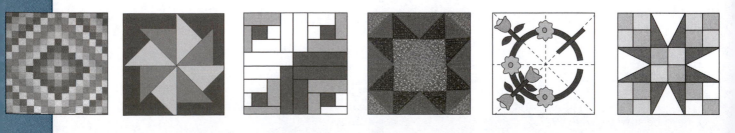

Chapter **13**

Setting Together the Quilt Top

You've made all your blocks and probably think you're almost finished. I'm sorry to say that you are only halfway there! You still have work to do—it's time to *set* together your blocks.

Consider the face of the quilt as a large block that you have to sew together. There is no set pattern to place the blocks in a design, so you have many choices on block positioning. You can move the blocks many different ways: place them side by side, frame each block with lattice, alternate a pieced block with a plain block, or even turn them on the diagonal.

In this chapter, we discuss the proper technique in sewing together the quilt top, and I will give hints on pressing. Just like a painting, the quilt top needs the correct frame. Borders and how to assemble them will be discussed. I'll also reveal the secret of mitering corners for the long sashing borders. Get ready to be demystified.

Solving the Quilt Puzzle

Before starting to lay out your blocks in the quilt top, you want to make sure the size of all the blocks is the same. All the blocks in this book should measure 12 inches square from seam line to seam line.

You would be surprised how uneven the blocks can get. How can this happen? I've found that fabrics with different qualities may stretch when handled or pressed during piecing. This is especially true of patches that have bias edges around their borders—for example, the triangles in the Eight Point Star. I have found that pieces of fabric can grow almost half an inch just by mishandling them. It also could be that you have not stitched exactly on the seam line. Being just $\frac{1}{16}$ of an inch off can grow to a half-inch mistake. So check your blocks and be sure to leave at least $\frac{1}{4}$-inch seam allowances all around.

Don't Get Stuck! _____

To check the size of your block, remember to measure from seam line to seam line, not from the raw edges of the block. People cut seam allowances inconsistently. Do not cut off any excess. You can cut away the large seam allowances after the blocks are sewn together.

When the size of your blocks is uniform, it's time to find their correct placement on the quilt top. As a beginner, you may have chosen to do a Sampler quilt to hone your skills. Sampler quilts are more of a challenge when it comes to getting your blocks to balance in color and pattern. This is one of my favorite times in quilt class because everyone has their say. We all stand around a table where the blocks are laid out and call out suggestions where to move them. It is really fun to mix and match block placement in your quilt. At the end, when everyone is satisfied, the quilt will be in perfect balance. Here are some hints on block placement, since you don't have my class with their boisterous suggestions to decide on your quilt face.

◆ Try not to have blocks with the same basic design next to each other. For example, don't put an Ohio Star next to a Churn Dash—there is too much similarity in the nine patches.

◆ Spread accent or bright colors throughout the quilt. Do not have too many dark colors in one area or your eyes will look only at the dark part and not appreciate the whole quilt.

◆ If you have a problem block, one that may have a different background fabric or has a unique design, you may have to move it to the center or make a block that complements it. Unfortunately, your last choice is not to use the block.

◆ Blocks that are similar (like Hearts All Around and Dresden Plate) should be placed opposite each other in a quilt so they will balance.

If you choose not to use a patch, you can always use it later in a pillow project!

Quilting Bee _____

If your block does not measure 12 inches from seam to seam, here is an easy way to make it right: Cut a 12-inch square out of cardboard; then turn the block to the wrong side, place the square on top, and redraw the lines as necessary.

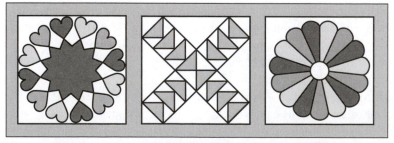

Look how you can balance your quilt with different designs.

Quilting Bee

I use the "squint method" to test balance. I put all the blocks in the designated order on my bed, step out of the room, then come in with my eyes squinted. First impressions make any unbalance obvious, and I can make changes.

Quilt Talk

Lattices are strips of fabric that separate and frame out each individual block. These are also known as **sashing**.

Side-by-Side Blocks

In this type of layout, the patches are sewn to each other rather than framed with *lattices*, or *sashing*.

The interplay of shapes and colors of the blocks forms new designs and looks very contemporary. Appliqué blocks are perfect for this method, since there is one large uniform background that basically frames out each appliqué motif.

I have seen Sampler quilts with the blocks pieced next to each other, but I think they appear too busy and confusing with the variety of shapes. In the case of the Sampler quilt, you may want to choose a different method of setting together. Let's look at some other ways.

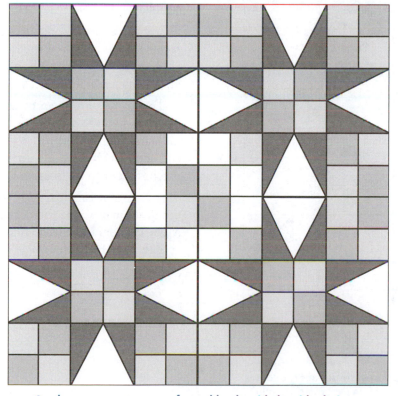

See how new patterns are formed by the side-by-side design.

Alternate with Solid Blocks

This is an easy way to separate your quilt blocks, alternating a pieced block with a solid 12-inch square of fabric. Your patches are really emphasized by the simplicity that surrounds them.

One nice thing about this method is that you have to piece fewer blocks to complete a whole quilt. Instead of piecing 15 blocks for a twin-size quilt, you need to piece only 8—the other blocks are solid fabric. The solid blocks, however, do need to have an intricate design quilted on them, so it really isn't a time-saver in the long run.

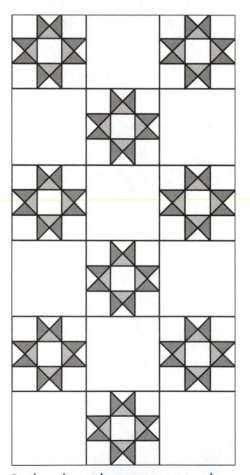

See how the patches are set apart and are more dramatic when separated by solid blocks.

Don't Get Stuck!

If you want to alternate pieced blocks with solid blocks, use this method on quilts with an odd number of blocks only, otherwise the overall pattern will look off-center. It's perfect for the quilt with three blocks across and five blocks in length, but not four blocks across and six blocks in length.

Lattice Alone

Sashing or lattice strips separate and frame the blocks in your quilt. Lattices can vary in size and complexity. Fabrics for the frame are chosen to complement your blocks, with a color taken from the color scheme, or you can use a neutral, solid-color muslin, or black. Proportionately, the lattices should be no larger than one-third the size of the block, in this case, 4 inches.

You can insert a solid lattice by cutting a rectangle the length of the block plus seam allowances (12½ inches) by the width decided upon plus seam allowances (3½ inches).

The lattices are sewn to the sides of the patches as you sew the rows together. Then measure the finished width of the quilt row and add ½ inch for the seam allowances. The patches seem to be floating on the lattice fabric.

If you want to add a little more interest, you can sew squares into the corner of each block. Many quilters use this technique to add the accent color from their blocks.

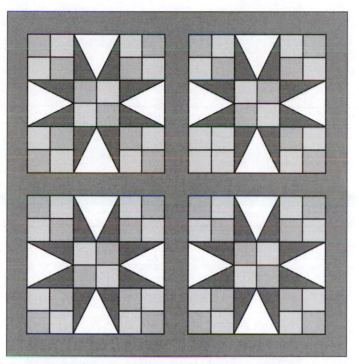

Notice how the solid lattice frames out the blocks.

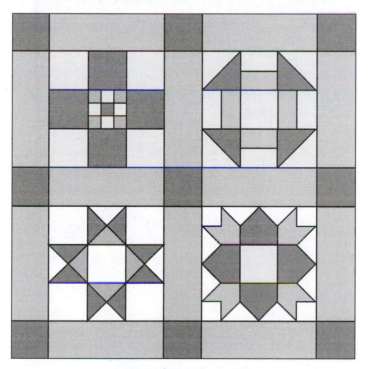

Lattice with corner squares.

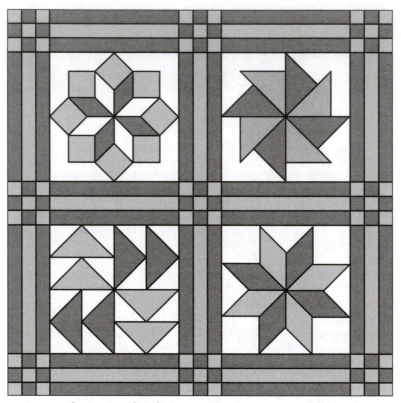

Intricate lattices can be almost as time-consuming as making your block, but look at the results!

The lattices will all measure 12½ inches in length by the chosen width (3 inches) plus seam allowances—3½ inches. To measure the corner squares, take the width of the lattice and add on the seam allowances (3½-inch square). Be sure to measure and count correctly.

When you become more experienced, you can try a complex lattice. The rectangle can be divided into three different color fabrics or have intricate piecing in each. Look at the preceding illustration of an advanced lattice.

Use a Different Slant

For a slightly different twist, you can use any of the previous methods of setting the blocks but turn the blocks on the diagonal. Look at the following figure to see how the blocks can change just by rotating them.

This design can be confusing to a beginner. Notice the sides of the quilt—there are side triangles that square out the quilt. I have used either solid triangles of the background fabric or even cut quilt blocks in half on the diagonal—yes, I did say cut quilt blocks—to fill in the open side areas. The plan of alternating blocks is probably the best approach because the solid blocks are easier to insert for a beginner.

Put all your patches in a pleasing order and let's sew them together.

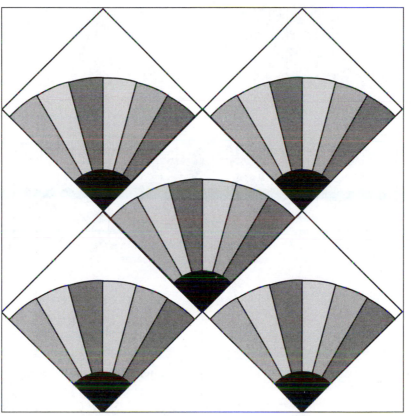

Quilt blocks set on the diagonal.

Joining It All Together

Consider your quilt top as one very large block. Once you have decided the block placement you need to analyze how to tackle sewing this together. Don't get overwhelmed—just divide the quilt face into rows, either horizontal or on the diagonal. You now have a plan of attack.

Quilting Bee

If you press all seam allowances toward the lattices, the seam allowances will butt against each other going in different directions, reducing bulkage.

Each quilt is unique so there are no set rules or instructions from now on. I can just tell you what to consider as you complete your quilt. Calculate how many, and measure the size of framing lattices needed for your quilt. Mark and cut out lattices or blocks making certain to add on the seam allowances. The blocks are alternated with the lattices and then sewn together in a horizontal row. If you have chosen the solid lattice, then one length of fabric is added above and below the row (see the following figure). Then the next row of the quilt is pinned and sewn to the first row unit.

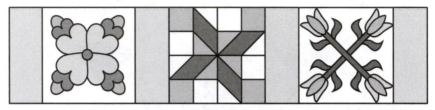

Sewing horizontal rows of a quilt and then adding either a solid lattice or a
lattice with corner squares.

In this stage of quilt making, even if I have
hand-pieced my quilt, I usually resort to using
the sewing machine. With all those long seam
lines, the machine is such a time-saver. However, you must be confident in using the sewing
machine because there are so many seam lines
to match up. Otherwise, slow and steady hand-
stitching is more accurate.

When you want to create a lattice with corner squares, you use the same technique of
alternating lattice and blocks across the rows.
The difference comes in sewing the horizontal
framing rows. You need to start with a square,
sew it to the short end of a lattice, a square,
and lattice all the way across the quilt.

Now it's time to sew these rows together.
Sew the lattice row to the top of the block row.
Do this for all block rows. Sew the lattices to
the top of the blocks only.

Then sew all the row units together, pinning
and sewing carefully, aligning all the intersecting seams. Soon you have sewn all these rows
together, and before you know it, the quilt top
is completed. Press all the horizontal seam
allowances toward the lattices. Finally, turn
the quilt top so the finished side is facing up
and press the right side; then cut off all the
threads—that in itself is an afternoon project!
Are you ready for the last piecing step?

Sewing the lattices and corner squares. Before sewing, press all seam allowances in opposite directions.

Don't Get Stuck!

It is tricky pinning and sewing so the squares and lattices align properly. Each intersecting seam is pinned and stitched to ensure they match. It helps to sew from one of the seams in the middle of the row to the outside edge.

It's Time to Cross the Borders

Can you imagine the *Mona Lisa* without a frame? Neither should your quilted work of art be without a *border*.

Quilt Talk

Borders are long continuous pieces of fabric that frame out the perimeter of your quilt.

Borders can be as simple as a solid fabric, or a series of bands of colors chosen from your color scheme. Expert quilters even create intricately pieced or appliquéd borders to surround

their quilts. It's all a matter of aesthetics. Balance, proportion, color, and the corner treatments are all variables you have to consider. You should think of borders as an essential part of the overall quilt design.

The corners of borders can be squared off, can have corner squares at the ends, or can even be *mitered*.

Quilt Talk

To **miter** is to join together the corner of two perpendicular edges with a 45-degree angle seam.

The first step is to decide on the fabric for the borders. I usually lay out my quilt top on a bed and fold pieces of fabrics from the quilt next to it. Then I use the "squint method" to see which fabric or combination of fabrics looks best.

Next, measure the finished edges of your quilt and be sure each parallel side is the same size. If they are accurate in length, then it's time to cut out your borders. For the side borders, measure from edge to edge, which is the length you need to cut.

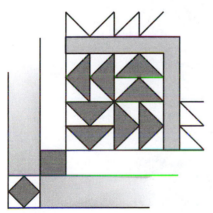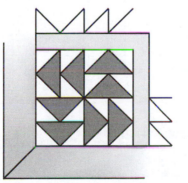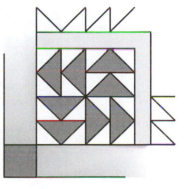

Simple, mitered, and expert borders.

If possible, avoid sewing seams—cut the border from a full length of fabric that runs down the straight of grain. If you don't have enough fabric, it is totally acceptable to use the crosswise grain and cut the border from selvage to selvage, creating one seam. Sew the side borders onto the quilt, open them out, and press the seam allowances toward the border.

Now it's time to work on the top and bottom borders. Measure from the edge of the left border across the quilt to the edge of the right border. This is the measurement for both the top and bottom borders. Sew on these borders. If you decide on attaching more than one band of color, repeat the process, measuring and adding on the side borders, then the top and bottom borders.

Don't Get Stuck!

When measuring your quilt, start your measurement 2 or 3 inches in from the outer edge. The outer edge tends to stretch, causing your measurement to be incorrect.

If your corner design includes squares, measure only the top and bottom of the quilt top; do not include the borders. Then cut four squares the size of the width of the side border and add one square to each end of the top and bottom borders (see figure b). Make sure to add seam allowances for the border and square pieces.

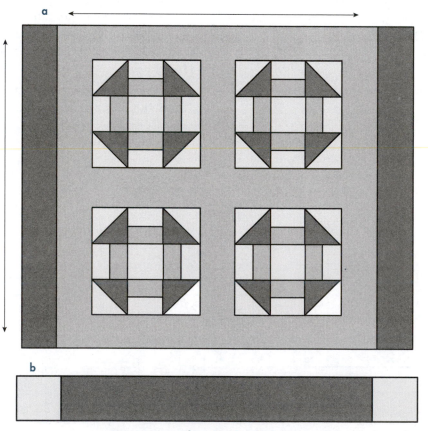

Measuring and sewing borders.

There are endless possibilities for border designs, so be creative and go into the borderline.

To Miter or Not to Miter

Mitering the corners of the border gives your quilt a smooth, professional look. This type of finish requires more fabric than the other borders, so if you are low on fabric, choose another method. When your border design calls for several bands of colors, cut all the fabrics the same size and sew them together into one unit, then proceed with the following directions. When making a mitered border it is essential to measure and sew accurately. These instructions will make mitering effortless.

1. **Measure and cut.** All border measurements are calculated by measuring the length of the quilt top then adding the width of both borders on each side of the quilt. If a quilt is 80 inches × 50 inches and the borders are 5 inches wide all around the perimeter, let's determine the measurements for the mitered border. The calculations would look like this:

   For the two side borders, add: 80" (quilt length) + 5" (top border width) + 5" (bottom border width) + 1" (fudge factor) = 91" × 5½" wide (remember to add on the seam allowance for the border width). For the top and bottom borders, add: 50" (quilt width) + 5" (left-side border width) + 5" (right-side border width) + 1" (fudge factor) = 61" × 5½" wide. I always add an inch "just in case"; you can always cut it off.

2. **Pin.** Pin the center point of the borders right sides together to the middle point of the quilt top. There should be an equal amount of fabric hanging off the ends. This really looks strange!

3. **Sew.** Start ¼ inch from the top edge of the quilt and backstitch. Then sew along the side edge of the quilt top on the marked ¼-inch seam line. Stop sewing ¼ inch from the end and backstitch.

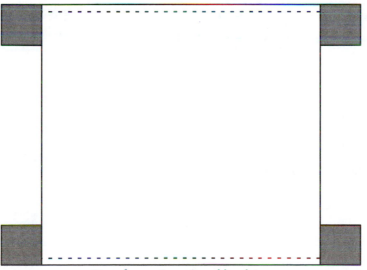

Steps for sewing mitered borders.

Sew all four borders, stopping at ¼ inch and backstitching. Try to get the stitches from both seams to meet at the same point.

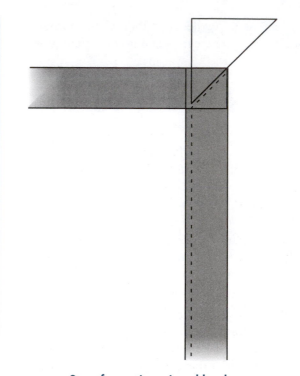

Steps for sewing mitered borders.

4. **Miter.** Most of my students get to this point and then bring me their quilt, with these ends hanging off, and say "Help!" Here's how to finish. Turn to the wrong side of your quilt. Cut off excess fabrics. Take a gridded plastic ruler, one that has a 45-degree angle, and draw a line from the backstitch point diagonally to the corner of the border. Pin and check to see if the border lays flat. If so, then sew on the drawn lines. Cut the excess from the border leaving a ¼-inch seam allowance.

Steps for sewing mitered borders.

5. **Press.** Press seam allowances to the borders and the mitered seam open.

Whatever border method you have chosen, I know that your quilt top is beautiful but, more importantly, it's finished! Next stop—quilting!

The Least You Need to Know

◆ If not all your patches are all 12 inches square, redraw the seam lines.

◆ Arrange your blocks so the colors and designs are evenly distributed around the quilt top.

◆ Set your quilt together by sewing horizontal rows of blocks and lattices.

◆ Borders frame your quilt and should complement its color and proportion.

◆ Mitered border corners are sewn together at a 45-degree angle.

In This Part

Part 5

Making the Quilt Sandwich and Keeping It Together

Your quilt is ready to be assembled and it is essential to hold the three layers together. Batting, backing, and basting are all-important factors to unite your pieces into a quilt to remember.

Then we'll breathe life into your quilt by adding the puffy inside to give your quilt warmth and dimension. You are going to build a quilt sandwich consisting of the quilt top, batting, and backing. Basting methods to hold all these layers together will be discussed. Quilt designs do not just serve the utilitarian purpose of holding your quilt together; the quilt design adds a new level of beauty. Let's give your quilt life!

In This Chapter

◆ Pros and cons of different kinds of batting

◆ Choosing backing for quiltability

◆ How to assemble the quilt top

◆ Various methods of basting for a wrinkle-free quilt

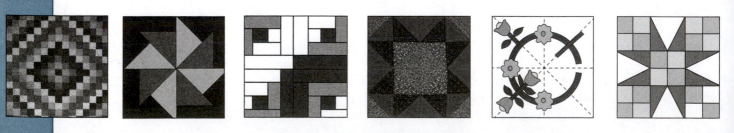

The Three Bs: Batting, Backing, and Basting

Now is the time for all good quilters to unite your quilt! Your quilt top demonstrates your artistry and creativity—now let's add dimension. When I first started quilting, I assumed that my quilt would turn out to be like a big puffy comforter. I quickly found out that the thicker the inside material, the harder it was to sew. The type of batting you choose will affect your ability to execute the quilting stitches. Most of the quilts with delicate quilting stitches use a very thin batting. I have since revised my thoughts about quilts and discovered that thinner is better for beginners.

The back of your quilt isn't always the back. Some quilters like to make their quilts reversible, so don't think that your fabric choice is insignificant. Besides looks, the "quiltability," or the ease of putting the needle through the fabric, is extremely important. Purchasing the wrong backing will make your quilting life difficult.

Your quilt is ready to be assembled and it is very important to hold the three layers securely together. Basting is essential. There will be weeks, months, or sometimes years of handling your quilt while you stitch and put on the finishing touches. There are several methods of basting that can be used to secure a stable unit. You can choose which method best suits your needs. But get ready to baste, baste, baste.

Don't Go Batty—Know All the Types of Batting

A quilt has three layers: the quilt top, batting (or filling), and backing. The middle layer is usually a soft, puffy batting, which adds dimension to your quilt. The type of batting you choose will dramatically change the quilt's appearance and your ability to quilt. Let's consider different types of batting and find out their good and bad characteristics.

Polyester Batting

This is the most popular and easy to use of all the fillers. It comes already cut in a variety of sizes and packed in plastic bags. All you have to do is open the bag and unroll the batting. These manufactured battings come in different *lofts*, or thicknesses, and are bonded to prevent shifting when quilted.

Quilt Talk

The **loft,** or thickness, of the batting can range from ⅛ inch to 2 inches.

The thicker the loft, the warmer the quilt. Each manufacturer has its own description of thickness: low loft, Fatt Batt, or Ultra-Loft. Ask to see samples to determine which thickness you prefer. Polyester battings are bonded by heat or a resin finish. Did you ever have a comforter that after you washed it, all the stuffing had moved around and formed uneven lumps? It would be really discouraging to have that happen after all the work you have done. So it is important to have battings that are bonded.

Quilting Bee

Some people have allergic reactions when using polyester battings that have been bonded with a chemical, resin finish. If you are one of those people, be sure to buy heat-bonded polyester battings.

Polyester Batting on a Roll or Bolt

This type of batting is found in many fabric or craft stores. It is the same quality as the batting found in bags, but the advantage is you can feel the weight and loft. Then the salesperson can unroll and cut off the exact amount you need. It is sometimes more expensive than the bagged batting though.

Cotton Batting

This type of batting works well in clothing and thin quilts. It is not as puffy as polyester batting, but is a more traditional thickness. Students who have used cotton batting have said cotton is very easy to quilt through, and your stitches can be very small. One disadvantage is that cotton shrinks—many brands of cotton batting need to be shrunk and some also need to have residual cotton oil washed out before use. Check to see if the cotton batting you are considering needs to be washed. (It is a messy project to wash this in a bathtub.) Some of the newer cotton battings are already washed, but please make sure. You do have to stitch your quilting lines closer together than with the polyester batting because it will shift in the quilt.

Other Fillings

The fillings discussed earlier are the most popular battings for quilts. Here are some unusual items that can be used for the inside layer.

Cotton flannel sheets or wool blankets add warmth but not fluffiness. I've used a flannel sheet in a quilted tablecloth where I wanted a thin batting. It would be horrible to put down a wine glass on a puffy tablecloth and have the glass not sit right—dry cleaner, here we come. A flannel sheet, which feels cooler than polyester, can be used in quilts meant for summer use. Many times old quilts were used as a batting. Open up one quilt and find another!

Scraps and Pieces

Quilters, being very resourceful, have filled their quilts with many unusual items. I've heard of women who, during the pioneer days, used cotton right from the harvested boles or carded wool. Antique dealers can authenticate a quilt by holding it up to a light and seeing if any seeds are visible in the cotton filling. Many times frugal quilters who had nothing else for batting pieced together sacks that held cottonseed, flour, or fertilizer products. During the Depression, women also used newspapers, rags, old clothes, or even feathers—anything to add warmth to the quilt.

Backing: It's Not Always the Wrong Side

Is the backing the wrong side of the quilt? Not always. Many times quilters use an attractive fabric for the quilt back so they can use the quilt on its reverse side. Traditionally a single length of fabric, the backing can be solid, printed, or pieced. It was expensive for pioneer women to purchase a solid length, so many times they pieced together feed or flour sacks that were opened and cleaned.

Don't Get Stuck!

Don't use a percale bed sheet for backing—the thread count is much too dense for a needle to pierce it. You should not use a muslin sheet either. There might be a finish that makes it unquiltable.

One trait that a backing should have is "quiltability," or ease of quilting. A backing fabric should have a low thread count and should be loosely woven. Traditionally muslin was used because it was the easiest to sew and inexpensive. You may be tempted to use a bed sheet because of its size. Don't do it! One time I made an octagonal wall hanging and I thought that a bed sheet would eliminate the necessity of seaming it together. What a mistake! I suffered with blisters through the whole quilting process.

Since quilting has become so popular, manufacturers have started marketing muslin that is 80 to 90 inches wide, perfect for quilt backing. Muslin and all fabrics for the backing must be shrunk before use, as were your fabrics for the quilt top.

Quilting Bee

Open up your bag of batting, unroll the batting carefully, and let it sit out for a few hours to relax the folds it accumulated from being in the bag.

What Size Should the Backing and Batting Be?

The batting and backing should be slightly larger than your finished quilt top. For the batting, it is easy to get the correct size—just measure the finished top and purchase a bag with the size that corresponds to your measurements.

Don't worry if your batting is too small or if you want to use up leftover pieces—there is a way of joining them together. Make sure that all the battings are the same loft or thickness. Then cut out as many pieces as you need to form the correct size, 1 inch larger than your quilt top. But do not overlap the battings that need to be united.

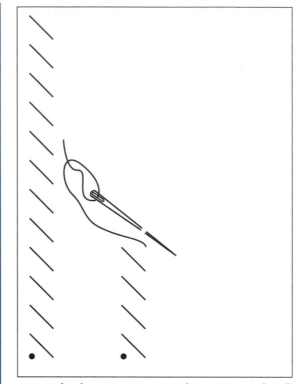

Don't let these Zs put you to sleep—your quilt will be finished soon.

If you are making a bed quilt, it is probably necessary to seam the backing. You can do this in several ways, and the method you choose depends on your preferences and the size of the quilt. Look at the following figure to see three ways you can seam together the backing.

> **Don't Get Stuck!**
>
> When basting battings together, don't overlap them or pull the stitches too tight because a lump will develop.

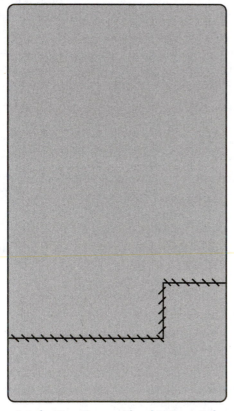

Join batting pieces with a basting stitch.

Using a needle threaded and knotted with quilting thread, baste the battings together. I use what I call a Z stitch. Take a horizontal stitch on the right batting to the left batting, then move your needle down ½ inch, taking another stitch in the right to left batting (see the following figure).

Determine how much fabric you need to buy. If you are making a small quilt, like a wall hanging or a crib quilt, measure the dimensions of the quilt top and add 2 inches all around the perimeter. If the quilt is large, a bed size for example, you will need to piece the backing. There are several ways to seam the backing together. Traditionally, the most acceptable way is to seam three lengths of fabric, of equal widths, vertically down the backing. This is used especially when the quilt is wider than two lengths of fabric sewn together. I am more practical and don't mind piecing together fabric of unequal widths as long as the seams run parallel to the sides and are not crooked. Depending on the size of your quilt and the amount of fabric you have, you may even seam the backing horizontally.

Whichever method you decide to use, measure the quilt top and compute how many lengths you need to purchase. Shrink the backing fabric and cut off the selvages. Remember that the selvage shrinks and puckers when washed, so remove it first. Sew together the seams and press. If you are sewing by machine, press the seams open. Press the whole backing. Now you are ready to layer your quilt. Some quilters want a traditional handmade quilt. Besides hand piecing, they will even hand stitch the backing.

Wrinkle-Free Basting for Your Quilt Layers

When each of the three layers is pieced, prepared, and cut to the correct size, you are ready to assemble your quilt. Remember, this is the last time you will be able to press the quilt top and the backing, so make them look perfect.

I use two different approaches to basting, depending on the size of the project. Find a large, flat working space (a dining room table, Ping-Pong table, or a hard floor) and, if possible, a friend to help you—an extra set of hands is a great time-saver.

Basting a Small Project

Follow these steps to baste a small project:

1. Put the backing fabric on the floor, wrong-side-up. It should be 2 inches larger all around the circumference of the quilt top.

2. Lift the batting carefully and put it over the backing fabric. (The batting is cut about 1 inch smaller than the backing and 1 inch larger than the quilt top.) Spread with your hands to smooth out the lumps.

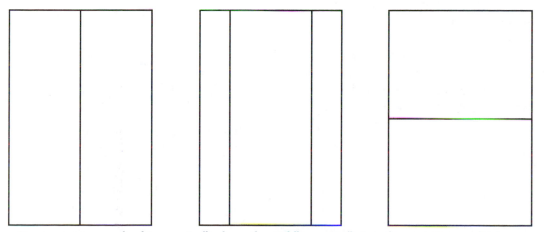

You can seam your backing vertically down the middle, vertically into three sections, or horizontally across the middle.

Don't Get Stuck!

This literally is a don't-get-stuck! When pinning together your quilt layers, be sure you can see all of the pins so you can remove them after you stitch up your quilt. I made a quilt for my niece and her husband, and a pin must have gotten lost in the batting. They soon learned pins and waterbeds do not get along. Use pins with large heads or safety pins that won't wander into the quilt.

3. Center the quilt face on top of the batting, right-side-up.

4. As you spread these layers, the fabric shifts. Cut off any excess of batting and backing: backing that is more than 2 inches all around the quilt top; and batting 1 inch all the way around the quilt top.

5. Pin through all three layers using extra-long quilting pins with very large heads.

6. Using a contrasting thread with a large knot, start stitching the Z stitch at the center of the quilt and baste parallel to the side of the quilt until you reach the bottom edge. Then start in the center and baste up. Each time, start in the center of the quilt and baste vertically, horizontally, and then diagonally. The basting lines should look like a sunburst. If there is any slippage, it may be necessary to baste more lines parallel to the sides.

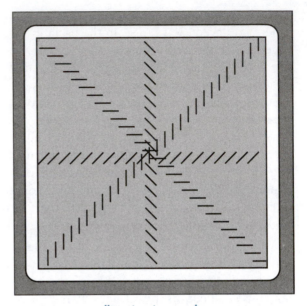

Baste a small project in a sunburst pattern.

Don't Get Stuck!

There are some problems to watch out for if you are laying out your backing on a rug. First, the masking tape will not stick to a rug, so the backing may be wrinkled. Second, you might baste through your quilt to the rug. I've done this and had to cut some of the basting stitches. You can purchase a 6-foot folding cardboard cutting board if there is no table or

Basting Large Projects

Follow these steps to baste large projects.

1. Lay the backing on the floor, wrong-side-up. Hold the edges down with masking tape so the backing is stretched taut against the floor with no wrinkles.

2. Place the batting on top of the backing and then spread it smooth with your hands.

3. Center the quilt face, right-side-up, on top of the backing and batting. Measure to see that the backing's seams are parallel to the sides of the quilt top.

4. Pin the layers together with extra-long quilting pins with large heads. Be sure to pin through all three layers.

5. Starting at the center of the quilt, run a line of basting stitches (Z stitches or running stitches) vertically and horizontally. On large projects, run the basting stitches every 4 to 6 inches parallel to the sides, forming a grid of basting.

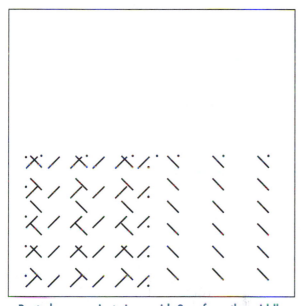

Baste large projects in a grid. Sew from the middle to the outsides.

There is an alternative method if you can't tape the backing to the floor. It takes slightly longer than the process I just showed you, because you have to baste in two stages. First, spread out the backing, wrong-side-up, and then put the batting on top. Baste the backing to the batting, making sure that there are no wrinkles in this unit. Then, starting at the center, run basting stitches on the unit, parallel to the sides.

Check to see that the backing is smooth. Then center the quilt top, right-side-up, on the basted unit. Pin and baste the quilt top parallel to the top edge. Start basting in the center, and form a grid with perpendicular basting stitches on the front and back of the quilt.

If you don't want to hand-baste your layers together, you can use safety pins. Quilting manufacturers have produced large nickel-plated safety pins that will not rust or tarnish on your quilt. Be careful: I once had a quilt that I was quilting at my leisure (in other words, very slowly), and when I removed the pins, they left holes in the fabric. Don't leave pins in for too long. The safety pins are great for basting projects that are machine-quilted. Sometimes the presser foot may catch on the Z basting stitches, but safety pins will make machine quilting easier.

Get your friends to help you assemble and baste the quilt top. Have your own quilting bee! Your quilt now has body. Next we will give it life by learning how to quilt.

The Least You Need to Know

- Prepare batting by letting wrinkles unfold and piecing similar lofts together, if necessary.
- Cut the batting 1 inch larger than the perimeter of the quilt top.
- Backing must be shrunk with selvages cut off, and sewn into a length of fabric that is 2 inches larger, all around, than the quilt top.
- Basting holds together all three layers with either a Z stitch or running stitch in a contrasting color thread.
- Small projects are basted in a sunburst design from the center out.
- Large projects are sewn in a 4- to 6-inch grid of basting stitches starting from the center and sewing horizontally and vertically.

In This Chapter

- ◆ How to mark quilt designs
- ◆ Steps to hand quilting
- ◆ Alternative methods of keeping a quilt together
- ◆ Hints on machine quilting

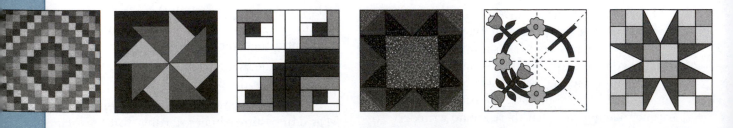

Quilting 101

It's finally time to quilt! Your quilting stitches will add dimension to your quilt by adding shadows and subtle designs while enhancing the motifs of the printed fabric. Before taking your first stitch you need to plan where those stitches will go. That decision will affect the overall look of your completed quilt. I suggest that beginners think fewer stitches—but don't skimp. Quilting can be tedious for novices. Consider this quilt as a learning experience and don't obsess over the size of the quilting stitches.

First decide on a quilting design and where to stitch. Then transfer your design to the quilt top. There is a dilemma ahead: You need to see your markings while quilting, but then not see the markings when you are finished. Today there are many modern quilting innovations—plastic stencils and wash-out pens, to name a few—that our quilting ancestors would be in heaven over. We'll discuss equipment to make marking your designs easy and worry-free.

Lastly we will learn how to bond our three layers into one quilt. I will give detailed instructions on how I was taught to hand quilt and then explain alternative methods of tying your quilt and quilting by machine. Each has advantages and disadvantages, so you can evaluate which is best for you. So relax, pull up a chair, and let's quilt.

Choosing Quilt Designs

With modern batting choices, where you quilt will be based on artistry, not necessity. When our ancestors used fillers such as cotton or wool batting, their lines of quilting had to be only 2 inches apart, otherwise the fillers would shift and lump. Because most of the batting manufactured today is bonded, it will not shift, allowing us to attach the layers every 6 to 8 inches apart.

The amount of quilting you do is up to you! You can make your designs simple or intricate. Let me suggest some ideas for quilting, ranging from the simplicity of outline quilting to the excessive echo quilting.

- **Traditional quilting.** The traditional method is to follow the outline of the block's design. Stitch ¼ inch from each seam line of your pieced or appliquéd patch. The amount of the ¼ inch is significant because it is just outside the pressed seam allowances.

- **Stitching in the ditch.** Doesn't that sound strange? This is another process of quilting that follows the pieces of the block's design—only this time you stitch right into the seam. The shape of the entire design then becomes distinct. The stitches are almost invisible because the fabric on each side of the seam will puff up around the stitches.

> **Quilt Talk**
>
> A **quilt stencil** is a plastic sheet that has grooves cut out in a specific design, sometimes hearts, flowers, or geometric shapes.

- **Design quilting.** You can also embellish your quilt blocks with a set design. There are many *quilt stencils* that you can purchase and simply trace onto your patch in the open spaces.

- **Echo design quilting.** Lines of stitching follow the outline of a block's basic design, then are repeated, like ripples in a pond, every ¼ inch. The concentric lines make waves of heavy quilting. This is a lot of work and not for beginners.

- **Overall design.** These lines of quilting ignore the block's pattern and use an overall design. You can quilt a grid of squares, diagonal lines, or a clamshell design.

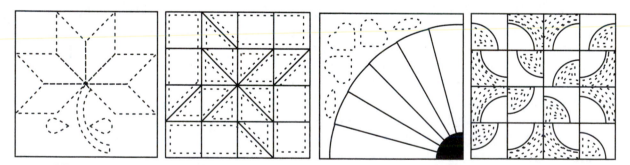

Four different ways to quilt your blocks, from left to right: stitch in the ditch, traditional, special design, or echo.

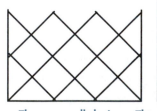

Three overall designs. These diamond, square, or clamshell overall designs add patterning to your quilt.

Quilting Bee

Two instances when you should quilt less: Don't waste time on an intricate design if you are quilting on a highly patterned fabric (the stitches will not show up). And, if you want a thick, puffy quilt, use less stitching because the quilting stitches compact the batting, making it flatter—goodbye, thick quilt.

For large solid spaces I suggest using a stencil of a quilt design. You can make your own with plastic sheeting and an Exacto knife, but I don't recommend it for beginners. Manufactured stencils come in a wide variety of shapes and are relatively inexpensive.

If you are determined to design your own patterns for quilting, trace common shapes and mark them in a specific order. Draw and cut out a cardboard heart or diamond or use a glass to trace a cardboard circle to style your own designs.

Look at pictures of quilts to get ideas on quilting styles that you like. Use your imagination! Decide on how you want to quilt and transfer your mind's creations to your quilt.

Got an Idea? Mark Your Quilt!

Some quilters mark their quilt top before putting all the layers together. I prefer to mark after the quilt is assembled. My quilts are usually a work in progress, and I often change my mind as I go along.

There are certain marking supplies you will need to purchase. So let's examine the different methods of marking.

If you have chosen to stitch in the ditch, you won't need any special supplies since your seams are your sewing guides. When marking for traditional quilting, however, you have several marking options:

Quilting Bee

When marking your quilt, draw as light a line as possible that you can still see easily. Don't use a number 2 pencil—it's so soft that it may smear and make your fabric look dirty.

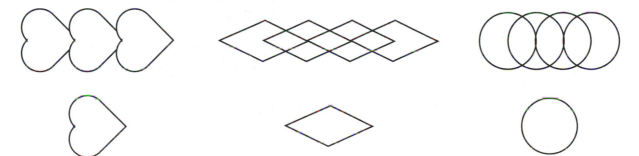

Cut out and trace shapes from cardboard to style your own designs.

◆ **A number 2.5 or 3 pencil.** You'll get a fine, sharp line that won't smudge.

◆ **Wash-out markers.** You draw a line to mark the design and then, when you've completed quilting, wipe the line with a wet cloth and the marks dissolve. There are two popular brands of markers on the market: One is blue and needs water to remove it; the other is purple and evaporates on its own in a day or two—by magic, the lines disappear!

Don't Get Stuck!

Always test markers on your scrap fabrics first. Students have used regular markers by mistake, and then there was nothing they could do to get rid of the marks!

◆ **Masking tape.** This is my favorite option for marking a ¼-inch seam line. Buy masking tape that is ¼-inch wide, cut off the amount you need, and line it up to the seam you are following. Then lift and move it to another seam. You don't have to get involved with any drawing or worry about erasing.

◆ **Tailor's chalk.** These lines can be brushed off when you finish quilting. The chalk makes thicker lines as it dulls, and thin lines are better for accuracy. You can purchase powdered chalk that rolls onto the fabric and comes in a variety of colors for marking dark and light fabrics.

◆ **Soap slivers.** This is one way our ancestors marked their quilts. It is a useful technique even today, especially on dark fabrics where a pencil or marker line will not show. Save all those old soap pieces from your bathtub, but don't use deodorant soaps because they have extra chemicals.

One hint on using stencils: The grooves are cut out in the design so you can trace it with your marking tool (not masking tape). Notice that the design is not continuous but that there is an inch every so often that is not cut. Many beginners stop at each end of the grooves and then start again, making a partial design. You are supposed to bridge these spaces with stitches. The manufacturer had to stop the groove or the stencil would fall apart!

Mark your designs, then get your needle, thread, and thimble. It's time to quilt!

Place the masking tape against the straight seam you are following. Then encircle your work with a hoop.

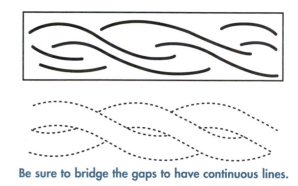

Be sure to bridge the gaps to have continuous lines.

Hand Quilting

Quilting is short, evenly spaced running stitches that are worked through all three layers of the quilt, adding strength and decorative textures. Let's proceed with putting our quilt layers together. I find hand quilting relaxing and enjoy quilting while my husband watches sports on television. I feel as if I'm spending time with him while I accomplish something.

Hoop or Frame?

Hoops and frames are specialized tools that help you hand quilt. Besides your quilting thread, quilting needles (sizes 8 to 10), and your thimble, you need something to hold your quilt taut. It is very important to stretch the fabric slightly to eliminate tucks on the backing.

Quilting Frames

When most people think of quilting, they picture women sitting around a *quilting frame*. I unfortunately have never had the opportunity to work my quilts on one. There just isn't enough room in my house and frames can be costly. Legs or wooden sawhorses support a large rectangular frame. The quilting frame holds your project so you can use both hands to quilt. Beginners should probably not work on a frame, since it is stationary and it takes practice to sew in the various directions of your quilting designs.

Quilt Talk

A **quilting frame** is a free-standing rectangle that holds a quilt, allowing several people to stitch a section, then roll the quilt to another section, quilting until the whole quilt is finished.

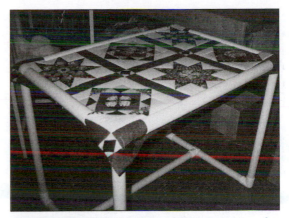

This PVC quilting frame is found in the classroom of my favorite quilting store—Acme Fabrics. Groups can work on quilt projects together with a frame like this one.

Hoops

I prefer using a hoop because I like to have my projects portable. A hoop consists of two round, oval, or square shapes that fit over one another and hold the quilt tightly between the two pieces. More basting is needed when you use a hoop because you will be moving and handling the fabric as you change the hoop's positions. Hoops come in several styles. The traditional wooden hoops have two round or oval hoops that fit into one another. The top hoop has a large screw that allows the hoop to open larger to accommodate the thickness of the batting.

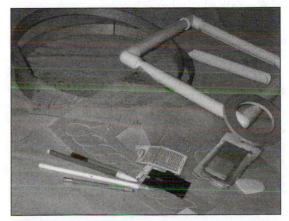

What's all the hoop-la? Here is the traditional hoop for quilting, along with other marking and quilting equipment.

There is a new type of hoop that is made out of plastic PVC piping. One of my students found that the PVC stretched and didn't hold the quilt tightly. So I suggest you don't use this type of hoop on quilts that have extra loft or thickness.

> **Quilting Bee**
>
> I like using a round hoop rather than an oval one—it's easier to move in any direction. Make sure your hoop has a large screw so you can open it to expand the hoop at least 1 inch!

Some quilters are able to quilt without a frame or hoop, but they increase the amount of basting. Also, continually check the back of the quilt for wrinkles or tucks. Choose the best tool for you and make your quilting experience great.

Rock Your Stitches

Gather all your quilting equipment, get comfortable, and let's quilt! Although quilting simply consists of running stitches, the trick is to catch all three layers in very small uniform stitches. Making small stitches is a matter of practice. My first quilting teacher said she didn't like her stitches sewn the first 20 minutes she quilted, so she always ripped them out! Remember, this is your first project and your stitches may be large. Never fear, practice makes perfect.

Take apart your hoop and place your project over the bottom part. Take the top hoop and unscrew it as large as possible. Position the top hoop over the bottom, trapping your quilt in between.

Give your quilt a face-lift—straighten your quilt to smooth out a wrinkle here and a tuck there.

Tighten the screw so that the fabric is taut but not stretched out of shape. Turn the hoop over and check that you have no folds or tucks in the backing. Tug on the backing slightly to straighten it out.

> **Don't Get Stuck!**
>
> When starting to quilt, be sure the needle does not go all the way through to the backing, but keep it parallel in the batting until it reaches the quilting line. Then bring the needle up.

It's time for your first stitch. Start with about 18 inches of quilt thread, and make the small knot that you have been using for piecing. Begin working at the center of your project and quilt toward the outside edges. Your hand with the needle is on the top of the hoop and your other hand is under the hoop, pushing up the needle and guiding where the stitches go. On the top side, put your needle about ½ inch from where you want to start quilting. I call this no-man's-land. Push the needle through the batting, but don't let it go through to the backing. Then bring the needle up on the line that you want to stitch. Pull the thread through.

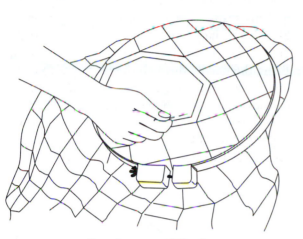

Start in no-man's-land.

Now I know you are thinking about the knot that is on the top of the quilt. Tug on the thread and the little knot will pop into the batting and be hidden. On the marked quilting line, take a backstitch and then start your running stitches, going through all three layers to secure them.

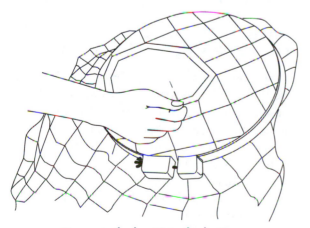

Pop goes the knot into the batting.

With your top hand, push the needle in perpendicular to the surface and, with your thumb, roll the needle to a 45-degree angle while your pointer finger holds down the fabric. Your stitches will be moving away from you. You will know you have gone through all three layers when the needle pricks your finger under the hoop. Ouch! Some people like to quilt toward themselves and use their pointer finger to push the needle and use their thumb to hold down the fabric. I usually alternate directions to give my fingers a rest.

Quilting Bee

You can use a leather thimble to protect the finger of your bottom hand, but I like to paint my finger with several coats of clear nail polish. It protects my finger but I can still feel the stitches. Don't apply nail polish if you have an open cut—that would hurt.

Pull the thread through and start another stitch, making sure the stitches are uniform in size. Eventually you will develop a rocking motion as you stitch. Move the needle down and then roll it up. Use both thumb and pointer finger to position the needle on the quilting line, then push with your pointer finger while the thumb holds the fabric down in front of the stitch. It may be more comfortable to push with your thumb and hold the fabric with your pointer finger. It's your choice.

Rock your stitches.

Take only one stitch at a time, especially around curves. As you get better you can take several stitches on your needle.

It's possible to move your line of quilting from one design to another by having the needle travel through the batting to get to another spot. When traveling, do not go all the way through to the backing. It's like taking one long stitch through the middle of the quilt.

Pack your thread and let your needle travel through the batting.

Stabbing Is a No-No

Try not to *stab* your quilt by pushing the needle into the top and pulling it out underneath with your other hand. The stitches may look right on the top of the quilt, but the stitches on the underside may be uneven and crooked. Use this method only when stitching is so hard that normal quilting is impossible—for example, when many seam allowances intersect or the quilt is too stiff to put your needle through with a running stitch.

> **Quilt Talk**
>
> You are **stabbing** when you insert the needle into your quilt with your top hand and pull it out the bottom with your other hand under the hoop. Then, with your bottom hand, you push the needle from the bottom to the top. When you stab, you are using both hands to quilt your stitches.

Securing Your Stitching

Now you are at the point where there are only a few inches of thread left on your needle. What do you do to secure and knot off the line of quilting stitches? Through the years, I have learned from my students several ways of finishing these quilting seams. The easiest way for beginners is this: Take a large stitch in the batting and then backstitch into the last two stitches of the seam. Bring the needle through the batting into no-man's-land and out the top of the quilt. Cut this thread so ¼ inch is showing. Insert the needle in the batting near the thread parallel to the top and move it back and forth catching the thread, making it disappear into the batting.

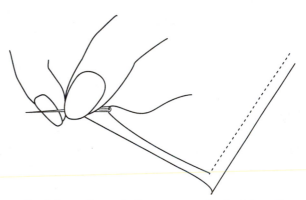

Don't be at the end of your rope—backstitch and make your thread disappear into the batting.

Tie Your Quilt into Knots

Sometimes you may want your quilt to be thick and fluffy. You may also be short on time. Because traditional quilting is time-consuming and does compact the batting, you may want an alternative. I have found the answer to both problems: Secure your layers with knots. Yarn or embroidery floss can be used to prevent your quilt from shifting. These quilts are called tied or tufted quilts.

Don't Get Stuck!

When you tie your quilt, you must use a bonded batting so the batting won't shift.

Here are some pointers for tying your quilt:

1. Pin and baste together the quilt top, batting, and backing.

2. Thread the embroidery needle with floss or yarn in a color that blends or contrasts with your color scheme, depending on your taste.

3. Decide on the arrangement of the knots. You can choose an overall pattern (such as every 5 inches in a grid) or follow the block's designs.

4. Starting from the center of the quilt, take a ¼-inch stitch from the top to the bottom through all three layers and up to the top. Don't pull all the way through but leave a 3-inch tail. Be sure you have caught all three layers.

5. With the ends, tie a square knot. Remember your scout lessons? Put the right end over the left end and under; then put the left end over the right end and under.

6. Pull the knot tight to secure it, and trim the ends to the desired length.

7. Repeat tying the knots in the designated design working to the outside edges.

Quilting Bee

When tying their quilts, some people like to leave a ½-inch tuft, while others leave longer ends and tie a bow.

Our quilting ancestors did not have all their covers quilted with complex designs. Many of their quilts were tied. For modern quilters, tying a quilt is great when you have to get a project done quickly; but make sure you use enough ties to hold your quilt together and that your knots are secure. Do get yourself tied up in knots!

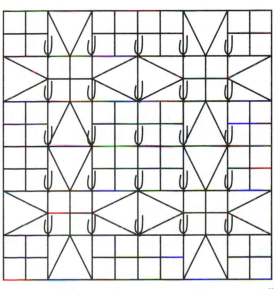
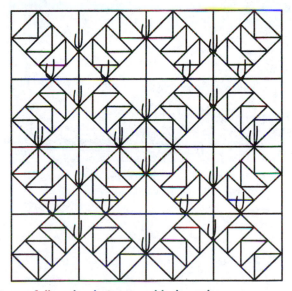

Where to tie or not to tie? Use an overall design or follow the design your blocks make.

Machine Quilting

Using the sewing machine is a quick way for quilting your projects. Beginners should start with a small project like a pillow or wall hanging to get familiarized with the technique. There are several strategies to consider to prevent the layers from shifting, making your quilt bumpy and lumpy. The first concern is that you are familiar and confident in using your machine. No novices please.

Plan your quilting design with your ability and machine in mind. Straight lines are easier to sew than curves. Overall designs of parallel lines or a square grid are easier than the clam shell pictured earlier in the chapter. Sewing in the ditch is good because the stitches are hidden in the block pattern.

This watercolor pillow made by the author has parallel lines machine quilted on the diagonal.

There are computerized sewing machines allowing you to program your own designs or ones that have a "free-arm" that allows you a full range of motion to make a *stippling* design or follow your quilting design.

> **Quilt Talk**
>
> **Stippling** is a random line of quilting usually done on the background of the block. The close together swirl of stitches makes the foreground design of the block stand out. The shapes are enhanced.

I've even seen books that have developed quilt patterns that are made up of one single continuous line of stitching. No constant stopping and restarting your machine lines.

Next use special equipment to assist you. A walking foot or a darning foot is a must. Accurate marking and basting are essential. Sometimes instead of basting with thread, some quilters use large safety pins. These can be removed as your machine needle quilts that area. There is also a no mark quilting paper in which you draw or trace your design onto one piece of this lightweight paper, then layer as many templates as you need, and sew (without thread) over the design. This makes perforations of the design through all the sheets. Position each piece of paper in the correct placement, and sew over the design. When done peel the paper away. Easy and accurate.

Lastly, practice on three layers using similar batting to try out your machine and dexterity. As you are machine quilting you may need to find solutions by tinkering with your machine. Here are some problems and I hope, some useful solutions.

Problem	Solution
The presser foot may push the top fabric along, making the top stretch move and pucker.	Use a "walking foot" (a special attachment to the presser foot that has rollers to the fabric); drop the feed dogs so you can maneuver the quilt though the seam; or loosen the top tension slightly.
You may quilt in tucks on the backing.	Baste more closely or use a hoop.
The stitches may be uneven and tension too loose.	Experiment with stitching through all three layers. Your machine may not be up to quilting, or you may have to choose a thinner batting.
There is too much fabric and bulk when you stitch a large-size quilt.	Try to roll up each end and secure it with safety pins. As you finish quilting an area, unpin and re-roll to another section.
The basting stitches get caught on the presser foot while you sew.	Sew smaller basting stitches on the quilt top, or if using a hoop, remove the basting inside the hoop area.

Thread, Bobbins, and Presser Feet

Use a straight or narrow zigzag stitch of 100 percent cotton or cotton-covered polyester thread. Choose a color that complements your color scheme. You can even choose a different color for the bobbin to give your quilt reversibility. Slide your quilt and the hoop under the needle. It can be difficult to accomplish this, and depending on your machine, you may have to remove the presser foot. Turn the hand wheel to lower the needle and start your first stitch. Hold onto the top thread, making the lower bobbin thread come up to the top of the quilt top. Make sure you lower the presser foot down. Don't forget because you would have nothing to move your quilt through the machine. Then sew on your marked lines. There is no need to backstitch, but sew slowly and carefully. Clip threads at the end of quilting.

Support and Seams

Set up your workspace for your convenience. Keep the bulk of the quilt lying on a table behind your machine, so the weight of the quilt won't pull and cause puckers or uneven stitches.

The best way for beginners to machine quilt is to use the stitch in the ditch method; remember that you sew right on the seam line following the block's pattern. The seams add strength to the quilt seam and the fabric won't shift as much. Please practice on a small project, like a pillow or crib quilt. Using your sewing machine can make your quilting quick.

The Least You Need to Know

- The three layers of the quilt must be held together with hand or machine quilting or knots.
- Quilting designs can follow the outline of your block's pattern, be an overall design, or be a specific design drawn from a quilting stencil.
- Mark your quilt with as light a marker as possible, but make sure you can still see the lines.
- Start quilting or tying from the center and work to the outside edge.
- Be experienced on handling your machine if you want to do machine quilting.

In This Chapter

- ◆ Finishing the edges of your quilt
- ◆ Making your own bias binding
- ◆ Signing your quilt
- ◆ The best strategy for cleaning your quilt
- ◆ Where to store your quilt

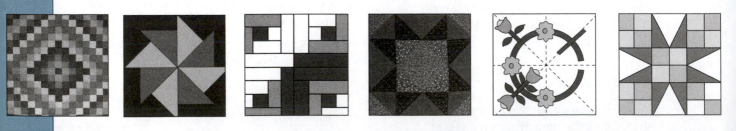

The first quilt (75" × 103") made by the author using only Dresden Plate, Churn Dash, Eight Point Star, and Ohio Star Blocks. Each block is repeated using different color placement and framed with muslin lattices.

Top block: Dutchman's Puzzle Pinwheel.

Middle block: Windmills.

Bottom block: Crazy Ann.

This quilt above was the first quilting project ever made by Maureen Mueller. After she made all the beginner blocks she realized she didn't like to appliqué, so we sought out different pieced blocks. They all seemed to be "spinning."

Top left: The top left quilt is a Blazing Star wall hanging. Each star contains identical fabrics but are placed in different positions.

Top right: A close-up of a Virginia Star quilt. My daughter Jessica wanted a "snowflake" quilt for her wedding. Notice how the center row of the diamond is the same fabric as the background so that section "fades" away.

Bottom left and right: Close-ups of the Blazing Star quilt. Notice how the color placement makes the stars look totally different.

The Patriotic Scrap quilts shown on these pages were created by Holly Ciccoricco. Look how each block has different fabrics.

Whenever Holly Ciccoricco makes a quilt, she always sets rules for herself. In these Tippecanoe twin-size quilts, each star block had to have different fabrics. She worked on these quilts simultaneously so they would be completed at the same time.

Purple and yellow squares and hearts.

Mari Garcia's Heart and Blocks lap quilt (48" × 56") was inspired by a package of precut hearts that she purchased at a quilt show.

Top left: Doris Bobek made her Yo-yo Flower block into a small wall hanging.
Top right: The author used the same patch and made her block into a pillow.

Bottom left: Yo-yos are very versatile. Here they are used in an appliqué picture of a flower basket.
Bottom right: The American Wreath pillow.

See how the Log Cabin block can be made into many configurations. This is an 18-inch square table runner made in the traditional Christmas colors.

These same 6-inch blocks are assembled to look like a Christmas tree. The 25" × 30" wall hanging is made by the author and used every year.

Top left: Robin Bogert made this Log Cabin wall hanging (24" × 24") when one of her friends gave her these fabrics as a gift. Look at the close-up on the right. Robin designed the robin of the fabric to take center stage in each Log Cabin block.

Maureen Fetcho started a block of the month club for this foundation-pieced Pineapple quilt (a variation of the Log Cabin). More than six years later she came to my class with more than 60 completed blocks. So far she has assembled five of these lap quilts for family members.

Turquoise baby quilt (28″ × 40″) made in the Trip Around the World style.

Left: Tippi Ulman prepared this 40″ × 40″ Trip Around the World wall hanging.
Aren't the colors dramatic? Right: The subtle green and tans of this lap quilt look
great with a shabby chic living room.

Top left: Robin Bogert made this Log Cabin wall hanging (24" × 24") when one of her friends gave her these fabrics as a gift. Look at the close-up on the right. Robin designed the robin of the fabric to take center stage in each Log Cabin block.

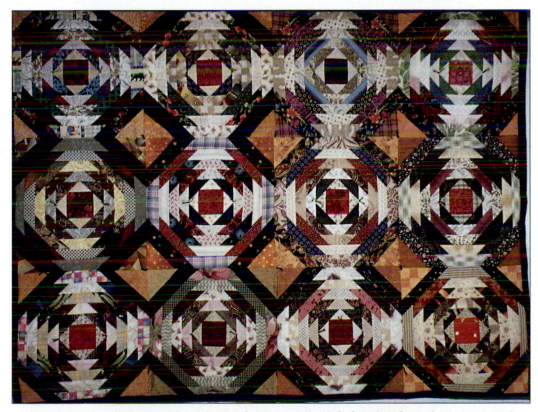

Maureen Fetcho started a block of the month club for this foundation-pieced Pineapple quilt (a variation of the Log Cabin). More than six years later she came to my class with more than 60 completed blocks. So far she has assembled five of these lap quilts for family members.

This traditional Amish Square design wall hanging was made by Laura Ehrlich. The fabrics exemplify the solid, bright colors and black accents of the Amish quilts.

Top: This 18-inch Square in a Square quilt block, made by Tippi Ulman, is basted and ready to quilt. **Bottom:** Sara Reiss made this Amish style quilt for her granddaughter in monochromatic purple tones.

Turquoise baby quilt (28″ × 40″) made in the Trip Around the World style.

Left: Tippi Ulman prepared this 40″ × 40″ Trip Around the World wall hanging. Aren't the colors dramatic? Right: The subtle green and tans of this lap quilt look great with a shabby chic living room.

This is a close-up of Maureen Mueller's Trip Around the World wall hanging. We call it her "psychedelic quilt." Look at that fabric—doesn't it look groovy?

Detail of a Log Cabin quilt purchased in Lancaster, Pennsylvania, the Log Cabin blocks are positioned in the Barn Raising design— this quilt is from the collection of Nita and Bud Munson.

Once you learn the basic techniques, you can let your imagination run wild. A friend of mine had collected her daughter's soccer T-shirts since she was in elementary school. For Kristy's college going-away present she asked me to make a quilt from these shirts. Thrown over her dorm bed it makes a great memory quilt.

Elaine Saigh received a whole bag of scraps from a friend and devised this Sunbonnet quilt. She loved the Sunbonnet Sue blocks and alternated a block made of four squares and one of the hats copied from several patterns. The embellishments of lace, beadwork, and ribbon are just charming. (Left: detail. Below: whole quilt.)

Here is a labor of love in progress. Holly Ciccoricco has again set rules for this flower-themed quilt. There is no appliqué. She would draw a picture on graph paper, then cut it up into templates. One 10-inch block has more than 250 pieces! This is not for the faint of heart. (P.S. Holly is an artist.)

Chapter 16

The Finishing Touch

Your quilt is beautiful! We're down to the last leg of the race. It's almost time to put it on your bed. I bet you can't wait to finish off those raveling edges with batting sticking out. There are several strategies for binding off the edges. Some methods use the quilt top border fabric, the backing, or a separate bias binding. Bindings can be purchased in a multitude of colors, or you can make them using a fabric from your color scheme.

Making your own bias tape can be confusing, but I'll show you the "molar" method that one of my first quilting teachers taught me. Follow the directions step by step, and you won't get into a "bind."

Every artist signs his or her work of art and you should, too. Whether with quilting thread, floss, or indelible ink pens, you can write your name, date of completion, the name of the quilt, and perhaps the occasion for giving it as a gift.

Throughout its lifetime, your quilt will need a bath and a rest, so where, and how you do this is important. When cleaning, the choices range from dry cleaning to hand washing to even vacuuming. We'll explore these methods. Where and how you store your quilt is important as well. You would feel horrible taking your quilt out of storage and discover it is faded, stretched out of shape, or has a musty smell. We want our children and our children's children to treasure your workmanship.

Finally Get Rid of Those Frayed Edges

You are probably tired of getting everything, especially your rings, caught on the ragged outer edge of your quilt. As soon as I finish quilting—and celebrating—the *binding* that encloses those ragged edges comes soon after.

Quilt Talk

Binding is a strip of fabric, usually cut on the bias so that it can stretch, that covers the outer edge of your quilt.

There are four ways to bind the edge of your quilt, and each gives a different look. There are advantages and disadvantages to each method. Read this chapter and determine how you want to end your ends.

Quilting Bee

Some people like to cut the batting flush with the quilt top, but I like to leave an extra half inch, to give the binding body and thickness.

There are some last-minute preparations you must make before neatly finishing the ends. Take out all the basting threads. Cut off all errant threads from throughout your quilt top. I don't know where they all come from—they just appear. Spread your layered quilt out and cut the excess batting to ½ inch all the way around the quilt top.

The backing will be cut off differently depending on the binding technique you use, so don't do anything until you decide how to bind the edge.

The first two methods I call the cheater's way, because they really are the easiest.

Don't Get Stuck!

Binding your quilt with a border fabric or the backing is often looked down on because the methods do not produce a binding that can be replaced. As a quilt is used, the binding is usually the first part to get worn. If that happens, the quilt top will be damaged—sometimes irreparably.

Turning the Border Fabric to the Back

This finish binds your edges so that the quilt border is the last color that frames the outside of the quilt top. The batting and the backing fabric are cut to 1 inch less than the border all around the quilt. Turn the border fabric under ½ inch; then fold about ½ inch of it around the quilt to the backing side. The back of the quilt will have ½ inch of the border fabric folded and sewn to it. Pin about 2 feet at a time of the border fabric folded to the backing. Use an appliqué stitch or a catch stitch. If you don't remember, check out Chapter 14 on how to sew invisibly.

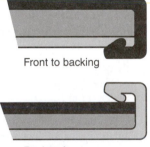

Front to backing

Back to front

You can fold the border from the front to the back or roll the backing to the front. Which way should you go?

Turning the Backing Fabric to the Front

This finish is very similar to finishing with a border fabric, just reversed. This time cut the batting about ½ inch larger than the quilt top. Then the backing should be an inch larger all the way around. Turn the backing fabric under ¼ inch so wrong sides are together. Then turn it over to the front, making sure the ¼-inch fold covers the edge. Pin so that the binding is even, about ½ inch, and sew with an invisible stitch. You have to make sure that the backing fabric coordinates with the quilt top because the binding forms a small frame on the front.

Attached Bias Binding

There are several steps to this method. Follow these step-by-step directions carefully:

1. Cut the batting and backing ½ inch larger than the quilt top. With a contrasting color, baste all around the outer raw edge of the quilt top at ¼ inch.

2. Purchase or make a bias binding. Open up one ¼-inch folded edge, and place the right side of the binding to the quilt top with the raw edge facing the outer edge.

3. Pin into the ¼-inch fold, turning the short end of the binding under to finish it off.

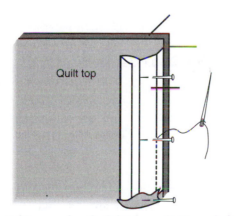

Doesn't this procedure look backward? Pin and align the raw edges of the quilt top to finish off the end.

Don't Get Stuck!

If you sew by machine, take care not to pull the bias binding—it has a tendency to stretch and pucker.

4. Stitch the bias binding to the quilt top in the ¼-inch fold, either by hand or machine.

5. Sew to within ¼ inch from the end of the seam, backstitch, stop the seam, and cut the threads. Now miter the corner. Make about a ½-inch pleat at the corner before turning. Pin the bias binding so that ½ inch is sticking up, and on the adjacent side put your needle where the other line of stitching ended and start sewing a new line of stitching.

Now this really looks wrong, but it's right. Pivot the binding and start stitching where the other line ended.

6. Stitch all around the perimeter of the quilt. Overlap the binding, ending where you began.

7. Fold the bias binding over the edge of the quilt and pin, making sure that the binding is turned evenly.

8. Sew with an invisible stitch until you get to the corner.

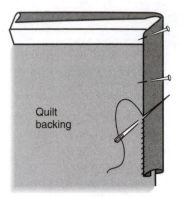

Be a magician and make your stitches in the binding disappear!

9. Now for the part of the binding that is sticking up—fold the right side of the binding up and then the top side down to form an accurate, mitered 45-degree angle.

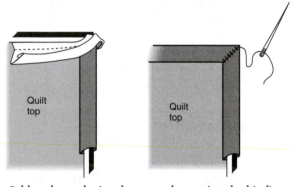

Fold under and miter the corner by turning the binding to the back and making a 45-degree angle at the corner.

10. Stitch to hold down the folded corner.

A bias binding adds a small border of color that can contrast with your quilt top, creating a frame.

Pillow Technique

One of my students uses this method regularly and it is very nice for baby quilts because you can insert lace into the edging. This finishing technique actually has to be done before the project is quilted. That's okay since I do not

recommend this method for beginners—it is very difficult to sew and manipulate the fabric. It is a problem to get the quilt to lay flat and it may look bunchy. If you use this procedure for your next quilt, here are the instructions.

Quilting Bee

If you use the pillow technique, you can insert lace before you sew the backing. Place the tape end of the lace against the raw outer edges of your quilt. You can check out Chapter 25 to see how to insert lace, piping, and ruffles.

1. Cut the batting and the backing even with the quilt top.

2. Place the quilt top right sides together with the backing. Sew by machine all along the perimeter of the quilt leaving about 2 feet open to turn it right-side-out.

3. Pin the batting evenly all around the outside edge. Hand-stitch this down on top of the same seam line. I know that the two steps seem repetitive, but it prevents the batting from stretching out of shape and getting caught on the presser foot as you sew.

Don't Get Stuck!

When sewing your quilt together using the pillow technique, don't forget to leave about 2 feet open so you can turn your quilt inside out.

4. Very carefully, reach your hand inside the quilt and turn it right-side-out.

5. Flatten and smooth out the three layers, pushing out the corners. Baste with a Z stitch in 6-inch grids.

6. Quilt.

The edges are finished and are inside the quilt.

Do Get into a Bind

Quilters have found that a bias binding or a bias tape is more durable than fabric cut on the straight of grain, and it can also bend to make finished rounded or mitered corners with 45-degree angles. Measure the perimeter of your quilt, adding about 5 inches for mitering the corners and finishing the ends. Once you have that measurement, you can plan the amount you need to buy or make. If you can find a packaged binding in a color that coordinates with the quilt top, buy it! A great deal of time will be saved. The rectangular packages come in a variety of sizes and widths, but the best to purchase is a double-folded quilt binding.

Making Bias Strips

Bias strips can be cut from the diagonal of one of your fabrics used in your quilt. It is great being able to have a coordinating fabric frame your quilt. The strips can be 1½ inches wide for a regular tape size or 2½ inches wide if you want to double-fold your binding. Cut the strips as long as possible. Remember to draw the diagonal and measure the width of each strip. Cut the strips carefully, and don't stretch them. Pin right sides together at a right angle; it doesn't look right, but it works. Open the binding to check if you pinned it correctly. Sew a ½-inch seam; then press it open. Sew the ends together with a ½-inch seam allowance.

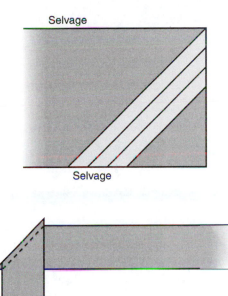

Angle your strips so they will stretch, and yes, I'm certain that's how to pin them.

Molar Method of Making Bias

There is another method of cutting the bias strips that is faster and easier, especially if you are cutting large amounts of binding. I call it the molar method, but its true name is the continuous-roll technique. One 36-inch square of fabric will make approximately 15 yards of ½-inch binding or 12 yards of 2½-inch binding. If you use the entire width of your fabric, 43 inches, you will make 22 yards of 1½-inch binding or 15 yards of 2½-inch binding. Isn't that amazing? The directions may seem puzzling, but I will describe them step by step.

1. Cut a square of fabric either 36 or 43 inches square, depending on how much binding you need.

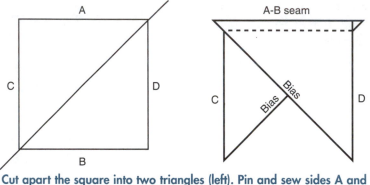

Cut apart the square into two triangles (left). Pin and sew sides A and B to make a big tooth—hence the molar (right)!

2. Cut the square in half on the diagonal to form two triangles. If you want, pin a paper with letters to each of the sides so you can figure out which ones are sewn together. Side A is opposite side B, C is across from D.

3. Sew sides A and B right sides together to form the molar shape. Make a ½-inch seam down the AB side.

Don't Get Stuck!

When sewing by the molar technique, check to be sure that the seam is on the straight of grain and does not stretch. Pull the roots of the molar and make sure they *do* stretch. I can't tell you how many times my bias did not stretch because I didn't sew the seams correctly.

4. Open up this tooth to form a parallelogram. Press open the seam.

5. On the wrong side of your fabric, use a see-through ruler to draw lines parallel to the bias sides. If you are using the binding for a full-size quilt, the width should be between 2 to 2½ inches; for a smaller project, measure 1½ to 2 inches.

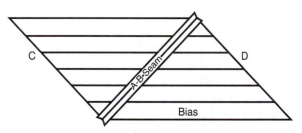

Draw parallel lines from side C to D.

6. Carefully hold together sides C to D; they are the straight of grain and will not stretch. This may seem backward because the seams are going in opposite directions. You will form a tube or sleeve, but shift the right side down one bias line so the top left side has formed a tail sticking up. Pin to match the drawn lines.

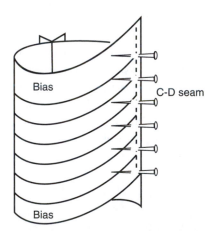

Be the boss of your fabric—form a tube or sleeve with a tail off the top the size of the bias width.

7. Pin and sew a ½-inch seam and be certain there is a tail on each end. Press this seam open.

8. Begin cutting at the top tail on the drawn line and spiral around the tube in one long cut.

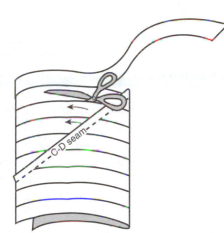

This is one long cutting line. Just start at the top and cut in a spiral around and around and around.

9. As I cut each yard of binding, I press it immediately and wrap it around a cardboard square. Can you imagine 20 yards of stretchy strips! It is so much easier to do a yard or two at a time. For a regular bias, press both sides under ¼ inch, then the entire strip in half down the center. When making a double bias, where the fabric is doubled, just fold the bias tape in half.

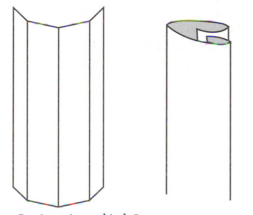

Don't get into a bind. Press as you go.

10. Sew together the bias tape right sides to the quilt top right sides, around the perimeter of your quilt. Fold over and whipstitch or use an appliqué stitch to secure.

I told you this method of making binding was tricky, but it is so efficient when making large amounts of binding that it's worth the effort.

Signing Your Quilt

Signing your quilt is the finishing touch to your quilting experience. Your work of art should be signed and dated. A running stitch of quilting thread signing your name can be sewn on the front or back of your quilt. If you want your name and date to stand out more, you can use embroidery floss and a decorative embroidery stitch.

Many of my students sign their quilts with labels placed on the back. One class assembled a wall hanging of different storybook characters for the children's room of a library. We signed the back of the quilt with all of our names on a label shaped like an open book. See this photo in the color photo section.

There are many terrific books that deal with calligraphy and styling memorable labels. Wash and shrink the fabric that you plan on using for the label. Practice writing with an indelible fine-point pen. Record your name, date of completion, occasion for making the quilt, and who you are giving it to. Some quilts are like cards hallmarking events and including memorable quotations. Turn under ¼ inch all around the label. You can hand- or machine-embroider the edges and designs around your insignia.

Attach your label with an invisible stitch to the lower corner of the backing. Sign your quilt and shout to the world that your quilt is complete!

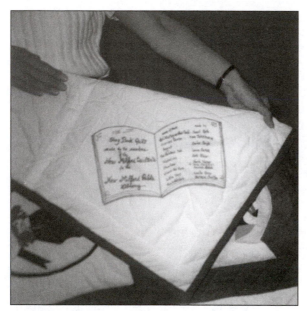

Hallmark events with your labels.

Scraps and Pieces

Those who collect quilts can date and follow a quilt's history with the information found from the signing. Many quilts were found with names signed on the front of special blocks. These were called Album quilts. Album quilts were often group projects that had each block signed by the designer. Blocks were even developed with a special space for signing your name. Our quilting ancestors took this signing seriously and developed special ink, quill pens, and patterned metal stencil plates. Calligraphy was practiced until their handwriting was perfected.

Drying and Dry Cleaning

I hate to even think about your quilt getting dirty, but the time will come when you will need to launder it. Before you choose how to clean your quilt, you need to know how different factors will affect it. Textiles are sensitive to light, humidity, and stretching or breaking of the fibers. In general, the less cleaning the better for your quilt. If your quilt is just dusty, you can air it outdoors when the humidity is low—but not in direct sunlight. You can hang the quilt on a line as long as the quilt is dry. For airing out my quilts, I'm lucky because I have a neighbor with three parallel clotheslines that I can drape my quilts over so they don't stretch. A quilt that is just dusty could also be placed in the dryer on "air" setting for 10 or 15 minutes.

Quilting Bee

If your quilt is just dusty and has no stains, you can vacuum it. Place a clean screen or netting over your quilt to protect it. Then use a brush attachment to carefully go over the quilt, removing the dust. The screening keeps the fabric from being sucked up into the vacuum. Wouldn't that be a horrible sight?

I hope your quilt never gets stained, but accidents do happen. Try to treat stains as soon as possible before they set. Examine the stain and spot clean it with an appropriate cleaner. There are charts that deal with specific types of stains on the cleaner bottle or packaging. Try not to rub too hard as you may destroy the fibers. If your quilt is made of silk or wool or if you don't know the origin of the stain, seek professional help. Check out several dry cleaners and choose one that is knowledgeable in quilt cleaning. If your fabric is colorfast, it is better to wash it by hand than to have it dry cleaned. Those chemicals and the way they affect the fibers always worry me.

Give Your Quilt a Bath

Always know the fiber content of the quilts you create. It should be 100 percent cotton or a cotton-polyester blend. Because you washed your fabrics before you assembled your quilt, you already know they won't shrink or run. I usually wash my fabrics in the washing machine and then throw them in the dryer. You can treat your quilt *almost* the same way. You can use the washing machine but I would not use the dryer, as it will weaken the quilting stitches and stretch the quilt out of shape. Place your quilt in the washer carefully and use a gentle cycle with cold water. Use Woolite or a mild detergent developed especially for quilt cleaning. If your quilt is an antique or is valuable, never use a machine washer.

Quilting Bee

Don't pick up a wet quilt from one end! Gently lift under it to remove it from the sink or tub. When the quilt is wet it weighs so much that the quilting stitches may break and the fibers can stretch out of shape.

For those of you who are too timid to throw your quilts in the washer, you can launder them in a large sink or the bathtub. Use lukewarm water with a mild detergent and gently press the water through the quilt—do not squeeze. Empty the tub of water and rinse out the soap. You may have to change the rinse water several times to ensure that all the cleanser is removed. Carefully pick up the wet quilt and support its weight from underneath.

Dry your quilt on a flat surface if possible. Go outside on a day with low humidity and spread out a sheet with towels over it to soak up the water. Place the wet quilt on top. Remember, do not put the quilt in direct sunlight; you don't want the colors to fade.

Fold Your Quilt the Acid-Free Way

Care for your quilt today and it will become tomorrow's heirloom. Sooner or later you will start accumulating quilts. It's great fun to be able to switch them around once in a while, so storing them properly is essential. Beware of dirt, creases, dampness, and sunlight. Find a cool, dry place to stash them. Don't use a basement or attic where your quilts may get water damaged or develop mildew or a musty smell. Fold them in a drawer or chest lined with *acid-free tissue paper* or a clean cotton sheet.

Quilt Talk

Acid-free tissue paper is a tissue paper made without chemicals that would destroy fibers. It can be purchased from craft catalogues or from dry cleaners.

Occasionally refold your quilt in a different manner so that crease marks will not develop. I have discovered it is not a good idea to fold a Lone Star quilt (one large eight-point star composed of diamonds) down the center of the star. It stretches the center where all the points come together. I like to fold that quilt into thirds. To remove wrinkles from incorrect folding or just from storing, you could put in the dryer with a damp cloth for several minutes. This is also a good way to fluff up the batting.

Here are two more last-minute thoughts. This first one is very important—don't iron your quilts. The heat of the iron will compact the batting and may even melt it into a gluey mess. If your quilt is wrinkled, don't worry, all the antique quilts have that wonderful rumpled, used look. Second, don't store quilts in plastic bags, especially garbage bags. The plastic traps any dampness and the fabric may mildew.

I'd like to tell you a frightening story (for a quilter, that is). One of my quilting ladies was storing this wonderful quilt she was working on in a large garbage bag. One day her husband took several bags of used clothes to the Salvation Army and deposited them in their collection bin. You can imagine what happened! Lucille made call after call to different collection agencies until luckily she found someone who had put the quilt aside. It seemed the woman was a quilter and realized that since it was a work-in-progress with pins and basting thread, it must have been put there by mistake. Lucille got her quilt back but now stores and transports her quilts in a large carryall. Please don't use plastic garbage bags!

Take care of your quilts and they will give warmth to your body and soul for your lifetime and more.

The Least You Need to Know

◆ Folding fabrics over the quilt ends will enclose the raveling edges.

◆ Bias binding is the most durable technique for finishing ends.

◆ Signing and dating your quilt should be done to make it permanent.

◆ Care must be taken when washing and drying your quilt.

◆ Store your quilt in a cool, dry area and wrap it in acid-free tissue paper or a clean cotton sheet.

In This Part

Part 6

Make It Your Way Projects

In the first quilting class I took, I found I really enjoyed the piecing. Each week we learned how to piece a specific block. I enjoyed piecing so much that by the end of the week's "homework" I had made two blocks, changing the fabric placement to make an entirely different looking block. Unfortunately, at the end of the course, I had a stack of blocks and didn't know what to do with them. I want you to have the know-how to put it all together. The directions for the projects are from start to finish. You won't be in the predicament of not knowing what to do next.

There are all types of projects and degree of difficulty. If you are a beginner, small projects like pillows and lap quilts may be a good start. Decide on something that you would love to make and remember you can select a color scheme that matches your home. Make your templates, buy your fabric, and get started. Before you know it the quilt of your dreams will be adorning your home.

In This Chapter

- ◆ Learning to identify easy blocks
- ◆ Strategies for piecing nine-patch blocks
- ◆ Understanding how to appliqué
- ◆ Preparing an applique block

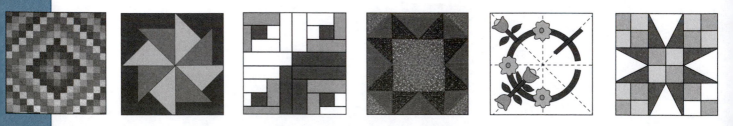

Chapter 17

Beginner Sampler Quilt

This project was my first real quilt. It is a Sampler quilt, a quilt which showcases one's expertise in piecing and appliqué. Each block is often framed by a strip of fabric called a lattice or sashing. Quilters have developed thousands of block designs. A Sampler is perfect for beginners to perfect their craft. Since each block is different, you can start with the easy ones and then choose blocks that are more difficult as you gain your confidence.

My original quilt includes four very basic 12-inch blocks that are pieced and appliquéd. They include the Churn Dash, Ohio Star, Eight Point Star, and Dresden Plate. These blocks are repeated but the fabric positions have been changed. If you feel like being adventuresome, I am also going to give you several more challenging blocks in the next chapter, if you want to interchange them. Remember you can substitute a block as long as it has the same dimensions, in this case a 12-inch square.

Beginner Sampler quilt.

Finished size: 75" × 103" (full size quilt)

Materials:

Fabrics

Full size batting

Backing fabric

Patterns and templates for the following blocks:

◆ Churn Dash

◆ Ohio Star

◆ Eight Point Star

◆ Dresden Plate

Fabric requirements:

3 yards muslin or solid fabric (white)—used in blocks and the lattices

6½ yards dominant fabric (dark blue)—used in blocks and the outer border

6 yards lighter dominant (turquoise)—used for blocks and inner border

1½ yards contrast color (brown)—used in blocks and corner squares

¾ to 1 yard each of two or three blender fabrics—used in blocks

6 yards backing fabric

The first thing that needs to be done is prepare fifteen 12-inch blocks from the four designs. In this quilt, there are four Churn Dash patches, four Ohio Stars, three Eight Point Stars, and four Dresden Plate blocks. Look at the picture in the color section and see how the block appearance can change with the placement of the fabrics.

Churn Dash

The first block to start with is the Churn Dash. It is the easiest. Make four for this quilt, changing the positioning of the fabrics.

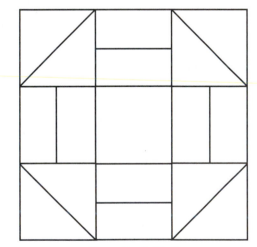

Churn Dash block.

It's a simple patch—great for beginners. There are three major pattern pieces: a 4-inch square, a 2 × 4-inch rectangle, and a large triangle—17 pieces in all. You can use either two, three, or four fabrics. The dark fabric is traditionally for the inner rectangles and triangles to form a "churn dash" motif. However, once I made this patch with the dark fabrics on the outside, giving it a totally different look.

Scraps and Pieces

Legend has it that a pioneer woman who was preparing butter in her churn inspired this patch. It is said that she looked down and saw the shape of the churn blade, known as the dash, and was "stirred" to design this energetic patch.

Notice how your eye is drawn in different directions when you use a variety of color values.

On your mark, get set, go! Do the Churn Dash and you will win the race by following these directions:

1. Prepare the templates.

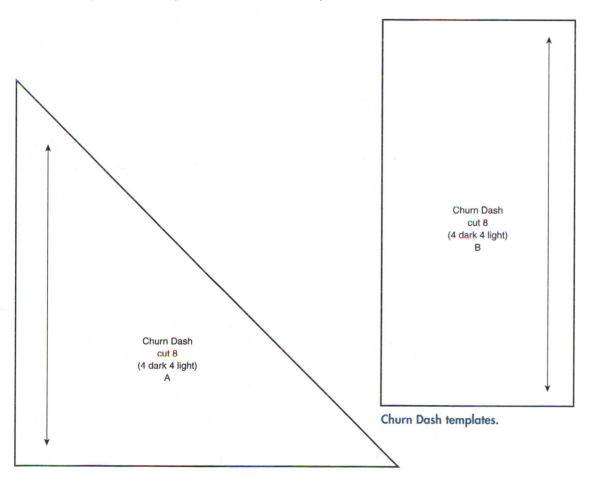

Churn Dash
cut 8
(4 dark 4 light)
A

Churn Dash
cut 8
(4 dark 4 light)
B

Churn Dash templates.

Churn Dash
cut 1
C

Churn Dash templates.

2. Decide on your colors and mark your fabric on the wrong side. Cut eight rectangles—four background and four dark; and cut eight triangles—four background and four dark. The square in the center of the block is usually cut from the background fabric.

3. Cut out the patchwork pieces, adding on seam allowances. Lay out the patches on the table in front of you.

4 Pin and sew together the dark and background triangles (template A) to form a 4-inch square.

5. Sew together the light- and dark-colored rectangles (template B) to form a 4-inch square.

6. Sew together the top row, the middle row by using rectangles and template C square, and the bottom row.

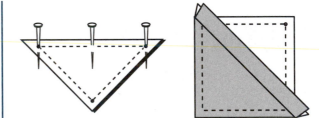

Triangles sewn together to form a square.

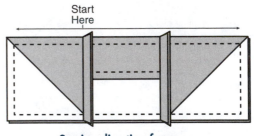

Sewing direction for rows.

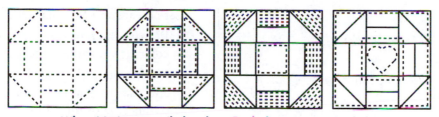

When it's time to quilt the Churn Dash, here are some ideas.

7. Sew the rows together starting with the middle square's dot and working across the center square to the outer dot. Then sew from the center square's dot to the end in the opposite direction.

8. Press the finished block.

Don't forget to pin carefully, check to see if the piece fits into the block laid out in front, and then sew. Be precise and systematic. Here's to never needing your seam ripper!

Ohio Star

The Ohio Star is a nine-patch design with the star motif built around a central square. This is one of my favorite blocks. It has such a clean look and can be harmonious with either modern or traditional decor. The Ohio Star has two pattern pieces: a 4-inch square and a small triangle (the 4-inch square is divided into four triangles). There are 21 pieces in the Ohio Star block.

Quilting Bee _____

Because the nine-patch blocks have similar pattern pieces, you can avoid confusion by making a set of templates for each block and storing them in separate zippered plastic storage bags. That way you can find the right triangle as soon as you need it!

You can use the traditional two colors, giving your patch a very definitive star motif. You can also create it with three colors, making the center square a different fabric. To add another color, change the color of the four inner triangles to make the fabric total four. You can go off the wall and make hourglass shapes by altering the placement of the darkest fabric.

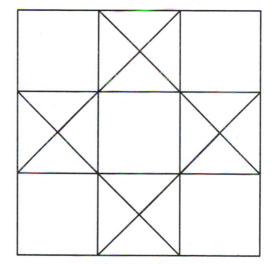

Ohio Star block.

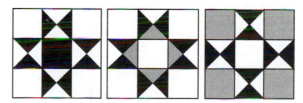

See how different placement of fabrics can change the look of the Ohio Star block.

Don't Get Stuck! _____

Be sure to pin the seam of the small triangles and open the pieces up to check. It is so easy to pin the wrong side of the triangle or, if you've chosen several colors, to pick up the wrong color. I can't tell you how many times I've made a boo-boo.

Let's create an Ohio Star block:

1. Prepare the templates and decide on the colors (two, three, or four fabrics).

2. Mark around the outside of the templates and add the seam allowance onto the wrong side of the fabric.

3. Cut out 21 pieces and lay out the design.

4. Sew together two small triangles (template A) to form a larger triangle.

Ohio Star
cut 16
(8 light 8 dark)

A

Ohio Star templates.

Ohio Star
cut 5
B

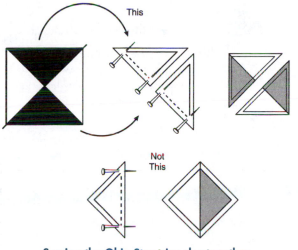

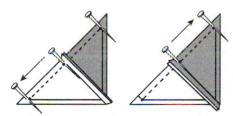

Sewing the Ohio Star triangles together.

5. Sew two sets of triangles together to form 4-inch squares. Make four squares made up of the triangles.

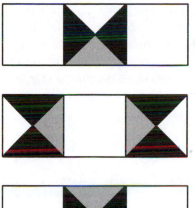

Sewing seams of triangles together to form a square.

6. Sew together each row of the Ohio Star, making sure that the colors of the triangles are in the correct positions. Stitch the rows together from the inside to the outside dots.

7. Press.

Rows of the Ohio Star.

Eight Point Star

This is the first block that is not sewn together in rows!

The Eight Point Star is drafted with eight diamonds sewn together to form a star. Squares and triangles are alternately sewn around the diamonds to square out the block. There are three templates, and you need to cut out 16 pieces in total.

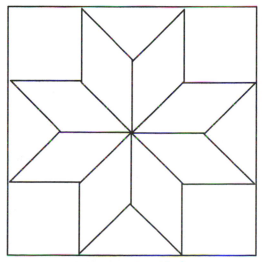

Eight Point Star block.

This block can be made with two coordinating fabrics and a background fabric—three altogether. Some students have used five fabrics (one fabric is used for the background, each remaining fabric makes up the star, cutting out two diamonds) to give the star a pinwheel look.

Be a stargazer and make this patch—you'll love it.

Don't Get Stuck!

Be sure to sew only between the two dots; I can't tell you how many beginners end up sewing the entire half of the diamonds together forming a nice little pocket.

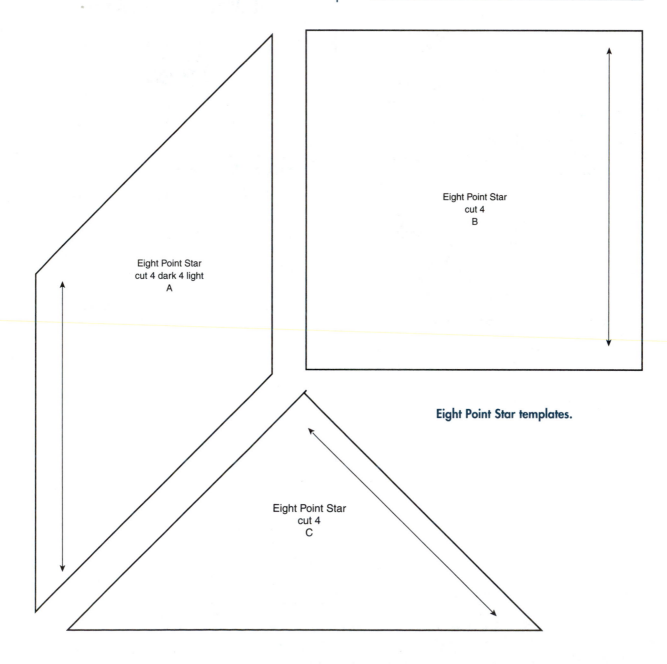

Eight Point Star
cut 4 dark 4 light
A

Eight Point Star
cut 4
B

Eight Point Star
cut 4
C

Eight Point Star templates.

1. Prepare the templates and decide on the colors.

2. Mark and cut out the fabric pieces, and lay out the block in front of you.

3. Start by picking up two diamonds (template A) next to each other. Flip over one diamond so the right sides are together. Pin into the dots of one side of the diamond (one fourth of the diamond). Sew between these two dots.

4. I like to sew all the diamonds together to form the star. Be extremely careful to match the dots perfectly, and always replace the pinned pieces to check that you pinned it correctly. If you pin the diamond to the wrong part of the star, you will end up with a herringbone zigzag. That's not a star.

5. Alternate sewing squares (template B) and triangles (template C) around the star. While the star pieces are in front of you, flip a square over a diamond so the dots match up with the right sides together. Pin into the two dots. Stitch from the widest part of the diamond to the tip of the star. Replace the block on the table and flip the other side of the square so that it matches the diamond it is next to. Pin and sew from the widest point to the tip of the diamond.

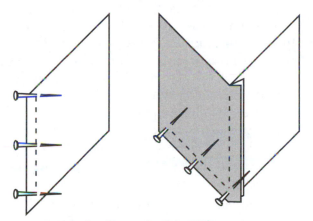

Sewing the diamonds of the Eight Point Star.

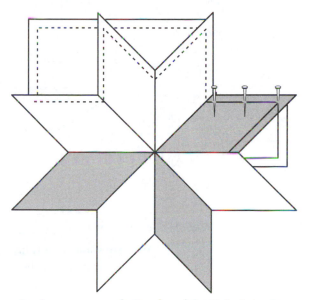

Sewing squares and triangles of the Eight Point Star.

Don't Get Stuck!

Be sure to alternate the squares and the triangles, otherwise your patch will be a very weird shape.

Don't Get Stuck!

Do not use a back-and-forth motion when ironing triangle patches—the triangles are bias and very stretchy. Blocks have been known to change even ½ inch in size. Use an up-and-down motion and a steam iron.

6. Press all seams of the star in one spiral direction. I like to press the seams of the squares and triangles toward the star, since it makes the star stand out as if it is stuffed. The center of the star may have a small hole, but this will usually press out. To press that mass of seams at the center of the star, put the point of the iron right into the middle and press them flat, spreading them out like petals of a flower.

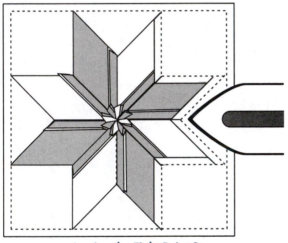

Ironing the Eight Point Star.

To reduce the bulk, you may want to clip off some long ends of the seam allowances but be sure not to trim too close because the fabric may ravel. Turn the block over and press the right side.

Dresden Plate

The Dresden Plate is one of the most popular appliqué blocks. It is believed that this patch was named for a china plate made from a factory in Dresden, Germany. This patch became popular in the 1850s. You can almost see a pioneer woman, needing a quilt pattern, take one of her dishes, trace around it, and then cut it into wedges. Instant quilt templates!

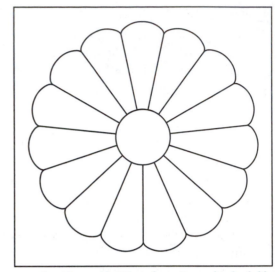

Dresden Plate with 15 wedges. Does this look like your china?

The Dresden Plate can be made in many different sizes and styles. I've seen as few as 12 wedges and as many as 20. The patches can be 10 inches to 24 inches in size. The colors can range from two, so that the plate looks like spokes of a wheel, all the way up to 20, with each wedge in a different fabric. Wedges can be rounded or pointed. If you have more than one type of Dresden Plate in your template collection, be sure to keep them separate. You don't want to confuse them and try to fit a 20-wedge plate for a 24-inch square onto a 12-inch block.

Our pattern for the Dresden Plate is 12 inches square, and the plate has 15 wedges of either three or five different fabrics. There are two templates: a wedge A and center circle B.

Quilting Bee

Before you start to sew, lay out your pieces on a square of flannel or felt as we discussed in Chapter 11. You will avoid picking up the wrong piece when it is sitting right in front of you. And you will to be able to clean up your work quickly by simply rolling up the flannel with your pieces safely

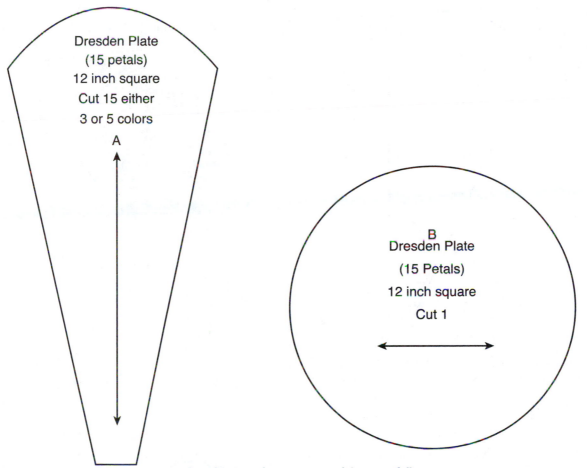

Dresden Plate
(15 petals)
12 inch square
Cut 15 either
3 or 5 colors
A

B
Dresden Plate
(15 Petals)
12 inch square
Cut 1

Dresden Plate templates. Cut your fabric carefully.

1. Prepare your templates made out of poster board and sandpaper as discussed in Chapter 9.

2. Cut a generous 12½-inch square out of your background fabric.

3. Mark and cut the wedges, adding on the seam allowances. If you are using three fabrics, cut five of each fabric; if you are using five fabrics, cut three of each one.

4. Lay the plate out on the table in front of you. Decide on the correct placement of your fabrics. There should be a set sequence in the progression of fabrics; for example, a yellow, green, and blue wedge, then repeating yellow, green, and blue wedges in the same order all around the plate.

5. Pick up two wedges that are next to each other and put their right sides together. Pin into the dots you marked at each end. Put the pins right into the dots perpendicular to the seam line.

Don't Get Stuck!

Remember, before you sew your Dresden Plate, check that you pinned correctly. Put the wedges back into the plate to make sure. If the color pattern is not correct, re-pin the wedge.

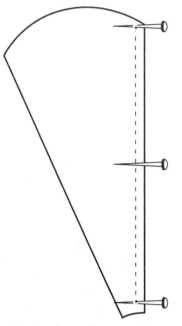

Pinning the wedges together.

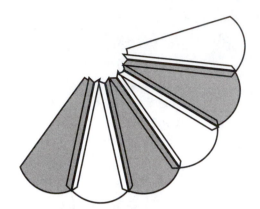

Press the seams open and baste on the outer seam line.

6. Sew from dot to dot, backstitching at each end. Do not sew the right-hand turn that goes through the seam allowance. This is one of the few times when the seams are pressed open.

7. Put the wedges back down onto your plate pattern and pick up the next wedge, pin, and sew. It is so easy to pick up the wrong wedge or pin it on the wrong side.

8. Sew the wedges all around, like spokes of a wheel, to form the plate.

9. Press the seams open. You should press these seams open because the square background fabric adds stability.

10. With a contrasting thread, baste along the outside rounded seam line. Your basting will show where to turn the raw edges under. Turn the edges under to prevent raveling, then baste.

Don't Get Stuck!

Be sure to use a contrasting thread when basting. It will be easy to see when you have to take the basting stitch out. There is nothing worse than ripping out your appliqué stitch by mistake!

11. Center the plate on the background block. You can easily find the middle by folding the block diagonally in both directions and finger pressing. If you hold or pinch the fabric, it will temporarily press it and an X should appear at the center of the open part of the plate.

12. Baste with a large stitch through the middle of each wedge up to within an inch of the outer edge. This will hold the plate securely in place to the background.

Quilting Bee

Try to take away any points on your rounded edge by pushing them in with your needle as you sew.

13. Now it's time to appliqué. Use lots of pins to hold down the rounded outer edge. I usually use at least five pins for each wedge. Turn under the seam allowance of one wedge and pin under each end where the dots are. Be sure to turn under right on the basting line. Then pin the center of the wedge at the top of the arc, and put one or two more pins on each side. Pin only two wedges at a time.

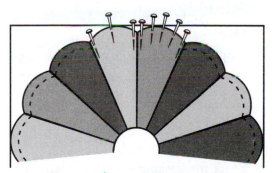

Pin your plate to the background.

14. Appliqué around the entire block. Refer to Chapter 11 to review the appliqué stitch.

15. Cut the center circle B. Be sure to add the seam allowances. The center circle can be any of the colors of the plate or the background fabric.

16. Baste on the sewing line with a contrasting color thread, then turn the seam under and baste again. Pin into position, and baste the circle onto the plate so it will not move. Appliqué around the center.

17. Remove all the basting threads.

18. Press.

The Dresden Plate is a wonderful block that uses both piecing and appliqué techniques. Many antique Dresden Plate quilts use the wedge shape pieces side by side around the border, giving the appearance of cones surrounding the quilt, hence the name Ice Cream border. Can you imagine piecing hundreds of the wedges for a border? When you see the scalloped-edge results, you will appreciate the workmanship even more.

Beginner Sampler Quilt Assembly

Take the following steps to assemble a beginner sampler quilt:

1. Prepare fifteen 12-inch blocks.

2. Position them in a pleasing arrangement, three across and five down. For hints on how to arrange them, refer to Chapter 13.

Don't Get Stuck!

Make sure all of the blocks are a 12-inch square or they won't match. Prepare a piece of cardboard that is a perfect 12-inch square. If it's not exact, then redraw the sewing lines on the wrong side of the block. Remember that the block will actually be 12½ inches including the seam

3. Cut out 38 lattices 12 inches × 3 inches. (Be sure to add on the additional ¼-inch seam allowances).

4. Cut out 24 corner squares in 3-inch squares. (Be sure to add the ¼-inch seam allowance.)

5. Join them together row by row. Corner square to lattice as in Chapter 13, and lattice to block.

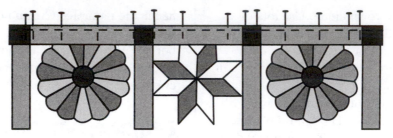

Sew the quilt top together row by row.

6. Sew each row together into your quilt top.

7. Since everyone sews slightly differently, measure the length of the sides of the quilt (be sure they are the same measurement). It should be approximately 75 inches in length and 60 inches in width. If so …

   ◆ Cut two inner borders 75½ × 6½ inches.

   ◆ Cut two top and bottom inner borders 60½ × 6½ inches.

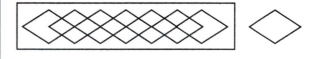

Quilting Bee

To prevent a quilt that is crooked, measure both sides of the quilt top and the middle. They should all be the same. If not, now is the time to re-sew some seams. Both opposite borders should be the same length.

8. Sew the borders onto the quilt sides, press open borders, and add the top and bottom borders. (See Chapter 13.)

9. Measure, cut, and sew on the outer borders.

   Cut two side outer borders 92 × 8 inches.

   Cut one bottom outer border 75 × 8 inches.

10. Press and take off all threads.

Quilting Bee

It is easier for beginners to apply the binding by rounding the bottom edges of the outer border corners. Take a plate and put it in the corner, draw around the plate and cut off excess point of border.

11. Layer the backing and batting with the quilt top. Baste.

12. Mark quilt designs.

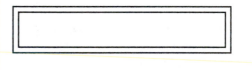

Quilt designs for lattices.

13. Start quilting in the center of the quilt top. Quilt blocks and then the lattices, making sure there is no buckling when moving to a new area.

14. Bind off the edges and take out basting.

You're done!

Don't Get Stuck! _____

Don't do a lot of quilting on a patterned fabric, it won't show up. Save the intricate quilting on solid fabrics where it will be appreciated.

The Least You Need to Know

◆ Lay the cut-out fabric pieces in front of you and pin two pieces together; be sure to lay the pieces back into the design to check for accuracy and then sew.

◆ Sew small pieces together to form a larger unit.

◆ Pieces of a block are sewn together horizontally in row.

◆ When you decide to appliqué, make sure you complete all the necessary steps to ensure the edges will not ravel.

In This Chapter

- ◆ Learn what makes a block challenging

- ◆ Special cutting techniques

- ◆ How to piece fabric pieces into units to make a four-patch or a nine-patch unit

- ◆ Piecing 90-degree angle seams

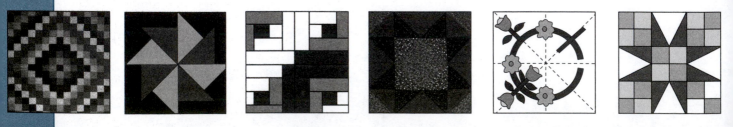

Chapter

18

Put a Spin on Your Sampler

If you want to put a new twist on your Sampler quilt, here is the quilt for you. Find the green Sampler quilt in the color picture section. This was, one of my newer students, Maureen Muller's first quilting project. It was quite an undertaking. She started out making some simple blocks as in the Beginner Sampler quilt, Ohio Star, Churn Dash, and the Eight Point Star. Then she wanted something more interesting. She also realized she didn't like the look or the making of appliqué blocks. So you won't see any curvy, flowery blocks, Maureen went for the angular, geometric designs. There is definitely a spinning motif, but these blocks won't make you dizzy!

Finished size: 96 × 65 inches full sized quilt.

Color scheme:

This quilt is a monochromatic scheme using all shades of green. Maureen kept the background of each block the traditional muslin. Choose one patterned fabric that you love and pull out several colors from that fabric.

Materials:

Fabrics

Full/queen size batting

Backing

Patterns and template for:

◆ Crazy Ann

◆ Dutchman's Puzzle Pinwheel

◆ Old Maid's Puzzle

◆ Pinwheel

◆ Rolling Star

◆ Star Flower

◆ Waterwheel

◆ Windmills

Fabric requirements:

2 yards muslin (background)

2½ yards light fabric (lattice)

4½ yards medium color fabric (blocks, corner squares, and outer border)

4 yards dark colored fabric (blocks, inner border)

6 yards backing

Start with the easy blocks in Chapter 17, Ohio Star, the Eight Point Star, and Churn Dash. Then twirl your quilt with these new blocks; they are grouped from easy to more complex. Let's get spinning.

Old Maid's Puzzle

I'm not sure why this block is known as the Old Maid's Puzzle, or Crosses and Losses in some parts of the United States. It is a four-patch block, the design is divided into two sections that are repeated. Although the pattern pieces are squares and two sizes of triangles, the trick is that sometimes the triangles form a square and other times a larger triangle.

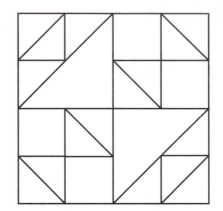

Old Maid's Puzzle block.

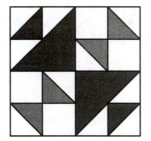 

Change the position of the dark color and the puzzle pieces sure change the Old Maid.

1. Make the templates and decide on the color scheme.

2. Mark fabric with the templates and mark ¼-inch seam allowances.

3. Cut out fabric pieces and lay out the design in front of you.

4. Take a dark and light small triangle of template A. Pin right sides together and sew the long side of the triangle, to form a square. Do this six times.

5. Pin a square (template B) to the side of the half square triangle to form a rectangle.

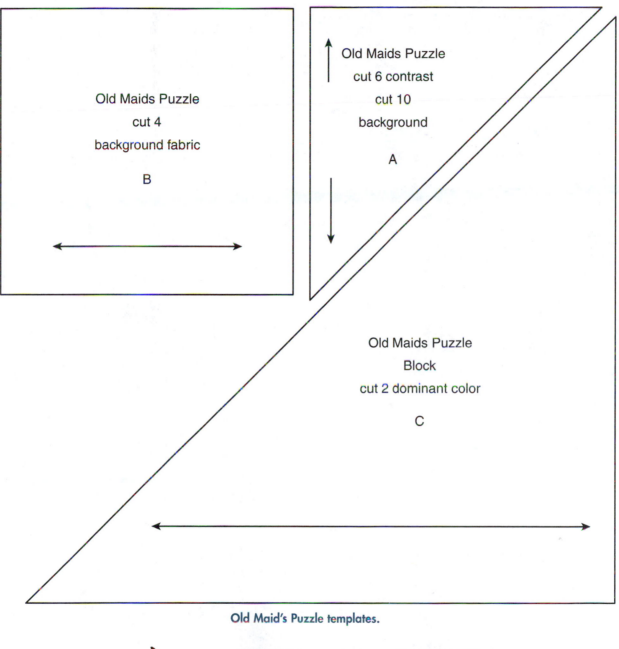

Old Maids Puzzle
cut 4
background fabric

B

Old Maids Puzzle
cut 6 contrast
cut 10
background

A

Old Maids Puzzle
Block
cut 2 dominant color

C

Old Maid's Puzzle templates.

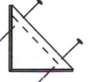 

Be sure to sew the plain square onto the correct side.

6. Sew two of these units together to form a 6-inch square (unit 1).

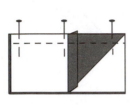
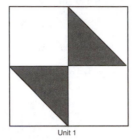

Unit 1

7. Take a *half square triangle* and pin two triangles (still template A) on each side to form a larger triangle.

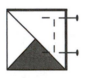

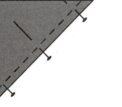

Unit 2

Take care to sew the short side of the triangle piece to the colored triangle on the square.

> **Quilt Talk**
>
> A **half square triangle** is a square that is made of two triangles on the diagonal.

8. Pin the long side of the large triangle (template C) to the pieced triangle to form a 6-inch square (unit 2).

9. Sew together unit 1 and unit 2 squares to form the top half. Make sure to pin the correct sides together; open pinned squares up to check the placement. Do this with the remaining units.

10. Sew top to the bottom. Don't forget that the tips of the large triangles should touch.

11. Press.

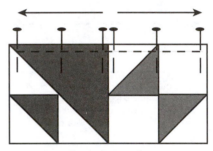

Sew from the inside out.

> **Don't Get Stuck!**
>
> Put a pin in the middle seam of the block to make sure the tips of the triangle match. First pin the ends of the sewing line and every few inches to keep the seam from shifting. Sew from the middle seam toward the outer edge.

Dutchman's Puzzle Pinwheel

This block has a spiraling effect, but with this variation, an inner pinwheel is formed. There are two pattern pieces: a large and a small background triangle. The difference from the normal block is in the cutting. When cutting the small triangles, four of them are in a different medium color and these are placed in the center. It is another four-patch square, meaning the block is divided into four sections. This block is not a puzzle at all, but you do have to take care to piece the inner pinwheel accurately.

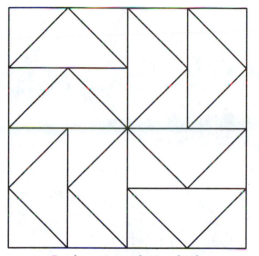

Dutchman's Puzzle Pinwheel.

1. Prepare templates and decide on the color combinations.

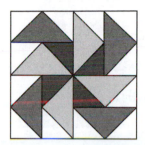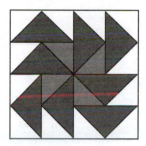

See how the inner pinwheel spins.

2. Mark the templates on your fabric, add ¼-inch seam allowances, and cut your fabric pieces.

3. Lay out the fabric pieces in front of you.

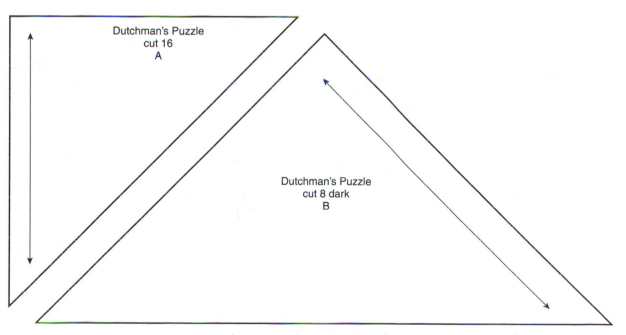

Dutchman's Puzzle
cut 16
A

Dutchman's Puzzle
cut 8 dark
B

Dutchman's Puzzle Pinwheel templates.

4. Pin together the longest side of the background small triangle (template A) to the smallest side of the largest triangle (template B).

Does that sound confusing? I hope not.

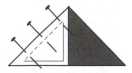 

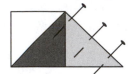 

Sewing triangles to the Dutchman's Pinwheel.

5. Pin the small triangle of the medium colored fabric to the other side of the large triangle. When the three triangles are combined, they form a 6 × 3-inch rectangle. Make four of the unit.

Sew the rectangle together with the medium triangle in the same correct position.

6. Prepare four more of this unit but with both triangles in the background fabric. You should now have eight units, four with background fabrics and four with the two colored triangles.

7. Put two sets of the rectangles together to form a 6-inch square. Make sure to have the medium colored triangle at the bottom right of this unit. Make four of these units.

8. Put the horizontal rows together, making sure you move each unit a one-quarter turn, to be in the correct position.

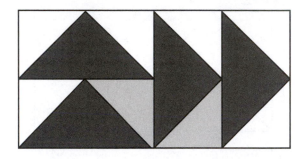

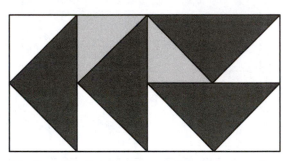

Flip the top half right sides together. Pin across the top seam; sew from the inside out.

9. Put horizontal rows together, making sure they are in their correct positions.

10. Press.

Windmills

If you haven't gotten enough of the spinning effects, here's another block to try.

This is a nine-patch block. There are nine 4-inch squares. Five of these squares have pinwheels in them. The construction is easy but there are 44 pieces in this block. When you look at this block, can't you just picture windmills on a hillside?

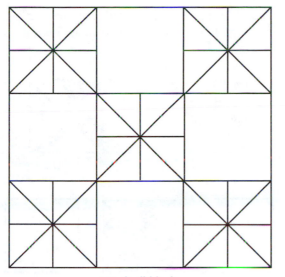

Windmill block.

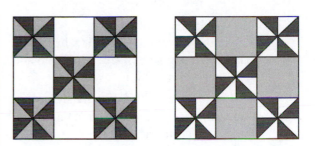

Color variations of the Windmill block—one light, one dark.

You can make all the pinwheels the same, or the center square can be a different set of colors. You can set all the pinwheels on a muslin background, or if you feel that is too light, the pinwheel squares can be two different colors. Usually three fabrics are used.

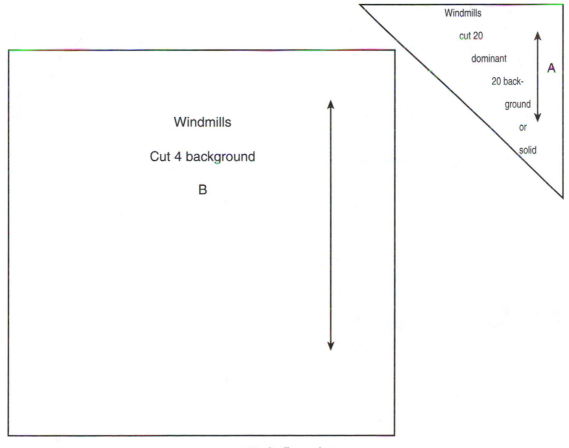

Windmills

cut 20

dominant

20 back-

ground

or

solid

A

Windmills

Cut 4 background

B

Windmill templates.

1. Make templates.

2. Choose the placement of your fabrics. Mark the wrong side of the fabric and add the ¼-inch seam allowances.

3. Cut 4 solid squares and 20 triangles in a dominant fabric and 20 in the contrasting or background fabric.

Quilting Bee

There are so many little triangles; keep them safe by placing them in a Ziplock baggie. Somehow, one always gets lost.

4. Pin a dominant colored triangle to a contrasting colored triangle, and sew along the long side to form a half square triangle.

5. Sew two half square triangles together, making sure the positions are correct. Then sew the bottom of the pinwheel by pinning two half square triangles together. Make five of these 6-inch squares.

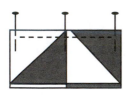

Put together eight triangles to form one of the "windmills."

6. Sew the windmill square to a solid square and another windmill, to form a row. Prepare two of these rows.

7. Then prepare the middle row sewing together the solid square to a windmill, to another solid square.

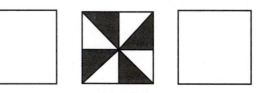

Sew the squares together row by row.

8. Sew the three rows together to form the 12-inch block.

9. Press by having all the seams of the windmill squares spiraling in the same direction, allowing the center of the square to press flat, like the pressing of the Eight Point Star.

Star Flower

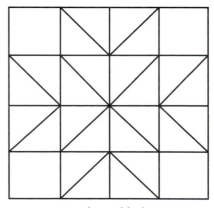

Star Flower block.

This block reminds me of a squashed Ohio Star but with a pinwheel in the center. The Star Flower is a four-patch. If you divide the block down the center vertically and horizontally, each section is the same. You need to make four of the same units.

There are two basic templates: a square (cut four) and a triangle. You need to cut 24 triangles of several colors: eight dark or the dominant color, eight background for the star, then four medium and four of the contrasting color for the inner pinwheel.

Play around with the color placement to suit your quilt. There are 28 pieces in this block. Is your head spinning yet? I told you this was a twirling quilt.

1. Prepare templates and decide on colors.
2. Mark the fabrics on the wrong side and add ¼-inch seam allowances.
3. Cut and lay out the pieces in front of you.
4. Start by making eight half square triangles for the star by pinning the long sides of the dominant and background fabric.

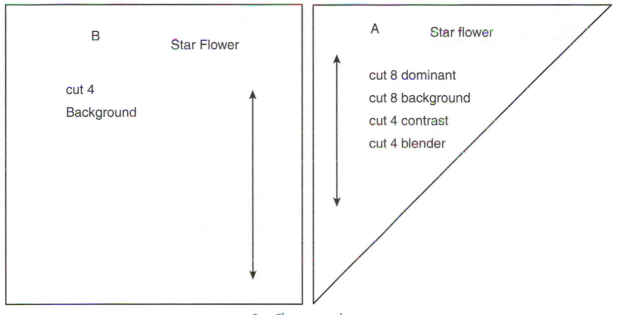

B

Star Flower

cut 4

Background

A   Star flower

cut 8 dominant

cut 8 background

cut 4 contrast

cut 4 blender

Star Flower templates.

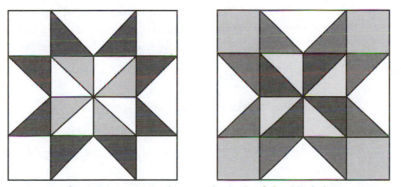

Varying the color positions changes the look of this block from a star to an X.

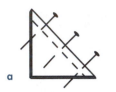 

Pin along the long side of the triangle to make a square, and then be careful to add the square onto the correct side.

5. Sew the four half square triangles for the center pinwheel.

6. Sew the solid square to the left side of the half square triangle.

Don't Get Stuck!

It is very easy to sew this square onto the wrong side; so please pin, then place the unit back into the block laid out in front of you.

7. Look at the following figure, sew a star half square triangle to the inner pinwheel half square triangle.

8. Sew unit a to b to form one quarter of the block. Make four.

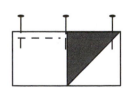 

Check that your pinning is correct when making this unit of the block.

9. Sew top two units together to form the upper half, then sew the bottom two together.

10. Sew the top to the bottom. Sew from the inside out to make sure the pinwheels match.

11. Press.

Quilting Bee

To make certain the center pinwheel matches, pin each end of the horizontal, center seam. Then pin the very center of the seam by pushing the seam allowance to one side and pin through the dot of the left side. Sew from that inside point to the outer edge. Backstitch to secure. Push the center seam allowance in the other direction, pin into the center dot of the right, and sew the other side of the seam.

Pinwheel

Don't get your head "spinning." This is a great patch but be careful—it's the first block with a *nonreversible template*. If you put a line down the center of the shape, each side of the line is different.

Quilt Talk

A **nonreversible template** is one that is asymmetrical. If the nonreversible templates are made upside down the piece will not fit in and is not usable.

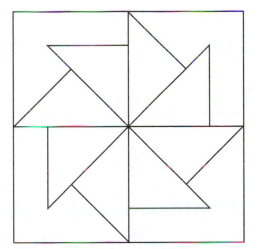

Pinwheel block. These spinning blocks are great for a child's quilt.

Some students have traced the templates and by mistake drawn the template upside down. When they try to piece the block, they are baffled that the pieces don't fit. I like to cut one of the tricky templates and make sure that it fits before cutting the rest.

This patch has only 16 pieces so it can be assembled quickly. There are two pattern pieces: a triangle A and the nonreversible trapezoid B. Don't get turned upside down—follow the directions for success.

1. Prepare the templates and choose the colors.

2. Mark and cut out your fabrics, adding on seam allowances.

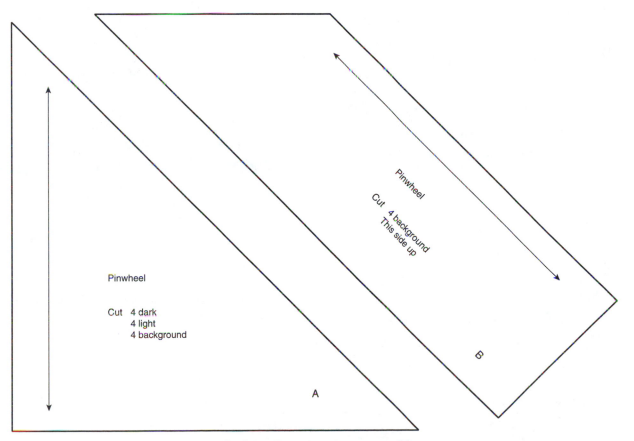

Pinwheel templates—one is nonreversible.

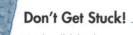

Don't Get Stuck! _____

With all blocks, remember to match up the dots, not the seam allowances. The seam allowances will hang over the edges. Don't worry, that happens with all triangles and diamonds.

3. Lay out the pieces in front of you, making certain that the trapezoid pieces fit.

4. Sew the colored triangle A to the trapezoid B, matching the dots. Then pin and stitch.

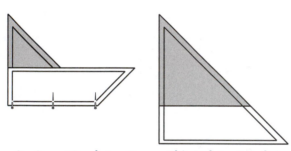

Sewing a triangle to a trapezoid (templates A and B).

5. Sew a colored triangle A to a background piece A. Match the short sides together, pin into the dots, then fit the pieces into the laid-out pieces on the table. Check that the colored triangle is in the correct place, otherwise your pinwheel won't spin.

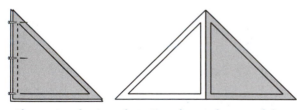

These triangles (template A) make up the rest of the Pinwheel block.

6. Sew these two pieced triangles together to form a 6-inch square.

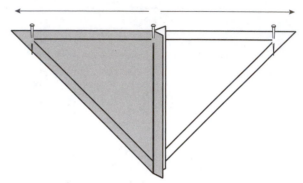

Making 6-inch squares of the Pinwheel.

7. Sew the top two 6-inch squares together, then the bottom two squares to form rows.

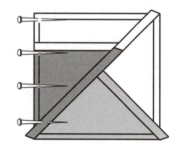

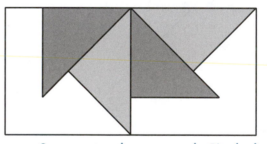

Sew rows together to create the Pinwheel.

8. Pin the top row to the bottom row matching the center seam. Sew from the center seam to the outside.

9. Press.

Rolling Star

If you want to take the Eight Point Star "up a notch," then you should make the Rolling Star. This block has a small central eight-point star, but instead of alternating squares and triangles, there are only squares. Remember how I said your Eight Point Star block wouldn't be squared off if you didn't alternate squares and triangles? This central part of the patch then has an octagonal shape and needs to be squared off with a background fabric to complete the 12-inch square.

There are three basic pattern pieces: a diamond, a square, and a four-sided shape that squares off the block. You will be cutting out 24 fabric pieces in all. This block always coordinates nicely into your quilt project because it combines three fabrics from your color scheme and the background. Be sure to use the darkest or brightest color in the part of the block you want to emphasize, either the diamond or the star or the squares.

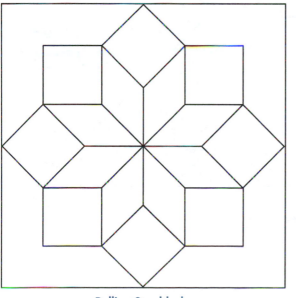

Rolling Star block.

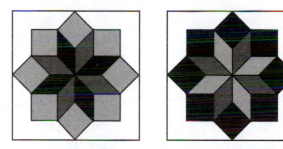

Notice how the placement of the dark color changes the appearance of the block.

If you like the Eight Point Star, go one step further. Check out the instructions and pictures for the Rolling Star. Then let's get rolling on the Rolling Star.

1. Make the templates and decide on the color combinations.

2. Mark, adding on seam allowances, then cut out the fabric pieces and lay out the block in front of you.

3. Start by picking up two adjacent diamonds (template A). Flip over one diamond so their right sides are together, and pin the dots. Sew from dot to dot only.

4. Sew all the diamonds together making sure to pick up the correct color diamond and pin it in the right position.

5. Sew the squares (template B) into the diamonds. Turn the square over the diamond with the right sides together. Match the dots. Sew from the widest part of the diamond out to the tip of the star. Sew in all eight squares.

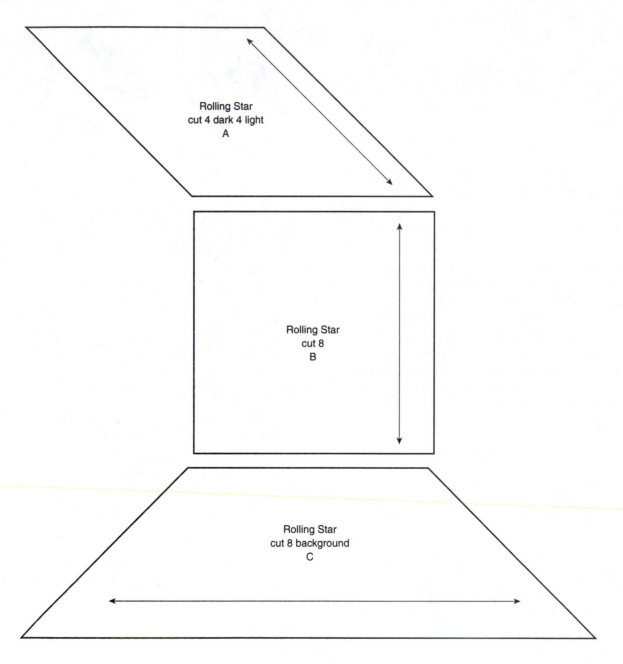

Rolling Star templates.

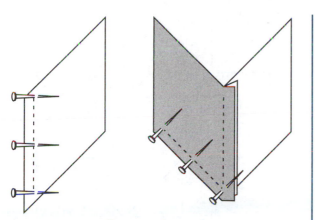

Rolling Star diamonds.

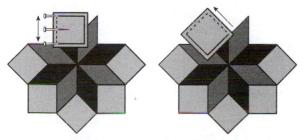

Put squares all around the Rolling Star.

6. Now for those weird-shaped trapezoids. Flip template C so that the "top" of the shape matches one side of the square (following figure, left). Pin and sew only between dots. There will be un-sewn ends at each side. Don't worry, we'll sew them next.

7. Fold the square in half onto itself, and pin one end of the background to the adjacent square. Sew from the inside dot to the outside of the block (following figure, middle).

8. Pin and stitch the center of another rectangle to the next square. Now we have to attach the two ends of the background that are hanging loose. Fold the square in half at an angle so that the background ends meet. Pin the dots and sew from the inside to the outer part of the block (following figure, right).

9. Sew in all the background pieces.

10. Press the inner star in the same way you would press the Eight Point Star. Iron the star and square seam allowances toward the background pieces to reduce bulk.

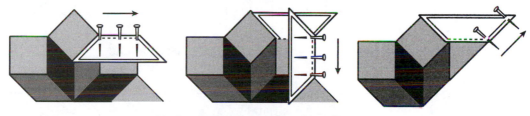

Sewing the background for the Rolling Star.

Crazy Ann

The inside unit looks very similar to the Dutchman's Puzzle Pinwheel, but this block is standing on its end. There are three templates: a square for the corners, a large triangle for the puzzle, and a small triangle for the background to the design.

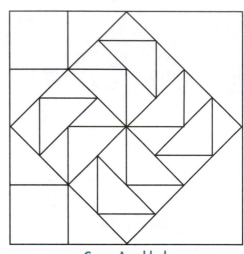

Crazy Ann block.

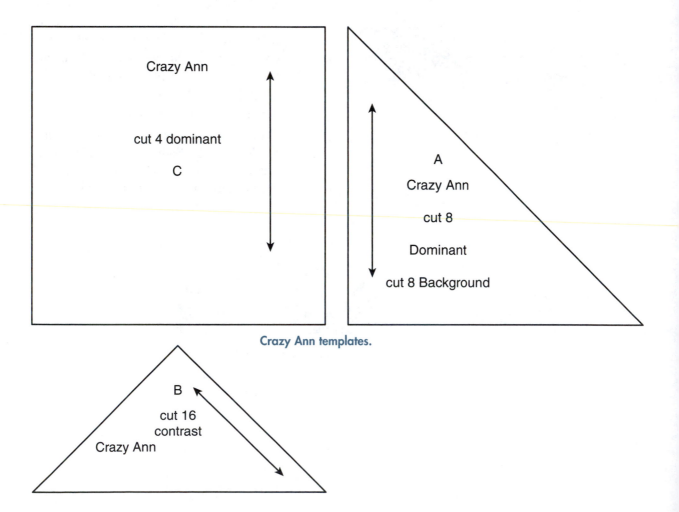

Crazy Ann

cut 4 dominant

C

A
Crazy Ann
cut 8
Dominant
cut 8 Background

B
cut 16
contrast
Crazy Ann

Crazy Ann templates.

Cut 8 large triangles (template A) in your dominant color, 16 small triangles (template B) in your light or background fabric, 4 squares in your contrasting color, and 8 large triangles (template A) in the background fabric.

Don't Get Stuck!

Because many of the pieces look so similar, to avoid confusion, keep the templates of each block in a separate envelope. I put them in Ziplock bags with the picture of the block facing so you can see it easily. The directions are copied and also put in there.

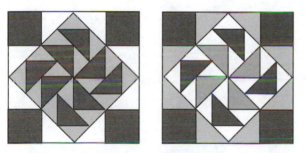

See how the background color of the "Puzzle" part can be the background color or a blender fabric.

1. Make templates, and plan color placement.

2. Mark the templates on the fabrics and add the ¼-inch seam allowance.

3. Cut out pieces and lay out the block in front of you.

4. First, make the inside "Puzzle" unit. (This is the same construction as in the Dutchman's Puzzle Pinwheel in the earlier part of the chapter.) Pin the short side of large triangle A to the long sides of two B triangles and sew to form a rectangle.

5. Sew two of the rectangles to form a 6-inch square. Make four of these sections.

6. Pin two of these sections together turning one quarter turn for the top of the Puzzle section. Pin and sew two sections for the bottom. Sew these units together.

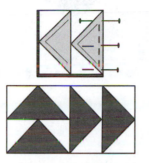
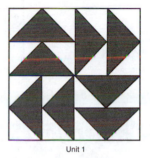

The center "Puzzle" part of the Crazy Ann block—unit 1.

7. Pin and sew two A triangles, in the background fabric, to the sides of the square C. Make four of these units.

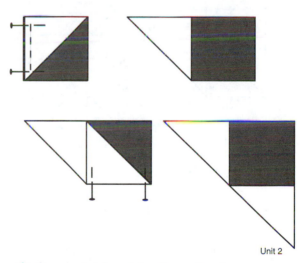

This larger triangle unit is what makes Ann crazy—unit 2.

8. Pin and sew these triangle units to each side of the Puzzle part (unit 1) to complete this block.

9. Press.

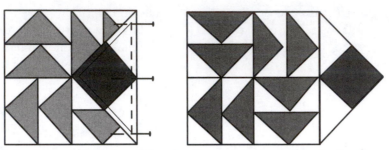

Don't worry if the tips of the triangle unit are longer than the Puzzle, as long as the dots match.

Waterwheel

This is the most difficult block to piece. It's that weird rhomboid, the shape that looks like a pointy rectangle.

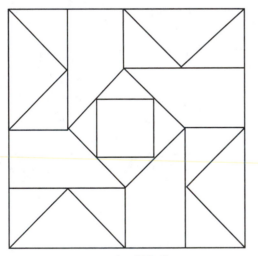

Waterwheel block.

This has the most number of templates to make. There are three different size triangles, a square, and that crazy rhomboid.

Depending on the position of the dominant color, you can really put a spin on this block. By now, you should have several blocks made. If you have muslin or a solid color around the outside of other blocks, then you would want to make the four large C triangles of that color.

Cut one square A, four rhomboids E, four small triangles B, and eight medium triangles C. There are 21 pieces all together. Don't let this wheel spin you around.

See how the wheels spin differently when the dominant color changes places.

1. Prepare the templates.
2. Mark the fabric and add the ¼-inch seam allowance.
3. Cut and lay out the pieces in front of you.

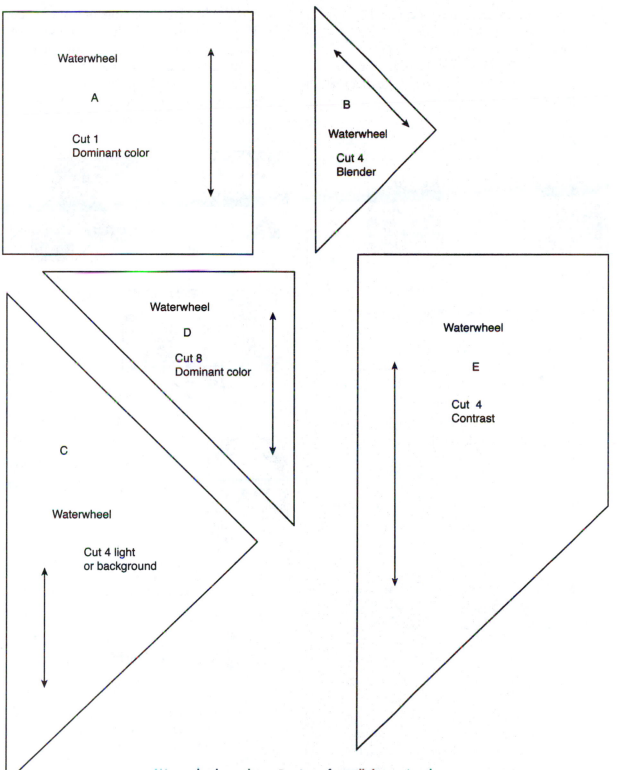

Waterwheel templates. Don't confuse all those triangles.

4. This time we start in the center with square A. Pin the longest side of the smallest triangle B to one side of the square. Sew. Then sew the other B triangles on to each side of the square (see the following figure).

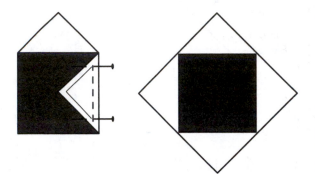

Sew a triangle to each side of the square to form the center unit.

5. Pin the small sides of the large triangle C to the long side of the two medium triangles D. When sewn, these form a rectangular unit. Make four of these.

6. Pin the long side of the rhomboid E to the triangles' "tip" side of the rectangle. Sew this onto each of the rectangular units.

Sew the three triangles together to form a rectangle, and then add that crazy piece E.

7. Now comes the tricky part. Pin the pointy part of the rhomboid to one side of the square. Sew dot to dot of this seam. Sew all four of the seams around the center unit. You now have two sides of each of these units that are flapping loose. How will you sew this block together?

8. Lay the block on the table in front of you. If you want to sew the horizontal seam of one of these units, fold the entire block right sides together so the seams you want to sew match up. Pin the dots carefully. Always sew these seams from the center of the block toward the outside.

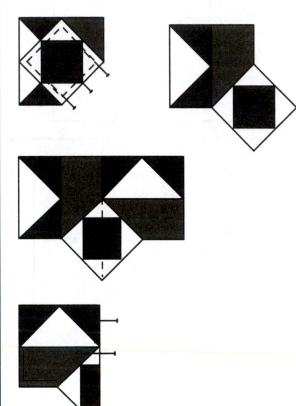

See how you have to fold the block in half to get the seams to match.

Don't Get Stuck!

Sew only from dot to dot on these seams. If you sew all the way through the seam allowance, you will not be able to manipulate to sew the seams, and when pressed they will not lay flat.

9. Pin the short sides of rhomboid and the rectangle unit together by folding the block in half through the center. Sew from dot to dot. Pin and sew all loose seams. Once you know this technique of piecing, it's not that difficult.

10. Press.

The Finishing Touches

When you have made 15 of all those spinning blocks, it's time to put your quilt together. This is how Maureen finished her quilt.

1. Decide on the position of your blocks.

2. Cut lattices and corner squares (seam allowances are included).

    ◆ Cut 22 lattices 12½ × 3½ inches.

    ◆ Cut two top and bottom lattice borders 50 × 3½ inches.

    ◆ Cut two side lattice borders 80 × 3½ inches.

    ◆ Cut eight corner squares 3½ × 3½ inches.

3. Sew lattices and blocks together in rows, and then rows of lattices and corner squares.

4. Sew the rows together in the correct order making the quilt top.

5. Cut the inner border.

    ◆ Cut two top and bottom inner borders 58 × 3½ inches.

    ◆ Cut two side inner borders 85 × 3½ inches.

6. Sew onto the quilt top. (See Chapter 13.)

7. Cut outer border.

    ◆ Cut two top and bottom outer borders 65 × 5½ inches.

    ◆ Cut two side outer borders 98 × 5½ inches.

8. Sew onto the quilt top.

9. Press and cut off all excess threads.

10. Baste the batting and the backing to the quilt top. (See Chapter 14.)

11. Mark and quilt designs. (See Chapter 15.)

12. Finish with a bias binding. (See Chapter 16.)

13. Use and enjoy your quilt!

The Least You Need to Know

◆ Lay out cut-out fabric pieces in front of you and pin two pieces together; be sure to lay the pieces back into the design to check for accuracy and then sew.

◆ Asymmetrical-shaped templates need extra care in marking since they are nonreversible.

◆ Some blocks are pieced on the diagonal.

◆ Be sure rows are sewn from the inside seam line to the outer edge.

In This Chapter

◆ Preparing the Tippecanoe block

◆ Hints in choosing fabrics for a scrap quilt

◆ Learning how to make and use a windowed template

◆ Special cutting techniques for making fussy cuts

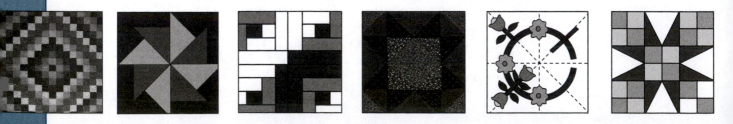

Chapter 19

Patriotic Scrap Quilt

One of my students gave me a bumper sticker that says "The quilter who dies with the most fabric wins!" (Find the red, white, and blue quilt in the color section.)

This quilt is a fabric collector's dream. Holly Ciccoricco had been searching for patriotic fabrics for several years. She had amassed quite a large assortment of red, white, and blue fabrics. Once she started piecing this quilt, people started donating their scraps. It is impossible to calculate how many different fabrics she used, but her plan was that no two blocks were the same. She has succeeded!

Scraps and Pieces

Tippecanoe may sound like a strange name but it has historical significance. Benjamin Harrison, famous for the battle of Tippecanoe, used as his presidential slogan, "Tippecanoe and Tyler too" because his running mate was John Tyler. These political and commemorative quilts were popular during the late 1890s.

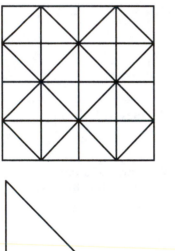

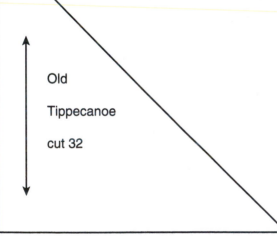

Old

Tippecanoe

cut 32

Old Tippecanoe block and template.

The name of the block is Old Tippecanoe. This block has only one template, a triangle.

However, there are 32 triangles. The fun in putting this together is how changeable the design can be with the variation of the color placement. The solid lattice frames each star to give them a definition of their own. Start your own challenge quilt, make each block appear different. Holly did and actually made two twin-size quilts—all with different color variations. That's very impressive.

Look at the close-up of Holly's Fabric Sampler quilt. Look how each block has different fabrics. Check out the "fussy cuts."

Fabric requirements:

8 yards of a solid dark fabric—for lattices, borders, and backing

1 yard contrasting color (red)—for inner border (border can be from selvage to selvage)

6 yards total of as many varieties of red and blue fabrics as you can find—fat quarters are great for this

Quilting Bee

Fat quarters are a great way to enlarge your fabric stash.

Holly's Hints

There are several hints that Holly discovered. Let me reveal them to you:

♦ Make sure there is a wide range of values, pattern, and variety in the scale of each color.

♦ When you make the center four triangles the same color, it will look like a large center square.

♦ Use striped, checked, plaid, patterned, or even fabric with words on it for your quilt. Take care in cutting the triangles in special ways. By matching up the stripes, patterns, or specific designs of a fabric you can get what is known as a "fussy." Take your template and line it up with a specific motif or strip. Check out the close-up of this quilt.

♦ You can cut a piece of a block with a specific design by using a *windowed template*. Draw your triangle in the center of an index card. Carefully cut out the triangle leaving the outside edge intact. You may need to use an Exacto knife for accuracy. Move this template over your fabric until you can see the design you want. This will show you how your marked piece will look. Then cut each of those pieces that same way.

Quilt Talk

A **windowed template** is made on a larger piece of plastic or cardboard, but the shape of the pattern is removed, leaving a hole in the paper. The opening shows how the block will look and masks the surrounding fabric.

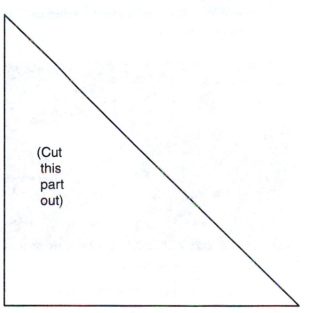

(Cut this part out)

Move your windowed template to find the same design in your fabric.

♦ You will need to ignore the straight-of-grain line when you cut in order to get a specific look.

♦ Because the edges of each piece may be bias and very stretchy, you need to take care not to pull or press these out of shape.

Putting It Together

We have suggested some ways to make this block preparation fun and easy. Follow these directions, and don't let this canoe tip!

1. Make templates, and decide on the position of the fabrics in the block. (See the following hints on color placement.)

2. Mark and cut out fabrics. Lay out pieces in front of you on a table to form the block.

3. Because there are 32 triangles in this block, it is easiest to first pair the triangles to form squares. Put the triangular pieces right sides together and sew on the long seam. Put all the triangles together to form 16 squares.

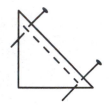

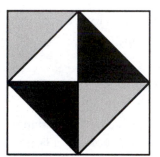

Pin the top half to the bottom half, making sure to sew from the middle of the block to the outside.

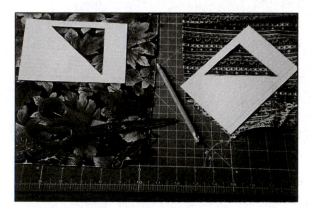

Pin the long sides of the triangles together to form a square and then four of these squares together to form a quarter section of the block.

4. Put four of these squares together to form one quarter of the block. Do this four times.

5. Sew the top two sections and the bottom two together. Then sew across the horizontal seam line.

6. Prepare 24 blocks for a twin-size quilt and arrange them to find a pleasing balance of colors for the quilt top. Spread your bright, light, and dark colors throughout the quilt.

7. To finish the quilt top, use 18 lattices in a solid color 12½ × 1½ inches, and 8 horizontal lattice strips, and the top and bottom strips are 54 × 1½ inches. The two side lattice strips are 62 × 1½ inches. Holly used a navy solid for framing each block.

Don't Get Stuck!

Remember to take your own quilt's measurements through the middle of the quilt (making sure each side is equal to that amount) so that you will have the same size quilt on each side. You want your quilt to line up. I did add a "fudge factor" to Holly's amounts.

8. Sew the lattices to the sides of the blocks making rows. (See Chapter 13.)

9. Sew the rows together with the horizontal lattice strip in between them.

10. Sew each side lattice strip from the top to the bottom.

11. Measure and cut the borders (remember that these amounts are estimates—everyone cuts and pieces differently):

Inner border (red):

- ◆ 2 strips 57 × 1½ inches
- ◆ 2 strips 81 × 1½ inches

Outer border (dark blue):

- ◆ 2 strips 88 × 3½ inches
- ◆ 2 strips 64 × 3½ inches

12. Sew the borders on. (See Chapter 13.)
13. Press.
14. Baste the backing and the batting to the quilt top.
15. Mark and quilt the designs.
16. Finish off the outside edge. (See Chapter 16.)

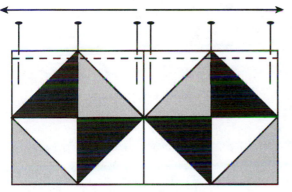

Here are some quilting ideas.

The Least You Need to Know

- ◆ In a fabric challenge quilt, you need a great variety of fabrics with a range of values and patterns.
- ◆ Each fabric piece can be cut in a particular way to make each section of the block look identical.
- ◆ Use stripes, checks and plaids to make each block unique.
- ◆ Make a windowed template to help these parts of the block.

In This Chapter

◆ Using diamonds to make a star

◆ Learning how to cut the fabric to manipulate its design

◆ Choosing successful placement of colors

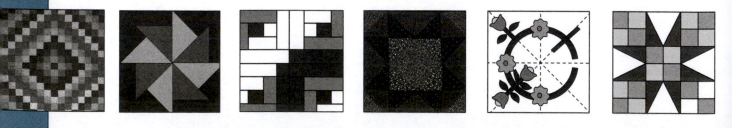

Chapter 20

Blazing Star Quilt Wall Hanging

I've always loved stars, especially the Eight Point Star. When I'd made these stars in all variety of colors and different shades of backgrounds, I then discovered a more challenging star: the Virginia Star and Blazing Star. The Virginia Star has eight large diamonds sewn together, but each of the diamonds is divided into four smaller diamonds, making 40 pieces in the block. This block is a 12-inch square.

The Blazing Star takes the star to another level; each of the eight large diamonds is divided into nine sections, making the total number of pieces 80! This block is 18 inches in size.

Virginia Star

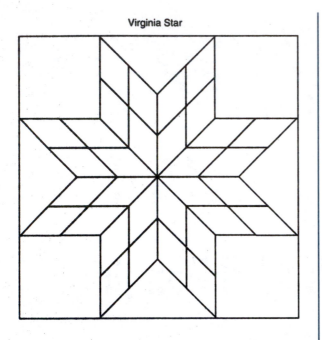

Blazing Star

Virginia Star and Blazing Star blocks. The colors can make them look like sunbursts.

Finished size:

Virginia Star: 34 × 34 inches

Blazing Star: 48 × 48 inches

Color schemes:

When I discovered these blocks, all I thought about was all the exciting color combinations I could make. I wanted to do a color study with the stars. If you look in the color photo section, find the Blazing Star wall hanging. I chose four different fabrics; brown was the dominant color, green was the accent, and there were two blender fabrics in lighter shades. (For the Virginia Star you should choose two or three fabrics.) You can have fabrics of all one color for a monochromatic scheme, or two different colors as I chose. You need a variety of values from dark to light for contrast.

Quilting Bee

Make several copies of the star layout. Take small snips of your fabric and arrange them in different ways to get a pleasing arrangement. Once you decide, glue the snips down. Just don't sneeze or move before you lose them.

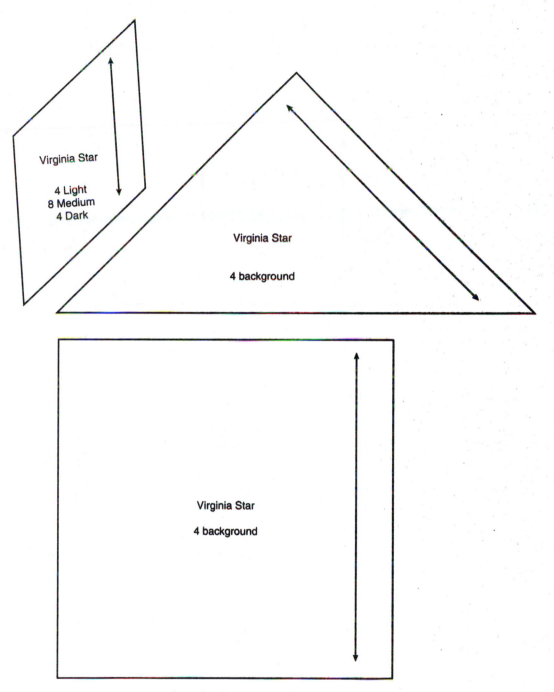

Virginia Star

4 Light
8 Medium
4 Dark

Virginia Star

4 background

Virginia Star

4 background

Templates for the Virginia Star.

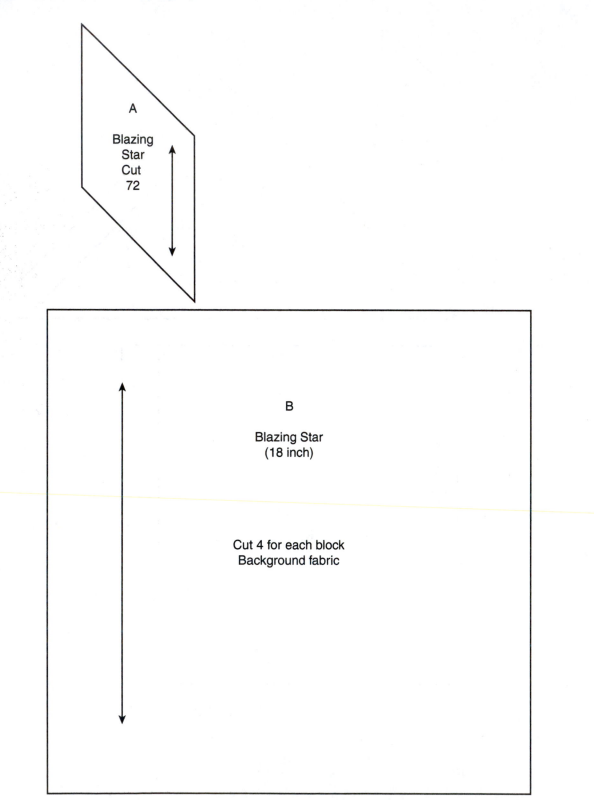

A

Blazing
Star
Cut
72

B

Blazing Star
(18 inch)

Cut 4 for each block
Background fabric

Templates for the Blazing Star; the diamonds are smaller, but the block turns out larger.

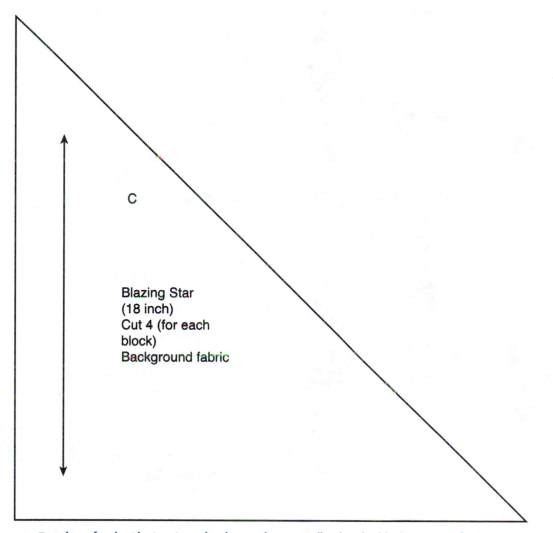

C

Blazing Star
(18 inch)
Cut 4 (for each
block)
Background fabric

Templates for the Blazing Star; the diamonds are smaller, but the block turns out larger.

You can combine the colors in a variety of ways: The Blazing Star is the most challenging. Start with the darkest value fabric at one tip of the diamond and go to the lightest at the other, or have the darkest at the center of the diamond and mirror the fabrics on either side.

The background fabric is essential to the color placement in the diamond. If a fabric is similar to the background, that part of the diamond will fade out. This is not always bad. My daughter Jessica wanted one that looked like snowflakes for her wedding quilt. After several tries, we found one that she liked, but the middle part of the diamond was the same color as the background. I hope to finish it on her first anniversary! Wish me luck.

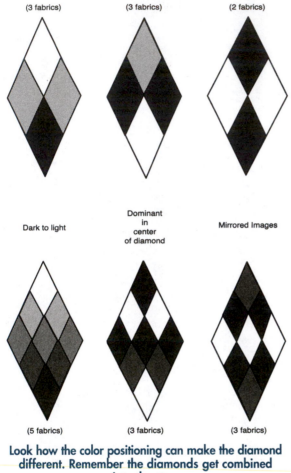

(3 fabrics)   (3 fabrics)   (2 fabrics)

Dark to light   Dominant in center of diamond   Mirrored Images

(5 fabrics)   (3 fabrics)   (3 fabrics)

Look how the color positioning can make the diamond different. Remember the diamonds get combined into the star.

See the different looks with the fabric changes on the background.

Materials:

3 to 5 fabric colors:

◆ Dominant fabric: 1½ yards—star and outer border

◆ Contrast fabric: 1 yard—star and inner border

◆ 1 or 2 (3) blender fabrics: ½ yard—star

Background fabric: 2 yards

Batting

Backing fabric: 1 yard

Don't Get Stuck!

Make sure you pin into the dots. Don't worry that the seam allowances do not match at the end, it's the dots that count.

Follow these steps:

1. Make the templates and choose the colors.

2. Mark and cut out the fabrics, adding on seam allowances.

3. Lay out the fabric pieces in front of you.

4. Piece the diamonds together. First flip the top diamond one to the center diamond two. Pin and sew dot to dot forming a row.

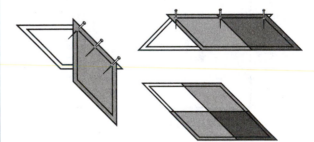

Sewing the small diamonds together into a large diamond unit.

5. Flip, pin, and sew diamond three to four forming another row (diamonds two and three are the same color).

6. Turn the right side of the diamond right sides together with the left side. I know this sounds confusing, but look at the following figure. Sew from the inside seam to the outside.

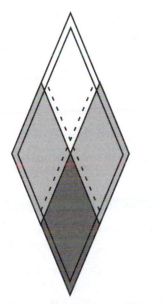

Press seams in one direction. It will be easier to quilt if the seam allowances are pressed consistently.

7. Sew all diamond units together like the Eight Point Star. Pin two diamonds, right sides together, matching seams of smaller diamonds.

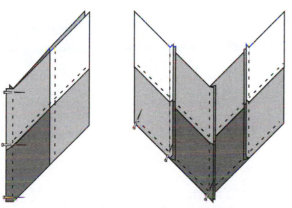

Sewing diamond units together in an Eight Point Star.

8. Sew the square template B around the star alternately with the triangle template C.

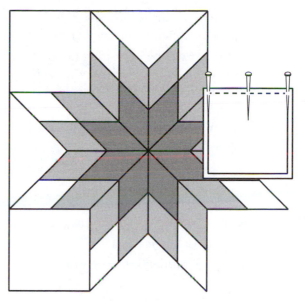

Sewing squares and triangles onto the Virginia Star.

9. Press the background seam allowances of the squares and triangles toward the diamonds. Now step back and you can gaze at your star.

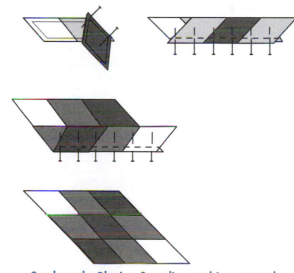

See how the Blazing Star diamond is prepared.

10. Prepare four star blocks. Sew together the blocks to make the wall hanging top.

11. Cut the borders by measuring through the inside of the quilt top. If you want to miter the corners, check out Chapter 13 for instructions. Here are the sizes for my borders, but be sure to measure your own:

Virginia Star quilt:

◆ Inner border: cut four strips 28 × 2 inches (all border seam allowances are included in measurements)

◆ Background border: cut four strips 31 × 1½ inches

◆ Outer border: cut four strips 36 × 3 inches

Blazing Star quilt:

◆ Inner border: cut four strips 42 × 2 inches (all border seam allowances are included in measurements)

◆ Background border: cut four strips 45 × 1½ inches

◆ Outer border: cut four strips 49 × 3 inches

12. Press quilt top.

13. Baste the batting, backing, and the quilt top together.

14. Mark and quilt designs onto quilt.

Once you have mastered this block, then you may be ready for the largest variation: the Lone Star. But instead of 80 pieces, there could be a thousand small diamonds.

Scraps and Pieces

The Lone Star quilt, also called the Star of Bethlehem, became popular in the 1820s. It has many, many tiny fabric diamonds making up a larger diamond; then eight of these larger diamonds are put together to form a star.

The Least You Need to Know

- The number of diamonds inside one of the points of the star can vary from four or nine, to hundreds, for a Lone Star quilt.

- The placement of the color of the fabrics will change the look of the star.

- Care must be taken when sewing the diamonds together because the seams are cut on the bias.

- The background fabric is integral to the contrast of the star colors of the diamond.

In This Chapter

- ◆ Choosing a "solid print" for your fabric
- ◆ Preparing your appliqué using freezer paper
- ◆ Learning the steps to mitering the borders
- ◆ Strategies for quilting alternating solid blocks

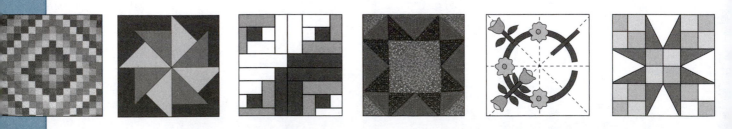

Hearts and Blocks Quilt

This quilt was made by Mari Garcia (see page 6 of the color section). She was inspired to make it when she bought a package of precut hearts in pastel colors. Look at the photo in the color insert; I think you will lose your heart over this quilt.

Finished size: 42 × 52 inches

Color schemes:

Mari has chosen pastel colors, but any combination of colors would look great. Bright, bold primary colors would make a striking baby quilt. To make a homespun looking quilt you could even use some plaid fabrics for the squares, and dark greens and reds for the hearts. That would give it a rustic quality.

Fabric requirements:

1¾-yards—dominant color of a *solid print* (purple in this quilt)

12 blocks and border

2¼ yards contrasting solid color (yellow)—for 12 blocks and backing

½ yard blue solid fabric—for 12 blocks

½ yard green solid fabric—for 12 blocks

¼ yard light solid fabric (light purple)—for the contrasting border

Fat quarters, four different colors (Mari used pink, blue, yellow, and green.)

Quilt Talk

A **solid print** sounds like an oxymoron. What it really means is that there is a subtle design so that there is depth to the fabric, not just the flat color.

Don't Get Stuck!

Sometimes you can substitute a fat quarter for ¼ yard, but if you are using the fabric for a border, you need the width so you won't have to piece.

Hearts and Blocks
Quilt

Cut 12 purple print

● (center point)

Cut 12 blue print

Cut 12 yellow print

Cut 12 green print

Template—5-inch square—seam allowance is included.

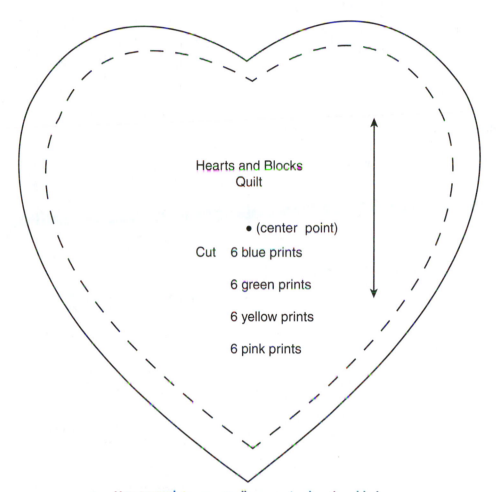

Hearts and Blocks
Quilt

• (center point)

Cut   6 blue prints

6 green prints

6 yellow prints

6 pink prints

Heart template—seam allowance is already added.

Cutting directions:

Cut 12 squares of each color of the "solid prints"

Cut hearts from as many scraps of each color of the printed fabric or from the fat quarters

Inner border:

Cut selvage to selvage—two strips 1½ × 44 inches

Two strips 1½ × 34 inches

(I've allowed a 2-inch fudge factor on the amounts.)

Outer border: Cut these parallel to the selvage on the straight of grain

Cut two side strips 5½ × 56 inches

Cut two top and bottom strips 5½ × 46 inches

(The fudge factor is included.)

Materials:

Fabrics

Batting

Freezer paper

Now take the following steps:

1. Cut "solid print" fabrics into 5-inch squares.

2. On the wrong side, mark hearts on scraps of fabric or fat quarters (into hearts).

3. Prepare heart for appliqué, using either the normal techniques (check out Chapter 11) or the freezer paper method.

Quilting Bee

You may think this is crazy, but you can use freezer paper from the supermarket to make appliquéing easier. This method is similar to the template method, but the background of the block is not trimmed out. Trace the templates onto the dull side of the freezer paper; do not add on any seam allowances. Cut the freezer paper on the traced lines. Pin all the shapes shiny side down on the wrong side of your fabric. Press these onto the fabric using an iron set at a low temperature. The freezer paper will stick to the fabric. Now add on the ¼-inch seam allowances around the outside edge and cut around the shapes. Press, turning under the seam allowances so that when folded the fabric sticks to the freezer paper. Pin the piece into position on the background of the block and start stitching the appliqué into place. When you are almost finished sewing the design, pull the freezer paper out through the small opening, and then complete appliquéing on the motif.

4. Appliqué hearts onto different colored background blocks. Center by folding two creases to find the center.

5. Lay out heart blocks alternately with the solid blocks, making sure that all the colors are evenly distributed.

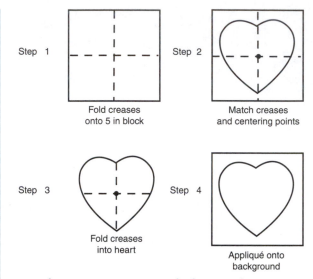

See how easy it is to center the heart in the proper position.

6. Sew three heart blocks alternately with the solid squares using a ¼-inch seam. Make four rows starting with the heart square.

7. Sew the next row together starting with the square block and alternating with the hearts. Make four rows.

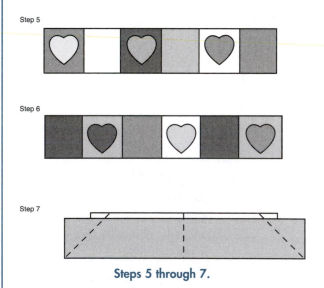

Steps 5 through 7.

8. Sew each of the rows together to form the quilt top.

9. Sew the light colored inner border to the outer border, matching the centers of each.

10. Pin the center point of the top border, right side together to the middle point of the quilt top, making sure there is an equal amount on each side of the quilt.

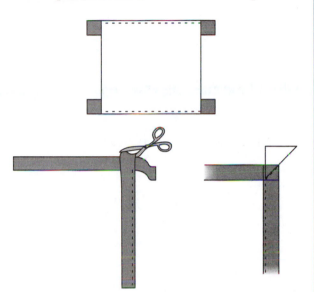

11. Start ¼ inch from the side edge of the quilt with a backstitch. Sew along the top edge on the marked ¼-inch seam line. Stop sewing ¼ inch from the end and backstitch. Sew the bottom and the side borders of the quilt in a similar fashion. Try to get the stitches from both seams to meet at the same point.

12 Miter. Turn to the wrong side of your quilt. Cut off excess fabrics. Take a gridded plastic ruler, one that has a 45-degree angle, and draw a line from the backstitch point diagonally to the corner of the border. Pin and check to see if the border lays flat. If so, sew on the drawn lines. Cut the excess from the border leaving a ¼-inch seam allowance.

13. Press seam allowances to the borders and the mitered seam open.

14. Attach batting and backing to the quilt top.

15. Mark quilt designs and quilt the patterns. There are several ways you can quilt:

    ◆ Stitch in the ditch around all the hearts and then stitch a heart in each solid square.

    ◆ Stitch ¼ inch around the heart and the squares.

    ◆ Stitch around each heart but then cross hatch across each square.

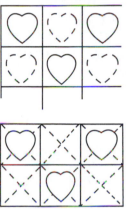
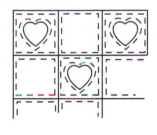
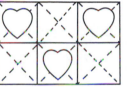

Three easy ways to quilt.

16. Bind off the outer frayed edges. The easiest way is to fold the backing toward the front of the quilt top. See Chapter 16 for directions.

The Least You Need to Know

◆ When you decide to appliqué, make sure you complete all the necessary steps to ensure the edges will not ravel.

◆ You can use freezer paper or dryer sheets to prepare your fabric for appliqué.

◆ Set your quilt together by sewing horizontal rows of blocks.

◆ Mitered border corners are sewn together at a 45-degree angle.

In This Chapter

- ◆ Preparing the Log Cabin table runner
- ◆ Sewing machine directions for chain piecing the Log Cabin block
- ◆ Changing the configuration of the Log Cabin block

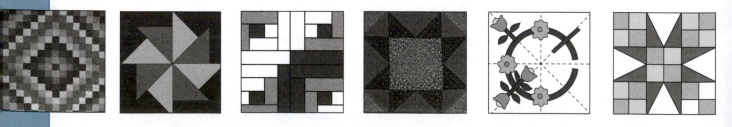

Chapter 22

Log Cabin Table Runner

The Log Cabin is one of the most popular patchwork quilts, and although it looks complicated, it's not. The combination of light and dark colors makes this block versatile in its ability to look either sophisticated, modern, or country.

This patch is formed by strips (logs) that are built around a center square. The strips get longer as they spiral around the center. There are 36 pieces to the 12-inch square Log Cabin block. Five templates, a square for the middle (template A) and four rectangles (templates B, C, D, and the longest E) are used to make a 6-inch square unit.

Four of these units are put together as in a four-patch block. The choice of fabrics is extremely important so that the darks and lights will create dramatic diagonal contrast. This half-light and half-dark combination can be turned to make many variations in your quilt. The Log Cabin can be changed very easily, so I have included two separate versions of a table runner, one a 16 × 16 inch square, and another 24 × 24 inch square.

Quilting Bee

If you have a lot of scraps, each template for the Log Cabin block can be cut from a different fabric.

Don't Get Stuck!

In order to make the light and dark colors go on the diagonal, careful planning is important. My first attempt at the Log Cabin was a disaster. I didn't follow the cutting directions for the colors. The darkest and lightest colors are cut from template A. Then each spiraling-out template is cut from both a light and a dark color. Careful placement of the light and dark colors is essential to get the diagonal effect.

This is the 24-inch layout for the Log Cabin table runner. Double the amount of fabric.

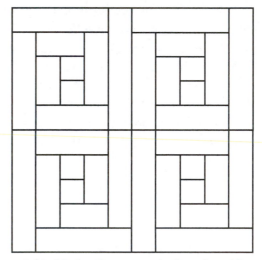

Log Cabin block—do you see the hearth and logs?

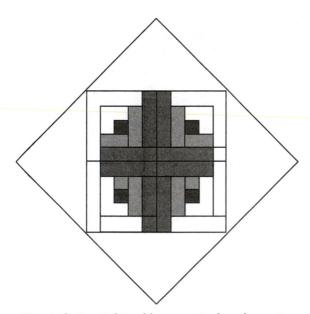

Here is the Log Cabin table runner. In the color section you can see I chose red and green Christmas colors.

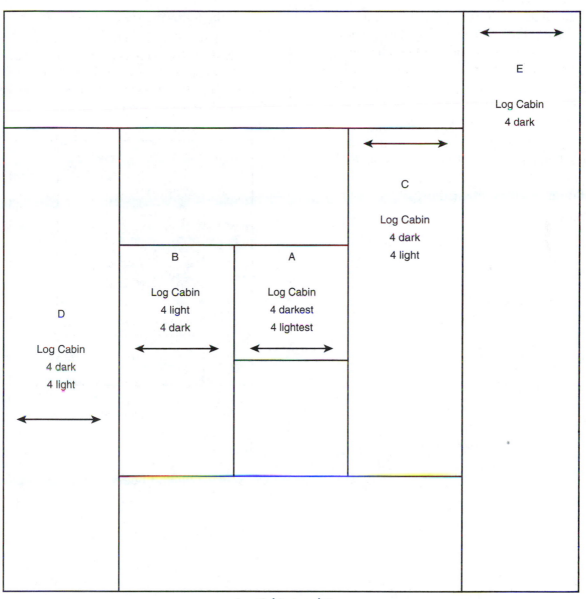

Log Cabin templates.

This is a really quick and easy project. You can make the runner for the center of the table or build an addition for larger sizes. The rotary cutter and sewing machine make this almost a one-day project.

Finished size: 16 × 16 inches or 24 × 24 inches.

Color schemes:

First, you need to realize that the Log Cabin block is a 6-inch square that is cut in half diagonally. Traditionally the center is red for the home hearth. This 6-inch unit can be turned different ways, so it is very conducive to color manipulation.

A monochromatic color scheme can work in two ways. First two extremely dark shades of the color are on one side and two lighter shades on the other, with a bright in the center; or two fabric shades can be on one side and shades of ecru or white can be on the other with a solid in the center.

You can also work with two or three colors: the dominant on one side, contrasting on the other, and a third in the center. Whichever you choose, it will be dramatic.

Materials:

>   Fabrics
>
>   Batting
>
>   Backing
>
>   Rotary cutter
>
>   Lipped ruler
>
>   Cutting mat
>
>   Bias binding
>
>   Sewing Machine

Fabric requirements:

16 × 16 inch table runner

- ◆ Four or five scraps or fat quarters of two light and three dark fabrics
- ◆ ½ yard for outside triangles
- ◆ ½ yard for backing

24 × 24 inch square table runner

- ◆ Four or five ½ yard pieces of two light and three dark fabrics
- ◆ 1 yard of backing fabric

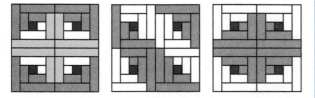

Look how you can turn the individual unit to change the design of the Log Cabin.

Take the following steps:

1. Choose colors so half of the square divided diagonally is composed of two light colors. The other diagonal half of the unit has three dark fabrics; the darkest one is the center square.

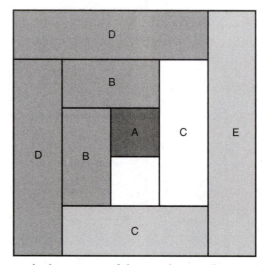

Study the position of the templates in the 6-inch square unit.

Quilting Bee

When using the quick strip-piecing method, cut a fabric strip 1¾ inch from selvage to selvage. That amount already has the seam allowance added on and you just have to cut off the correct length, measuring the unit as you sew. Don't even mark.

2. Make the templates and mark the fabric. Cut out the fabric pieces adding on ¼-inch seam allowances.

3. Lay out the design on the table in front of you, or use the chain-piecing method described in the beginning of the chapter.

4. Pin the right sides together of both A templates (darkest and lightest color fabrics).

5. Pin the right side of the lightest color of template B to the combined As unit. Sew the seam down the left side. Sew the other three units in the block.

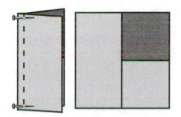

Don't Get Stuck!

Before you sew the Log Cabin block, make sure you open up the pieces to see if they fit into the layout. The darkest A should be on the top, otherwise the colors will spiral in the wrong direction.

6. Pin the dark piece B to the top of the AB unit. Then sew and open the piece flat.

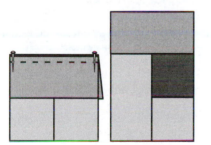

7. Pin the dark piece C to the side of the AB unit and sew.

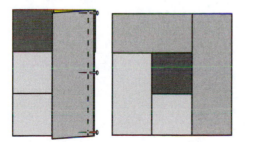

8. Pin the light piece C to the bottom of the ABC unit. Sew and open.

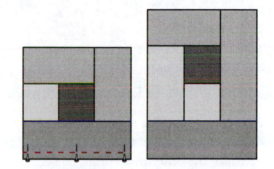

9. Pin the light piece D to the left side of the unit and sew.

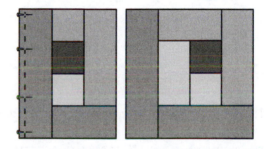

10. Sew the dark piece D to the top of the unit.

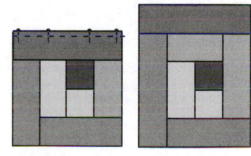

11. Finally, pin and sew the dark piece E to the right side of the unit.

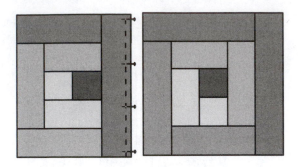

12. Open the last log and press the seams to the outside of the unit.

13. Make the other three units, and decide on their position.

14. Sew two units together to form the top row. Then sew the bottom two units together.

15. Pin the ends and the center seam together. Then stitch from the inside seam line out.

16. Now that your 6-inch blocks are completed, press them.

17. Cut four outer triangles using template F.

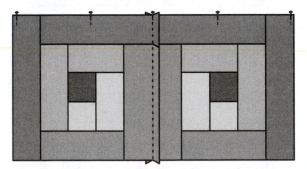

The Log Cabin is assembled as a four-patch, sewing the top to the bottom row.

18. Pin the long side of the triangle to one side of the block, making sure not to stretch the edge because it is bias. Sew.

Quilting Bee

Use the sewing machine method of chain piecing the logs (see Chapter 12).

Scraps and Pieces

It is believed that the Log Cabin design started in the 1860s as a tribute to Abraham Lincoln, who was born in a log cabin. Traditionally, the center square was a red square that represented the home fires or the hearth of the cabin. It is not surprising that this patch was unpopular in the South during the period of the Civil War.

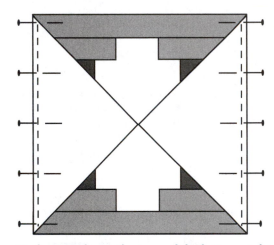

Pin the triangles on the top and the bottom, right sides together. You can sew from the center to the outside to prevent stretching.

19. Pin and sew the opposite triangle on and then sew the other sides.

20. Press open.

21. Pin batting and backing to the runner. Baste.

22. Quilt the logs in the ditch and a design on the triangles.

23. Finish edges with bias binding.

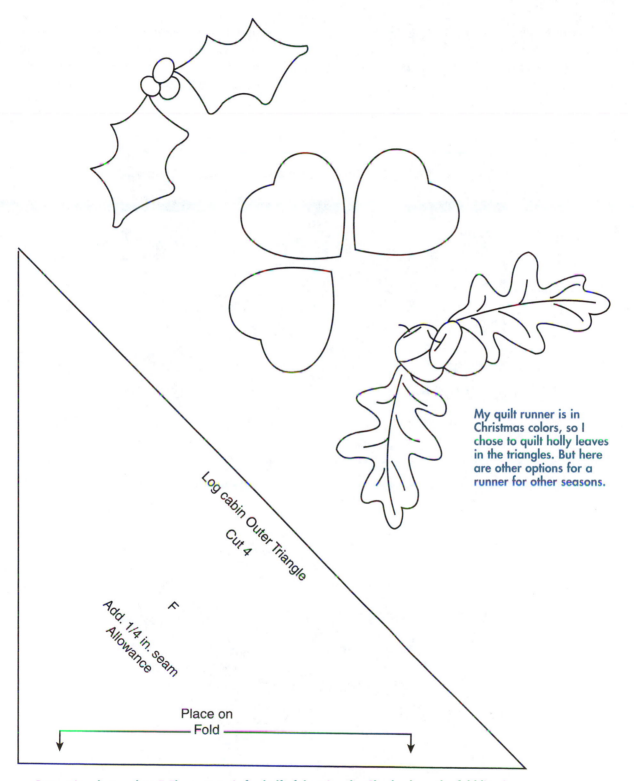

My quilt runner is in Christmas colors, so I chose to quilt holly leaves in the triangles. But here are other options for a runner for other seasons.

Log cabin Outer Triangle
Cut 4

F

Add. 1/4 in. seam
Allowance

Place on
Fold

Outer triangle template F. The pattern is for half of the triangle. Check where the fold line is.
Be sure to add the seam allowance around the outside edge.

You can easily change the configuration of the runner by making 12-inch square blocks and combining them to make the size and shape you desire.

Put four blocks together to form a square table runner, or six for a rectangular one. Look at the way the Log Cabin blocks, when put together, can form different designs. Some examples are Barn Raising and Straight Furrows. The Barn Raising has the diagonal lines of the block forming a square on point.

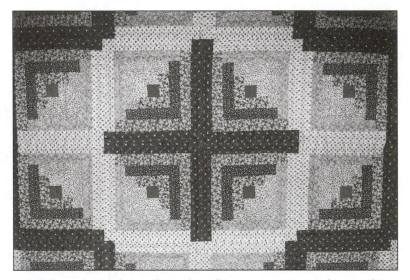

Detail to a Log Cabin quilt purchased in Lancaster, Pennsylvania. This quilt is from the collection of Bud and Nita Munson. The blocks are positioned in the Barn Raising design. The Straight Furrow pattern has all the colors of the log cabins lining up diagonally. It almost looks like the farmer has just plowed his field.

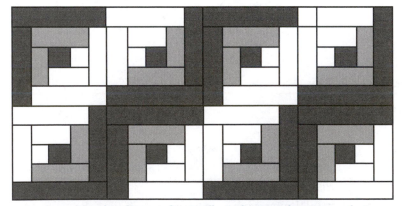

See how the colors line up diagonally in the Straight Furrows design. Keep your home fires burning on your Log Cabins.

The Least You Need to Know

- The Log Cabin block can easily be assembled into a variety of quilt configurations.
- Careful placement of fabrics is important to form the diagonal appearance of the block.
- When chain piecing a quilt with the Log Cabin, you can sew all the patches together at the same time in a production line.
- The blocks can be rotated in the quilt to form many different designs.

In This Chapter

◆ String piecing many fabrics together to form a new "fabric"

◆ Reviewing appliqué techniques

◆ Instructions for chain piecing borders

◆ Preparing a pieced heart quilt

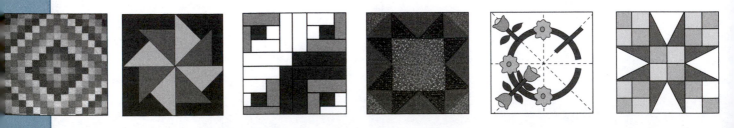

Strippy Heart Baby Quilt

If you want to "kick your hearts up a notch" you may want to string piece your hearts. This will get your sewing machine revved up. If you look at the picture of this quilt in the photo section, you'll notice there is a top and bottom section of the heart. The bottom of the hearts and the triangle corners are *string pieced* and the border is made of every color in your quilt.

Quilt Talk _____

String piecing was developed by frugal quilters who wanted to use up small strips of their fabric. These leftovers were sewn together to form a new fabric which could be cut apart for patches.

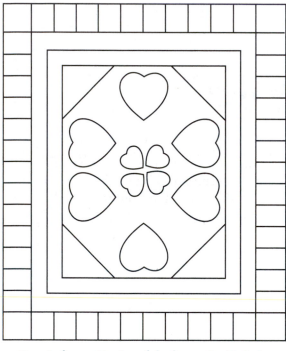

Here is the positioning of the hearts in this baby quilt.

Finished size: 30 × 36 inches

Materials:

Fabrics

Batting

Backing

Rotary cutter

Sewing machine

Dryer sheets

Don't Get Stuck! _____

Even though the directions call for ¼ yard pieces, don't use fat quarters. You need the length from selvage to selvage.

Fabric requirements:

13 pieces ¼ yard or less of pastel fabrics cut from selvage to selvage

Half in the dominant color (purple) for hearts and border

3 yards of solid or muslin for top and backing

Cutting directions:

Six heart tops (B) of six different fabrics

Four small corner squares (D) of dominant color

Four small hearts (F) of four of the fabrics used in the heart tops

♦ 6½-inch square (G)—background fabric (muslin)—cut eight

♦ 6½-inch triangle (A)—background fabric (muslin)—cut four

Borders:

Inner border:

Dominant color:

♦ Two strips 22 × 1½ inches

♦ Two strips 26 × 11½ inches

Middle border:

Background fabric:

♦ Two strips 28 by 2½ inches

♦ Two strips 30 by 2½ inches

Outer border: 58 rectangles (template E) of all colored fabrics except background

String pieced fabric: One strip of each of the 13 fabrics—1¼ cut selvage to selvage (about 42 inches)

Take the following steps:

1. Cut 13 pastel fabrics into strips from selvage to selvage; the strips are 1¼ inches wide.

2. Arrange the strips in a pleasing progression of colors, light and dark values alternating.

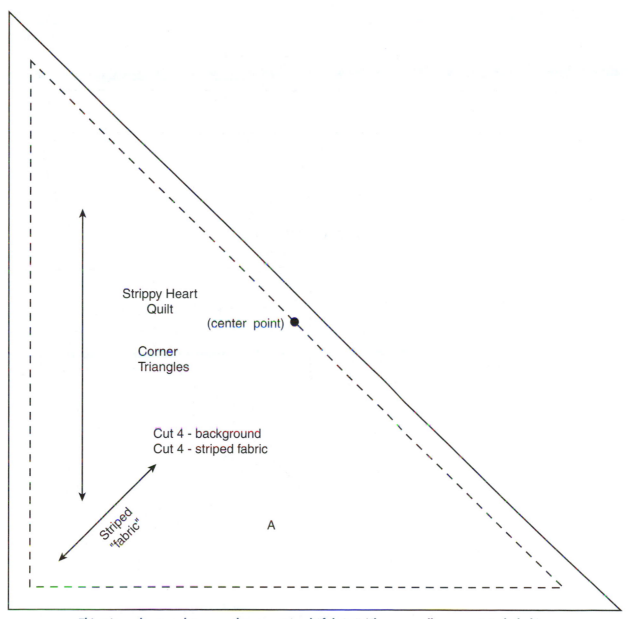

Strippy Heart
Quilt

(center point)

Corner
Triangles

Cut 4 - background
Cut 4 - striped fabric

Striped
"fabric"

A

This triangular template uses the new striped "fabric." (The seam allowance *is* included.)

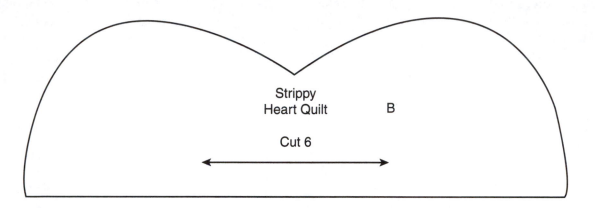

Strippy
Heart Quilt   B

Cut 6

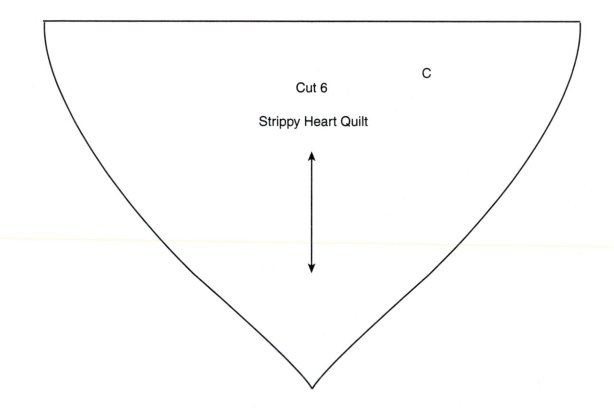

Cut 6

Strippy Heart Quilt

C

Strippy Heart templates. (The seam allowance is *not* included.)

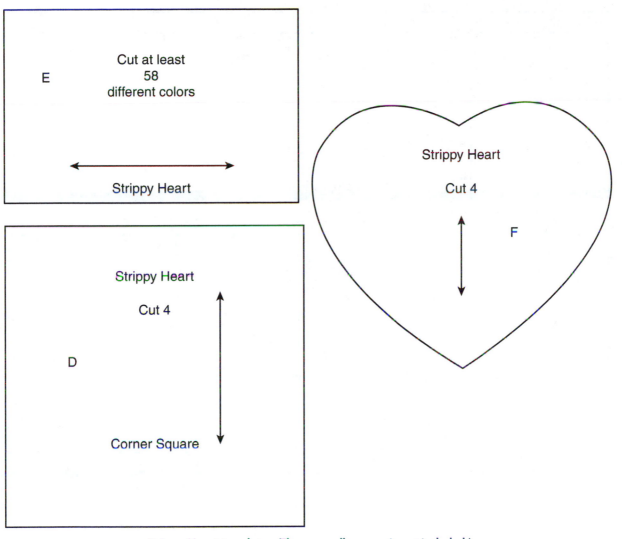

E

Cut at least
58
different colors

Strippy Heart

Strippy Heart

Cut 4

F

Strippy Heart

Cut 4

D

Corner Square

Strippy Heart templates. (The seam allowance is *not* included.)

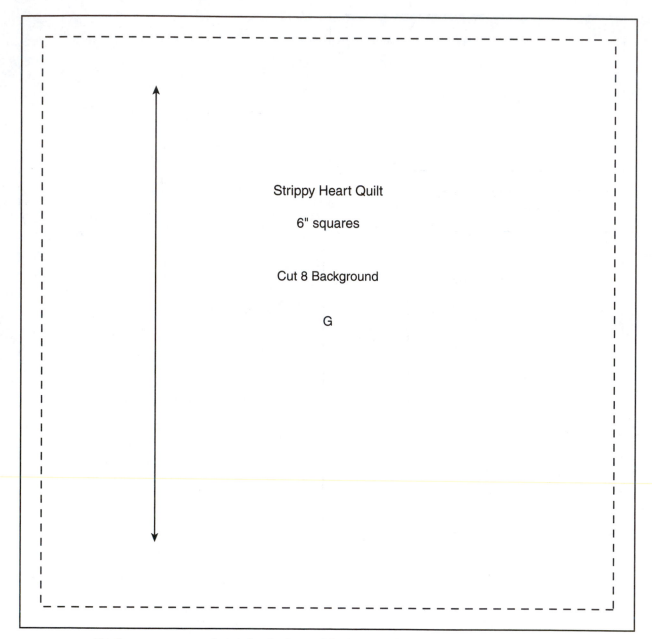

Strippy Heart Quilt

6" squares

Cut 8 Background

G

This large square template is for the base of the hearts. (The seam allowance *is* included.)

Don't Get Stuck!

As you string these pieces of fabric together, put your favorite colors in the center of this arrangement. Add more strips if your triangle does not fit.

3. Sew the strips together by sewing machine with a ¼-inch seam. Be certain that there is enough fabric to fit the triangle and the seam allowance.

4. Press all seams in one direction.

5. Cut four triangles (template A) from this striped fabric. Follow one stripe, lining up the point of the triangle and the center point on the long side making sure this stripe runs perpendicular to the long side.

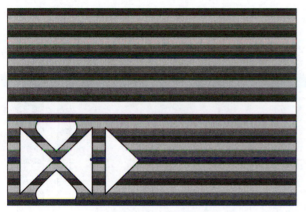

Make your striped fabric; cut out the corner triangles and heart bottoms.

6. Sew background triangles to each of the striped triangles forming a square.

7. Sew each striped heart bottom (template C) to the heart top (template B).

8. Prepare heart for appliqué, using the normal method (see Chapter 11) or dryer sheet to finish the edges.

Quilting Bee _____

Mark the wrong side of the fabric with the templates. Cut out, adding ¼-inch seam allowances. Pin the right side of the fabric to a dryer sheet. Sew by machine on the marked seam line. Clip and trim the seam allowances. Carefully pull the dryer sheet away from the fabric and put a small cut into the sheet. Pull the right side of the fabric through the dryer sheet cut, turning it inside out to form the heart. Press using a pointer, a sewing tool, or an orange stick to poke out points.

9. Center each of the six pieced hearts and appliqué them in the middle of each 6-inch square G.

10. Appliqué two small hearts onto each remaining 6-inch background square.

11. Sew together quilt top into rows.

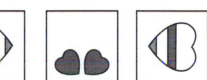

Look how the hearts are placed in the blocks, and then sewn together in rows.

12. Sew together the quilt top. Press.

13. Pin the inner borders to the long sides of the quilt top. Sew. Press border out.

14. Pin the top and bottom inner borders, sew all the way across from side to side. Press.

15. Pin and sew the background border along sides and then top and bottom. Press.

16. Now it is time to prepare your pieced outer border. It may take some manipulation to make it fit.

Chain piece together pairs of rectangles, then sew the pairs together until you have two strips with 12 rectangles and two strips with 16 rectangles.

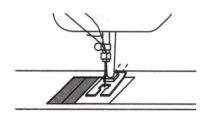

Chain the piecing rectangles until you have the correct measurement.

Pin and match up the side borders to the quilt top. Fold out and press these borders open.

Now comes the challenging part, making sure the corner squares match up to the side borders. Add a corner square to each end of the borders. Pin the borders onto the quilt top and bottom, making sure the corners match up.

Quilting Bee

If these corner squares don't match up to the side borders, you may have to increase the size of some seam allowances.

17. Press well.
18. Add backing and batting. Baste. Quilt and bind off.

Besides the pastel colors, primary colors would look great also. When you have finished this quilt all I have to say from the bottom of my heart, "Hearts off to You!"

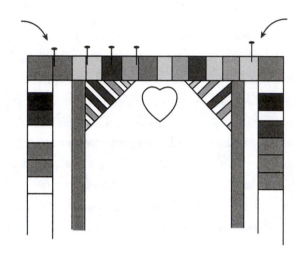

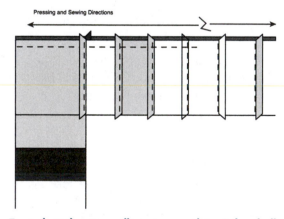

Try to butt the seam allowances so there is less bulkiness on the corner squares.

The Least You Need to Know

◆ String piecing is a technique that uses up leftover scraps and makes a "new" fabric.

◆ The string pieced fabric can be used to cut out templates.

◆ A dryer sheet can be used to finish up the raw edges of an appliquéd piece.

◆ Using a sewing machine to chain piece is a quick and easy way to sew similar pieces together.

In This Chapter

◆ The Trip Around the World quilt is designed from many small squares radiating around a center square.

◆ Learning to press alternately to decrease bulky seams.

◆ Directions for using the machine strip method of piecing the Trip Around the World quilt.

◆ A rotary cutter will make cutting the strips more efficient.

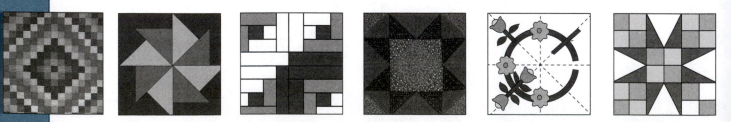

Chapter 24

Trip Around the World Quilt

As a quilter, it is now time to take a voyage. Let's travel around the world. The Trip Around the World quilt is made up of many squares of similar colors pieced on the diagonal around a central square. The lines of similarly colored squares surround one center square, and the contrasting light and dark fabric squares give the impression of orbiting the world.

When I first started quilting, Blanche and Helen Young developed a quick method of making this attractive but sometimes tedious quilt. They used strips sewn together by machine, cut apart, and then sewn together again. That technique opened up my eyes. This quilt project is small and is prepared in a slightly different method. But look up their book to make full-, queen-, or even king-size quilts.

This is a small baby quilt. Look how the colors encircle the center square.

Scraps and Pieces

In the old days, when a women used small, recycled pieces to make a quilt she was considered an accomplished quilter because of her frugality and patience.

Finished size:

The pictured quilt has a finished size of 22 × 40 inches.

The shape and size can easily be changed by increasing the size of the squares, or adding more rows of squares. You need to add a row to each side of the quilt top thereby adding on 6 inches. You can also make this quilt a 40-inch square for a wall hanging, or a lap quilt 40 × 52 inches.

Color schemes:

The baby quilt pictured has a monochromatic color scheme. A full range of shades from dark to light of one color is necessary because you need six different fabrics. Color schemes of shades of two colors (I once made a baby quilt using pink and blue), or many colors can be used. (See the pictures in the color photo section.)

The shades can progress from dark to light. Then there is a dramatic color contrast when the darkest color is put next to the lightest. You can also position the values of the colors so they increase in intensity and then get lighter again.

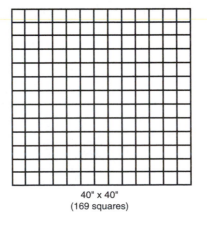

22" x 40"
(117 squares)

40" x 40"
(169 squares)

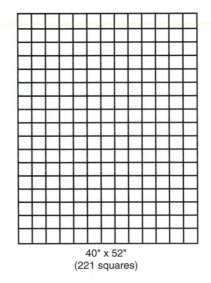

40" x 52"
(221 squares)

Look at how the size can change.

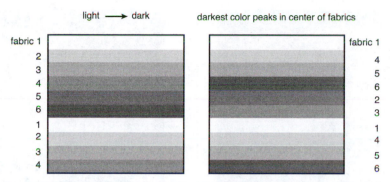

See how the shades of the fabrics can flow from dark to light or can peak with the dark color in the center.

It has a more subtle flow of shades. I personally like to end with a dark fabric as the last row for the corners, it kind of circles the design. If you look in the color section, you should find a sage green and beige quilt. I made this for my daughter Jamie's apartment that was decorated in shabby chic. Several muslin or ecru fabrics make a subtle shading of colors.

Many colors can be combined as long as there is variety in darkness and intensity.

Quilting Bee _____

Try not to alternate every other square with dark and light colors—it gives it a choppy and disjointed look.

Requirements:

Six fabrics—⅓ to ½ yard each

Rotary cutter

Cutting mat

Lipped ruler

Sewing machine

Batting

Backing: 1½ yards

Don't Get Stuck! _____

The required amount of fabric listed is more than you need, but when I told my class to buy ¼ yard, we found that the shopkeeper who measured the fabric cut it so crooked that there wasn't enough to make the rows. It's better to have too much than too little.

Before you can start this quilt, you should know the principles of rotary cutting. I realize that these "scissors" look like a pizza cutter, but remember it is very sharp and cuts you and your fabric equally well. Here are some steps to help you.

After washing your fabric, fold it so that the selvages are brought together, and then fold it again bringing the folded edge to the selvages. Brush the fabric flat, so there should be no wrinkles.

Next you need to straighten the raw edges—lay the folded fabric on the cutting mat along a crosswise line of the grid. Align the ruler (with the lip leaning on the mat) along a vertical grid line, parallel to the edge with about ½ inch of the ragged edge of the fabric showing.

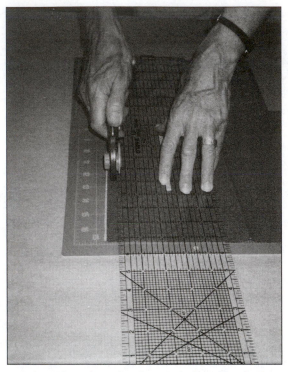

See how the ruler is lined up with the ragged edge showing.

Press the ruler down with one hand, open the blade of the cutter, and cut away from yourself leaning the blade against the ruler.

Turn the cutting board half turn around. (I sometimes walk around the table so as not to disturb the fabric.) The freshly cut edge is now on your left. To cut the strips, find the line on the ruler to match the width of the strip. Put this line directly on the cut edge and cut the strip. Hooray! One strip is done. It is really so easy.

Quilting Bee

Put a piece of thin masking tape on the line that needs to be matched up. It will save time and mistakes.

See how to line up the raw edge with the correct measurement line. We used masking tape to indicate the correct line for cutting.

Follow these steps:

1. Wash and prepare fabrics. Cut three 3½-inch strips (from selvage to selvage) of each of the six fabrics.

2. Arrange the strips of the fabrics in a pleasing order.

Quilting Bee

I usually take graph paper and cut little squares of all fabrics. Then I start to position them in the correct placement to decide what look is best. I glue down the design I like the best. But do this quickly before you sneeze or move all those squares.

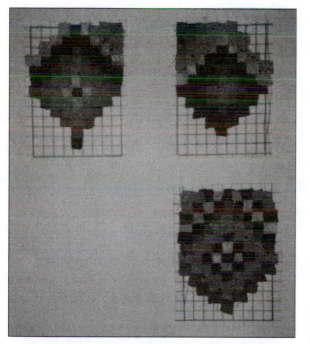

Look how the color placement can change the look of the quilt.

3. Sew the strips with right sides together, until all the strips are joined.

4. Press the seams alternately toward every other strip.

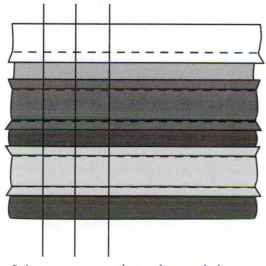

Strips are sewn together and pressed alternate directions.

5. Using your rotary cutter, cut 3½-inch strips from the sewn fabric—make sure the cut is perpendicular to the sewn strips.

6. Take these new strips of squares and lay the correct number (9 rows for the small quilt, 13 for the larger size) of them side by side.

7. Now comes the crazy part; working on the top part of the quilt, we leave the first left side row the same, but the second row we are going to remove the top square and sew it to the bottom of the strip (moving the design "up").

8. Remove two of the squares on the next strip, and sew them to the bottom of the squares. Continue the square removals through the middle strip and on the next strip (the sixth strip or for the larger quilt, the eighth strip), reverse this procedure sewing the squares to the top so the design shifts in the other direction. Re-sew each of the strips so that there is a mirror image of the pattern.

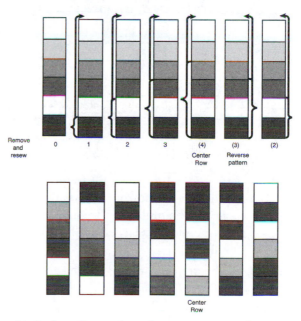

Notice how the number of squares sewn to the top increases as you go to the center of the quilt, then the pattern reverses.

9. Sew each of these strips together being careful not to pin the incorrect side of the strip to the row. Pin the row and open up into the pattern.

10. Press the seams all to the outside from the center. Half the quilt is done!

11. Prepare another side exactly the same, now having two halves.

12. When you put them together, you'll notice the two center rows are the same. I have seen the quilt sewn together in the pattern, but I prefer making a separate row of individual squares to fill in the correct square to complete the design. Press this row with the seam allowances toward the center.

Prepare the center row.

13. Sew the top half of the quilt to the center row and then the bottom half on the quilt, completing the quilt top. If you want, you can sew a 3-inch or larger border, to add to the size.

14. Baste the quilt top to the batting and the backing.

15. Tie or quilt designs through all three layers.

16. Bind off edges.

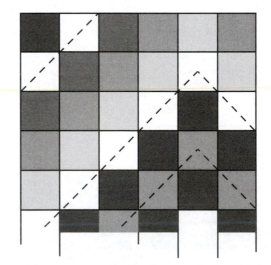

See how you can tie or quilt your Trip Around the World quilt.

This quilt design is so versatile that you can change the size and shape by manipulating the size of the squares, the number of rows, or by adding borders. Look at the color photo section and discover how many trips you can take.

The Least You Need to Know

◆ A Trip Around the World quilt has many squares positioned concentrically around a center square.

◆ A rotary cutter, cutting mat, and lipped ruler can cut strips easier and faster than regular scissors.

◆ The Trip Around the World Quilt is made in three sections: the top, bottom, and center row.

◆ Pressing the seams in alternate directions makes sewing easier.

◆ You can quilt designs or tie this quilt.

In This Chapter

◆ Understanding Amish Quilts

◆ Learning to piece a quilt with a medallion center

◆ Applying a hidden sleeve for hanging the quilt

◆ Templates and directions for 16-inch Amish Square in a Square block

◆ Preparing a pillow back with an overlapped or Velcro closing

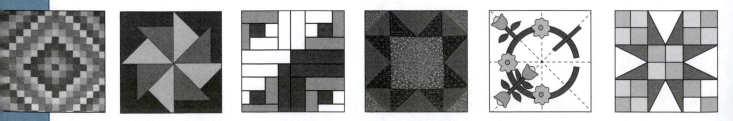

Chapter 25

Amish Square Patterns

Isn't it surprising that members of the Amish and Mennonite communities in Pennsylvania, Ohio, and Indiana, who only wear dark, somber clothes, can make quilts that are so graphic and colorful. Amish women, because of the dictates of their religion, used black, dark brown, or other solid dark fabrics for their clothing. However, there are no rules for quilt colors. The most intense colors and values are combined.

The Amish women were inspired to design quilts by what they saw around them: stars, rows in the fields, wedding rings, houses, or log cabins. There are many traditional quilt patterns and the Square in the Square is one of the oldest and most simple of the designs. The center square is surrounded by triangles and a series of borders. This pattern is conducive to using a machine to piece.

Amish Square in a Square Wall Hanging

There may be five colors or as little as two. This quilt's graphic design is embellished by decorative quilting. So get your bright colors and quilting needles out. Let's start.

Finished size: 30 × 30 inches

Fabric requirements:

Dominant color: ½ yard for the large outer border and squares

Black: ¼ yard for the center square, large outer squares, and small squares

Contrasting color: ¼ yard for the narrow borders

Light color: ½ yard for the triangles

Backing: 1 yard

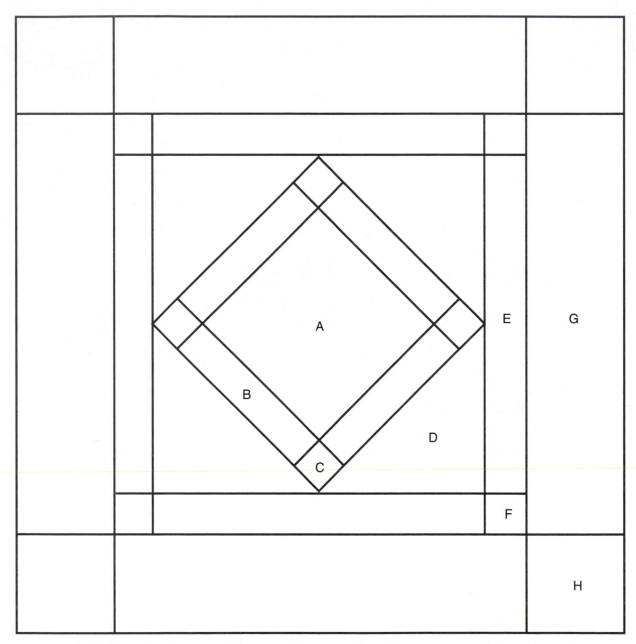

Amish Square in a Square wall hanging. (You will need to enlarge on a copier by 125 percent.)

Cutting directions:

When you look at this list, there seems to be a lot of pieces of the pattern; but cut them one section at a time, and lay them out in front of you. To ensure these strips and squares are right angled, use graph paper to cut out patterns. All of the cutting templates below have the seam allowances included, and if you use a sewing machine you just need to line up your presser foot with the edge of your piece.

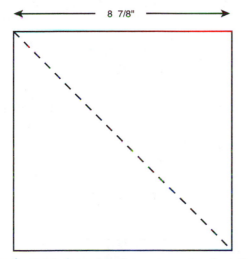

← 8 7/8" →

Cut the 8 7/8-inch square, then cut apart to form the triangles.

Scraps and Pieces

Because Amish women have to follow so many rules concerning their religion, clothing, hairstyles, housework, and behavior, it is believed that quilting is one of their creative outlets. Although quilts were considered strictly utilitarian bed clothes, and being "prideful" was a sin, there was and continues to be great competition among Amish women as to the choice of quilting patterns, number of spools of thread used, and the number of stitches counted to the inch.

Quilting Bee

Measure this square on graph paper and cut out the fabric this exact size. Fold the square in half, corner to corner on the diagonal. Finger press or carefully iron this crease. Open up the fabric and cut on the fold forming two correct sized triangles.

Piece A—cut one (center square) 7½-inch square

Piece B—cut four (short borders) 7½ × 2½-inch squares

Pieces C and F—cut four of each color (small corner squares) 2½-inch squares

Piece D—(triangles)—8⅞-inch square cut in half on the diagonal; cut two of these squares, then you will have four triangles

Piece E—cut four (middle border) 2½ × 16½-inch squares

Piece G—cut four (outer border) 5½ × 19½-inch squares

Piece H—cut four (outer squares) 5½-inch squares

Materials needed:

Two to five different colored solid fabrics

Batting

Backing

Rod or dowel for hanging quilt

Quilting Bee

I usually cut the center first then the rest to make sure the size of each piece is correct and matches up. If one is slightly larger, then the borders will not fit, so cut carefully.

Follow these steps, keeping in mind that it's easiest to start at the center medallion and work to the outside edges:

1. Sew two of the B borders across from each other on each side of the square A (top left of the following figure). Press these seams toward the square.

2. Sew squares C onto each end of the remaining two B borders and press the seam allowances toward the small squares (top right of the following figure).

3. Sew the top and bottom borders to the center square.

Don't Get Stuck! _____

Carefully match up both the seams of the large and small squares. The seams should butt up, each going in a different way. If the square at the second end doesn't match, you may have to take in or let out the seam to be able to pin the intersection of the squares.

4. Pin the triangle pieces D to the center section (bottom of the following figure). Notice that the ends of the triangle will not match up but the triangle piece will hang over some on each end. Sew opposite sides together, then the top and bottom triangle.

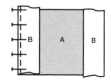

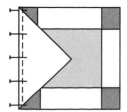

5. Combine the pieces E and F together for the next border. Pin and sew them onto the center medallion as in steps 1–3. Do not lose the tips of the triangles when sewing this seam.

6. Lastly, put the outer borders G and H on using the same method. Now your quilt top is done!

7. Center the quilt top over the batting and backing. Baste.

8. Mark and quilt with designs. To individualize your quilt, you can go to the store and buy stencils for quilting designs, or you can use the feathers and heart design putting four together for the center square, and two together for the triangles. Use the small hearts for the small corner squares. The triheart pattern is used for the large outer border; start with one in the center of each border, dovetailing them out to cover the entire section. Look at the detail in the color photo section.

Scraps and Pieces _____

The Amish and Mennonite quilts are known for their intricate quilt designs. Traditionally hearts and feathered designs of all shapes are used; long curved lines for borders, circles, squares, and even wreaths.

9. Finish off raw edges with binding of contrasting color. (See Chapter 16.)

10. Apply a hidden sleeve to the backing for hanging your quilt.

You can go to the store and buy stencils for quilting designs or use these hearts and feathered heart. Trace each section of these on opaque plastic and cut out. Then just trace them onto your quilt.

Hidden Sleeve Method

Measure the horizontal width of your quilt, and subtract 2 inches from that amount. You want to have enough room at each end of the sleeve to have the rod hang on a nail. If your quilt is very wide, you may want to divide the sleeve in half, forming two pockets. Then you will be able to hang the rod on three nails, one at each end and then one in the middle. You don't want your rod to bow under the quilt's weight.

Quilting Bee

Do not sew with the tube stretched flat against the backing. Allow an excess on the top half of the tube to hang loose, making more room for the rod to slip into the sleeve.

Cut a strip 3 to 4 inches wide, depending on the size of the rod and the length of the horizontal measurement of the quilt. Finish each short end of the strip.

Then fold the length in half and sew a ¼-inch seam. Finger press the tube so that the seam runs down the center. Center this casing and pin it across the backing about ½ inch from the top of the quilt. Invisibly stitch the top of the casing, then sew the bottom length of the sleeve.

Put your sanded dowel or rod through the sleeve and hang your work of art.

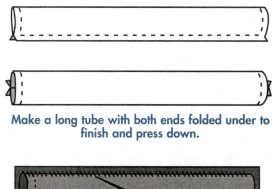

Make a long tube with both ends folded under to finish and press down.

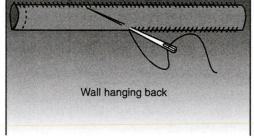

Put on your sleeves. Use an appliqué stitch or whip-stitch to sew the tube into place. Sew the back of the sleeve flush against the backing, but leave the sleeve loose.

Fabric Loops

This method has visible fabric loops to hold the rod. Let's find out how to make those loops that look so beautiful.

1. Decide on the width of the loops. I like about 2 inches. Double that amount and add ½ inch for seam allowances. I cut my strips $2 \times 2 \times ½ = 4½$ inches wide, and from selvage to selvage for the length, making the strip 4½ inches by the fabric width.

2. Fold this strip in half lengthwise with right sides together.

3. Sew a ¼-inch seam down the length and press the seam down the center, forming a tube (left side of the following figure).

4. Cut the tube into sections, double the size you want for each loop, and then add ½-inch seam allowance to determine the amount. If you want a 2-inch loop, cut the tube into 4½-inch sections (middle of the following figure).

5. Sew the ends of each section together to form a circular loop (right side of the following figure).

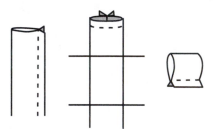

Don't get loopy! Sew and press the seam and then turn the tube right side out. Cut it into sections.

6. Evenly space and attach loops to the top of the backing and whipstitch or invisible stitch.

This quilt hanging looks like a banner that announces your quilt artistry. If your quilt bottom ripples, you may want to put a sleeve on the bottom of the backing so that the rod will hold your quilt flush to the wall.

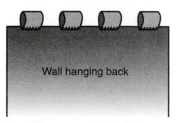

Sew loop to loop to loop to hang your quilt.

If you like this pattern, you'll love the next one. With slight variations you can make this Square in a Square design into a quilt or a pillow.

Pillow and Quilt Version of the Amish Square

If you liked the Amish design Square in a Square, then you will love to make it for a pillow or quilt to accompany your wall hanging. This pattern makes a smaller block than the wall hanging but is very versatile. When my students Tippi and Sara saw the wall hanging we found the smaller block. Look in the color photo section and see the variety of color combinations my students have used in the past.

Tippi and Sara are excited when Sara's blocks are pieced together. All Sara needs are her borders to make it a twin-size quilt.

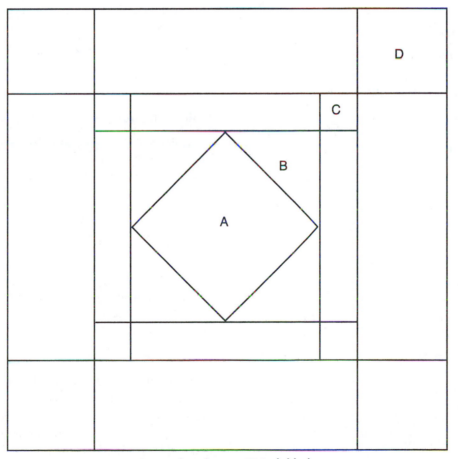

Square in a Square 18-inch block.

Finished size: Block is 18 inches

Twin-size quilt using a dust ruffle: 68 × 97 inches

Full/queen-size quilt using a dust ruffle: 92 × 100 inches

Materials:

Pillow:

- Three to five fabrics of solid prints
- Backing
- Thin batting
- Velcro
- Pillow form

Quilt:

- Fabric
- Backing
- Batting
- Binding

Fabric requirements:

Pillow:

- Four to five solid or solid print fat quarters

Quilt:

	Twin	Full/ Queen
◆ Lightest fabric (blocks)	1 yard	1½ yards
◆ Medium fabric (blocks, outer border)	3 yards	3½ yards
◆ Medium-dark fabric (blocks and outer border for full/queen)	1 yard	2½ yards

Quilt:

	Twin	Full/ Queen
◆ Dark fabric (blocks and pieced inner border)	1½ yards	2 yards
◆ Backing	5½ yards	6¼ yards

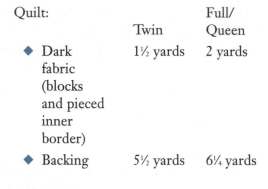

Don't Get Stuck!

Make sure you have enough fabric for the borders. You can measure and set aside those areas, plus a little "fudge factor" so you won't cut the small pieces from there. I don't like to cut the borders out before the quilt top is completed because everyone sews and cuts differently. You don't want to end up trying to match your fabric on your last leg of your quilt.

Color schemes:

Amish quilts traditionally used solids, but if you look at Sara's purple quilt in the color section, she used solid print fabrics.

Quilt Talk

A solid print sounds like an oxymoron but it is a fabric that has a subtle pattern of monochromatic colors giving the impression of a solid when seen from a distance.

These are fabrics that "read" a solid. They can be small-scaled prints or a tie-dyed mottled fabric. Each block has the fabrics in different positions making it fun and challenging to make. The challenge comes when you put together the quilt top. Remember, you can have bright colors next to each other so that the graphic design just pops out at you. If you look in the color photo section, you can see the results of class projects with an unbelievable array of color. Now let's get started.

This block has a slightly different configuration, having the triangles attached before the borders. First we'll learn how to make the block, then you can build your quilt, block by block, and decide if you want to make a pillow, twin, or full/queen quilt. Follow these steps:

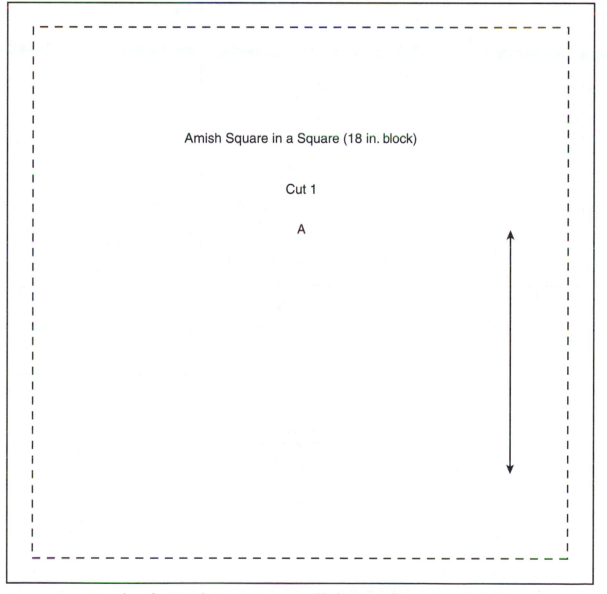

Amish Square in a Square (18 in. block)

Cut 1

A

Templates for 18-inch Square in a Square block. (Seam allowance is included.)

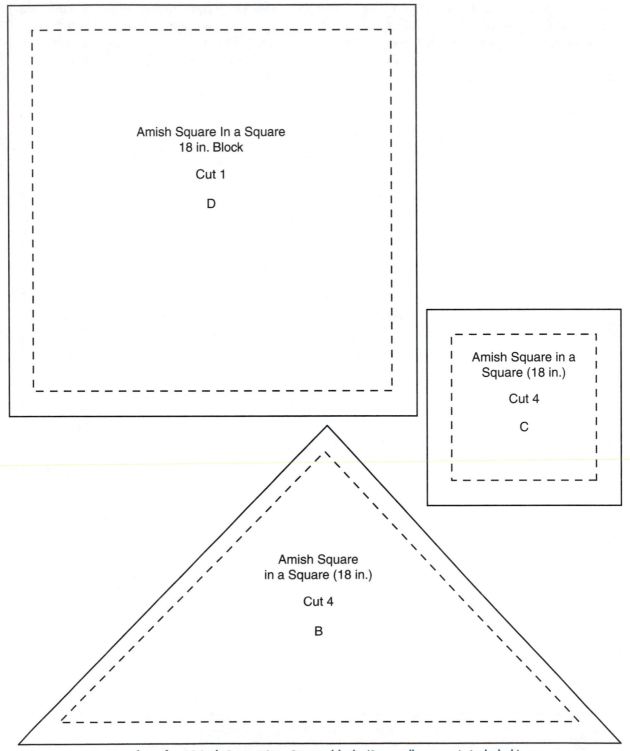

Amish Square In a Square
18 in. Block

Cut 1

D

Amish Square in a
Square (18 in.)

Cut 4

C

Amish Square
in a Square (18 in.)

Cut 4

B

Templates for 18-inch Square in a Square block. (Seam allowance is included.)

1. Make template (templates already have the seam allowance included) and prepare fabrics.

2. Cut out pieces from templates and cut out borders:

   ◆ Cut four inner borders 8½ × 2 inches.

   ◆ Cut four outer borders 11½ × 4 inches.

3. Sew the triangle pieces (B) onto the center large square (A), first sewing two triangles opposite each other (left side following figure), then sewing the top and bottom triangles. Press triangles open.

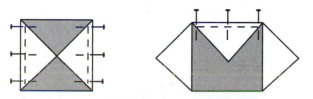

Sew two triangles across from each other, press open, and attach the top and bottom triangles.

4. Sew two of the borders that are 2 inches wide onto each side of the center and then press out (top of following figure).

5. Sew the small squares (C) to each of the ends of the inner, narrow borders (bottom of following figure).

6. Sew these borders to the top and bottom of the center. Put your pin right into the seams that intersect. Sew from that seam of the square to the outer edge, and then sew from that same seam to the other edge.

7. Pin two of the outer borders on the center across from each other. Press out.

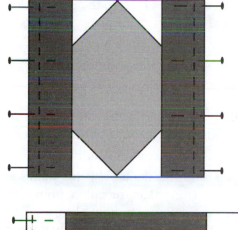

Sew the narrow borders onto each side of the center, then add the squares to the remaining border.

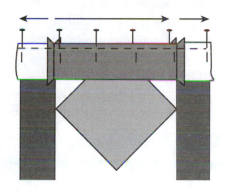

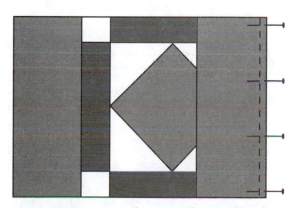

Put your pins next to the seam allowances and check out the direction you should sew.

8. Sew the squares (D) to the ends of the outer borders, and apply as in step 6.

9. Press and your block is complete.

Now it's time to finish our projects.

Pillow:

1. Baste your block with a thin batting and muslin for the backing of the front section.

2. Mark your pillow and quilt the designs.

3. You can make the back with a solid square 1 inch larger than the pillow front, but because you may want to clean your pillow you'll want to divide the backing into two overlapping sections or two sections held together with a zipper. (The zipper application is for experienced sewers only.) Make sure the pillow backings are large enough. There should be enough of a lap so that the backing doesn't pull open when the pillow is inside.

4. Measure the size of your pillow, and add 1 inch to the horizontal side. However, you must add considerably more in the other direction: Calculate half the size of the pillow, and then add 4 inches for a fold. Cut two of these pieces. For example, if your pillow is 15-inches square, the horizontal size is 16 inches. For the other direction, divide 15 by 2, making 7½ inches. Add 4 inches for a total of 11½ inches.

5. Cut two backing sides, 16 × 11½ inches. Fold down ¼ inch to finish off the edge, and then press under 1 inch all the way across.

6. Overlap these folded edges so that they are the same size as the pillow top. Baste both ends of the lapped pieces together to hold securely.

7. Turn this lapped backing right side to the right side of the pillow top. Pin the pillow top and backing together and sew at ¼ inch all the way around the outside edges.

8. After you sew together the pieces, pull the right side of the pillowcase through the opening of the lap. Insert your pillow form, and you have a pillow.

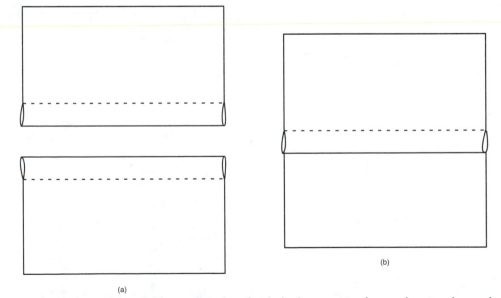

(a)

(b)

Fold ¼ inch under and then fold 1 more inch to finish the lap. Position by overlapping these edges.

Don't Get Stuck!

Use a plain muslin for this part of the process. This is not the attractive back of the pillow but just the lining to allow you to quilt.

Quilt:

Each of the Amish Square blocks, made for the quilt-size projects, should have the colors in a variety of positions. This way when the blocks are combined in the quilt top, each of the squares is impressive on its own.

For the twin bed, make 15 blocks, full/queen make 20. The twin quilt has one 5-inch border, the full/queen has a narrow inner border in addition to the outer border.

Twin Size (64x95)
15 blocks
1-5 in. border

Full/Queen Size (86x97)
20 blocks
inner border - 2 inches
outer border - 5 inches

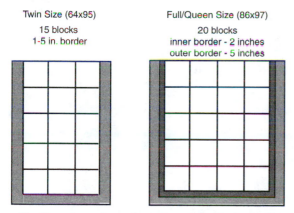

Check out how the quilts are made with the blocks and borders.

1. It's time to find the correct placement of your blocks in the quilt top. Start mixing and matching where they all go. Make sure to spread the accent and bright colors throughout the quilt.

2. Sew the blocks together in rows and then the rows together making the quilt top. (See Chapter 13).

3. Measure the sides of the quilt and for the twin quilt, cut two outer border the side length by 5½ inches. For the full/queen quilt measure the side of the quilt and

first cut two of the inner border—the length by 2½ inches. Cut out.

4. Sew these borders onto the sides and press open.

5. Now measure the width of the bottom of the quilt top (including the side borders). Cut out either the 5½ inch border (for the twin) or the 2½-inch inner border (for the full/queen).

6. Sew the bottom border onto quilt top. The twin-size quilt is completed!

7. For the full/queen quilt—proceed by measuring the side borders, cutting them that length by 5½ inches, and sewing them onto the sides. Press out.

8. Then measure the bottom width of the quilt and cut the border that length by 5½ inches.

9. Finish the quilt by basting the batting and backing with the quilt top (Chapter 14), quilt designs (Chapter 15), and bind off the raw edges (Chapter 16).

You are done! Whether you've made the pillow or built a quilt from all these blocks, it is a great accomplishment.

The Least You Need to Know

◆ Amish quilts are colorful and graphic with a considerable amount of quilting.

◆ Start piecing from the inside square.

◆ Press the seams of the borders so that the allowances butt against each other.

◆ A quilt can be hung on the wall by using a hidden sleeve made from a tube of backing fabric.

◆ One Square in a Square block can be used by itself for a pillow, or add many together for a quilt.

◆ When you quilt a pillow front, use muslin for the backing, not your good fabric.

In This Chapter

- ◆ Understanding an appliqué block
- ◆ Steps for applying fabric motifs to your blocks
- ◆ Preparing bias strips
- ◆ Applying a piping to a pillow

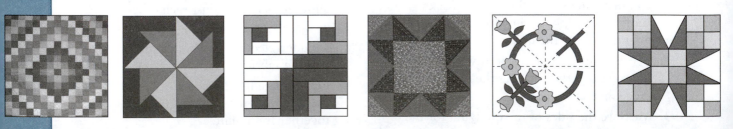

Chapter 26

American Wreath Pillow

The American Wreath pillow is prepared by the appliqué technique. We have used this method when we sewed the hearts onto our quilts in Chapters 21 and 23. This pattern was probably a beginners' block for a Baltimore Album quilt.

Around the 1850s, a group of quilters from the Baltimore area became famous for their appliqué workmanship. The quilt tops were a series of appliquéd blocks, picturing amazing details of flowers, trees, animals, or fruit that almost come alive. Each block was a work of art. These quilts are so intricate and astonishing that many are hanging in museums.

See if you are able to duplicate this technique. This wreath pattern uses bias tape and is symmetrical but in a mirrored image. Let's get started.

American Wreath block, a circle of tulips and flowers.

Finished size: 16 inches

Materials:

Fabric

Piping (2 yards if you make your own or one package if you purchase)

16-inch pillow form

Zipper or Velcro

Fabric requirements:

Muslin or light colored solid fabric (appliqué base) ½ yard

Solid green or dark color (stems) fat quarter

Dark green or other color (leaves and pillow back) ½ yard

Dominant color (tulips, buds, centers, and border) fat quarter

Contrast color (flowers, tulip accents, corner squares) fat quarter

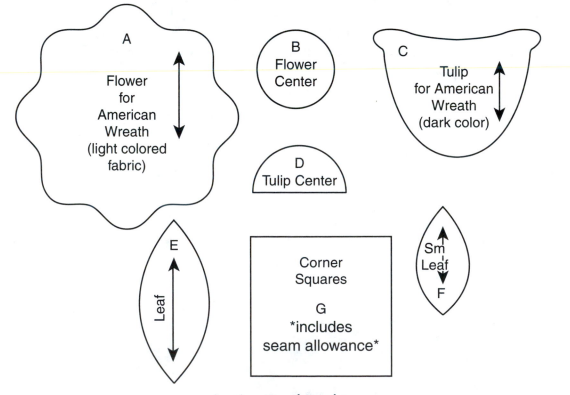

American Wreath templates.

Scraps and Pieces

During the 1800s, Baltimore, not New York, was the major seaport, thereby receiving all the newest, most innovative fabrics from Europe.

Follow these steps:

1. Prepare templates and fabrics.

2. Cut muslin, or light colored fabric in a 14-inch square (seam allowances and fudge factor are included) for the appliqué base. Fold this in half horizontally, vertically, and diagonally. Baste on these folds.

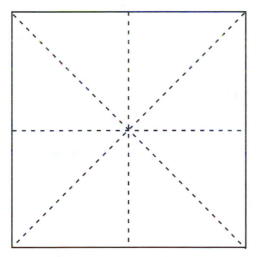

Fold and baste your pillow base.

Don't Get Stuck!

Use a "strange" colored thread to baste these lines. If you baste with a thread that matches your fabrics, when you try to take it out you may remove the actual appliqué stitching.

3. With a wash out pen or lightly with a pencil, mark a 7½-inch circle following the pattern.

4. Prepare a bias binding for the stems and wreath.

   Small strips of fabric, cut on the bias, are used for stems of flowers. It is easier to appliqué *bias strips*, or fabric that is cut on the bias, because they curve and bend without puckering.

   Measure and cut on the bias the amount designated for the stem. For most, cut the length of the stem 1 inch wide.

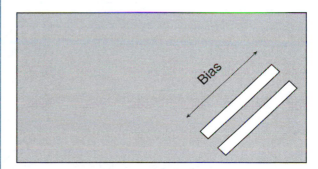

Quilt Talk

Bias strips are cut on the diagonal of the fabric. Find the finished selvage and fold it up on a perpendicular angle. The diagonal that is formed is the true bias.

Cutting bias stems.

5. Fold the fabric in half all the way down the length, wrong sides together, forming a long tube, matching the raw edges. Sew by hand or machine ¼ inch down the long side with the raw edges. Shift the seam line so it is in the middle of the tube. Press flat so the seam doesn't show.

This is a half block motif. To transfer this pattern, use a light box or bright window to trace these markings. (You will need to enlarge on a copier by 125 percent.)

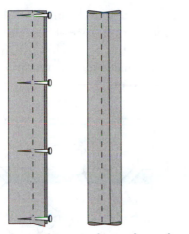

Sew down the long edge to make a tube and press.

6. Position the stem so the seam does not show, then pin and appliqué. This way makes appliquéing easy because the tube that is formed will not change size or ravel. Now you can draw your stem lines with bias and they will stretch whichever way you want.

7. Cut bias strips into:

   Four 5-inch pieces for wreath

   4-inch pieces for double tulip stems

   Two 2½-inch pieces for single tulip stems

   3½-inch pieces for bud stems

8. Position the bias strips for the wreath, so the inner edge is on the 7½-inch mark from the center point. Pin these four pieces in place. Steam press these curves to get a gentle curve. Slip the double and single tulip stems under the wreath bias strip so they lie on the diagonal basting line.

Quilting Bee

It is easier to work with smaller sections of the bias strips so leave spaces where the flowers are going to be placed. This will also cut down on the bulkiness under the flowers.

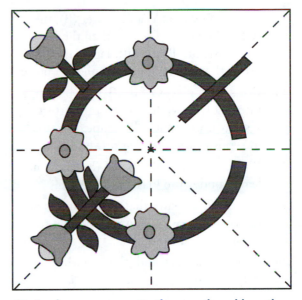

Notice the open spaces on the wreath and how the stem strips are positioned on the diagonal. The tulips and flowers are next.

9. Cut and prepare the flowers (A), flower centers (B), tulips (C), tulip center (D), and leaves (E and F). Be sure to add on the seam allowances. (You can use the basic method of appliqué described in Chapter 11, or the freezer paper technique in Chapter 21.) Clip curves, turn down the tips, and then baste.

Clip curves, turn under the tips of the points, and baste. You don't need to baste all around the tulip center, it will be slipped under the tulip.

10. Pin the flowers (A) and center (B), tulips (C) and centers (D), and then the leaves into position. Baste with large stitches down the center of each appliquéd piece.

11. Press both pieces of the 3-inch bias tape into a soft curve following the pattern. Use steam to block the shape. Pin this into position under the flower. Baste.

12. Pin the buds (F) on top of the stem and leaves under the bias strip.

13. Once you are sure that everything is in the correct position appliqué down the whole kit and caboodle.

14. Remove basting, and it's everywhere.

15. Trim block so that it is 13 inches. Redraw the seam lines if necessary.

16. Cut the four border strips 2 × 13 inches. Sew two of them to opposite sides of the wreath center. Press them out.

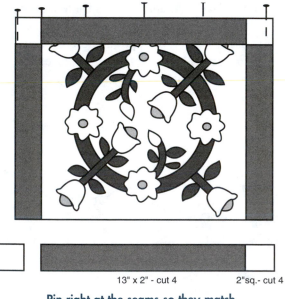

13" x 2" - cut 4   2"sq.- cut 4

Pin right at the seams so they match.

17. Sew two blocks to each end of the remaining borders. Pin these to the top and bottom making sure the seams of the block match the border. Attach them by sewing from the inside out. The pillow front is done!

18. Add batting and a muslin backing to the pillow front. Baste all together. Quilt pillow front either by stitching in the ditch, the traditional ¼ inch around the designs or by echo quilting.

Here are some quilting ideas: quilt in the ditch or echo it. Echo quilting: ¼-inch waves of quilting lines or ¼ inch around all figures.

Sometimes you want to add a contrasting color but want a more tailored edge to finish your pillow. This is when you'd use piping. Measure the sides of the pillow and add about 2 inches more to the length. The round fabric cording can be purchased at fabric or craft stores in a variety of colors. The piping is applied in the same manner as lace, placing the piping's raw edge next to the pillow top's edges with the bulky cord facing to the center. Pin to the corner; then clip the tape up to the cord, allowing the tape to open. Turn the corner, continuing to pin up the next side. Sew along the piping's line of stitches. Use a *zipper foot* if you need to, securing the piping onto the pillow top.

The Least You Need to Know

- Preparation of bias tape strips.
- Understanding how to prepare fabric pieces for appliqué.
- A pillow top must be quilted with a batting and backing before the pillow back is attached.
- Know how to attach piping to the edge of a pillow.

Quilt Talk

The **zipper foot** is a presser foot that can slide to one side and is used to sew in zippers. But it can also let you sew very closely to the piping cord. Use it when sewing the piping to the pillow back.

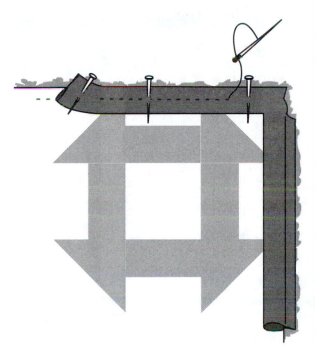

Clip into each corner to turn the piping around the pillow corner.

Finish your pillow back as we did in Chapter 25.

Your pillow is done. I hope you feel like an artist painting your wreath with fabric.

In This Chapter

- ◆ Piecing stems and leaves of the pillow front
- ◆ Preparation of half square triangles into units
- ◆ Understanding what a Yo-yo quilt is
- ◆ Preparation of yo-yos

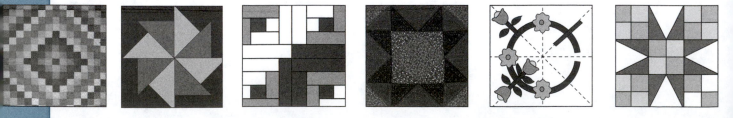

Yo-Yo Flower Pillow

One of my students, Nita Munson, on a trip to visit family in Texas found this cute wall hanging. She loved it and wanted me to draft up the pattern. So I did but also made it into a pillow for the class to prepare. The pillow base is pieced and then the *yo-yos* are applied. Yo-yo quilts were popular during the 1920s to 1930s. Scraps were used to make these round yo-yo shaped circles. They were then invisibly stitched together to form a "quilt." The completed yo-yo spread is used over a solid-color blanket or sheet and is used purely for show and not warmth because there were holes between each circle.

I have a friend who started to make a Yo-yo quilt and cut 100 2-inch circles. After gathering many of them into yo-yos, she decided they were too small and went on to cut 100 3-inch circles. She has been making them ever since. But she is not upset about her unfinished project—she has all her yo-yos sitting in a pretty basket in her living room where they look very decorative indeed! Before you start such a large undertaking, start with this pillow and see how much you enjoy your yo-yos.

Yo-yo rose block. This wall hanging was made by Kathy Stehleh.

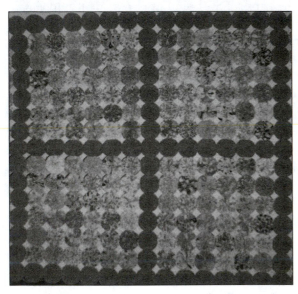

Pictured is a section of a Yo-yo quilt. The round, gathered pieces of fabric are whipstitched together.

Quilt Talk

Individual **yo-yos** are made from small round pieces of fabric that are gathered around the outside edge. Yo-yo quilts are novelty quilts. Technically they are not really quilts because there is no backing and batting.

Finished size: 12×12 inches

Materials:

> Fabrics
>
> Pillow form
>
> 1 package of piping

Fabric requirements:

> Muslin or light colored fabric—fat quarter
>
> Dominant fabric (yo-yos)—fat quarter
>
> Contrast fabric (stems, border, and back of pillow)—½ yard
>
> Medium contrasting fabric (leaves)—fat quarter
>
> Blender fabric (corner triangles)—fat quarter

Follow these steps:

1. Prepare template and fabrics. Cut out fabrics, adding on the seam allowances. We'll cut out the yo-yos later.

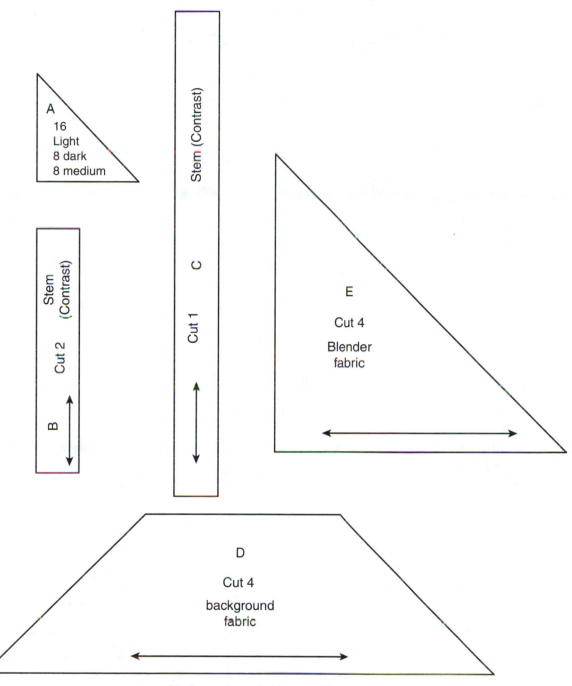

Rose block templates. (Add seam allowances.)

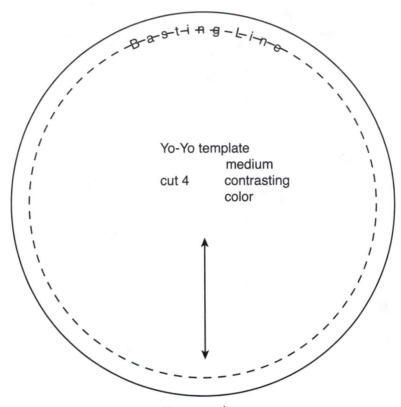

Yo-Yo template
medium
cut 4   contrasting
color

Yo-yo template.

2. Sew the long sides of template A triangles in the background and the contrasting fabric (triangle). Make eight half square triangles in the lightest and darkest fabrics.

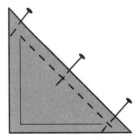 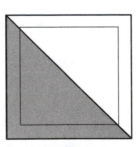

Make eight half square triangles of the dark background fabrics and eight of the medium background fabrics.

3. Sew another eight half square triangles combining the background and the medium contrasting fabrics. Stitch along the long side of the triangle to form the half square triangles.

4. Sew two of the dark background fabric squares together to form the bottom of the leaf making a rectangular unit.

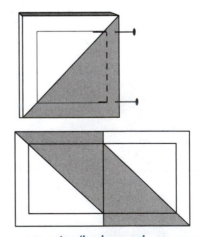

Sew two contrasting/background squares together to form the bottom of the leaf. It kind of looks like a diamond shape.

Don't Get Stuck! _____

Keep the pieces laid out on the table in front of you. Be sure to pin and open up these pieces to make certain that it is the correct configuration.

5. Sew two of the medium/background fabric squares together to form the top of the leaf. This time the rectangular unit will look like a larger triangle.

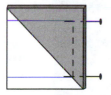 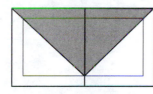

Sew two of the medium contrasting/background half square triangles to form the top of the leaf.

6. Pin and sew the bottom and top of the leaf to form a square leaf section. Make four of these leaf section that all look the same.

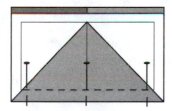

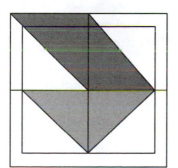

Sew four leaf sections together.

7. Stitch the short stems (template B) between two of the leaf sections.

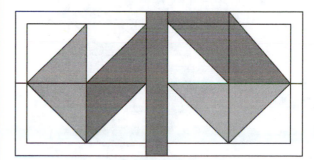

You've completed half the leaf section.

8. Sew the long stem (template C) between the two halves to form the center of the block.

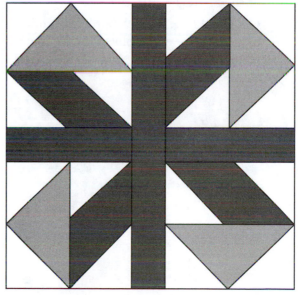

Center unit.

9. Pin together the background rhomboid (template D) to each corner.

10. Sew the blender fabric triangle (template E) onto each corner. Right now it looks strange because we haven't positioned the yo-yos.

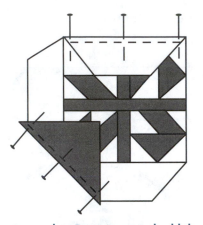

First sew on template D, open up and add the triangles. Notice how the triangles are placed. The ends will stick out on each side.

11. Cut two 9½ × 2½-inch rectangles for the borders. Pin these to the top and bottom of the block. Press open.

12. Cut two 12½ × 2½-inch borders to the opposite sides of the block. Press open.

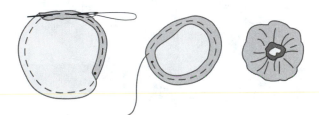

Sew the edge down and draw up the yo-yo.

13. Now it's time for the yo-yos. Cut out four 4½-inch circles.

14. Turn over ¼ inch around the raw edges, toward the wrong side of the fabric, and sew with a thread that blends in with the fabric.

Appliqué the yo-yos onto the end of the stem.

15. Carefully, draw this thread so that the fabric pulls up, making the yo-yo.

16. Knot it off and hide the thread.

17. Appliqué the yo-yos onto the ends of the stems.

18. Baste the backing muslin to batting and the pillow front.

19. Quilt.

20. Prepare the pillow with piping and backing, as in Chapter 26.

Now you are done!

The Least You Need to Know

◆ A Yo-yo quilt is not truly a quilt because it has no backing and batting.

◆ A half square triangle can be combined in many configurations.

◆ A yo-yo is made by turning down the outside of a circular piece of fabric, basting, and drawing up the threads.

◆ A yo-yo can be appliquéd onto blocks or whipstitched together.

Index

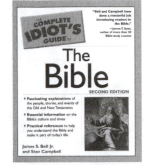

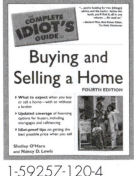
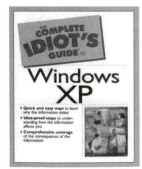